The
Multiple Staff
Ministry

The
Multiple Staff
Ministry

MARVIN T. JUDY

With the cooperation of

MURLENE O. JUDY

Nashville   ABINGDON PRESS   New York

Standard Book Number: 687-27298-X

Library of Congress Catalog Card Number: 69-18442

The quotation from an article in *Church Management,* vol. 39, May 1963, by Carroll B. Fitch is used by permission of *Church Management.*

The section entitled "The Church Business Administrator" by Carroll B. Fitch and the section "Personality in Church Administration" by Ordway Tead are from *The Appropriate Functions and Relationships of the Church Staff in the Protestant Church* and are used by permission of the copyright owner, Marvin T. Judy.

The Everett C. Hughes quotation is reprinted with the permission of *Daedalus,* Journal of the American Academy of Arts and Sciences, Boston, Mass., Fall 1963, "The Professions."

The quotation from James D. Smart is from *The Teaching Ministry of the Church,* by James D. Smart. The Westminster Press. Copyright 1954, Walter L. Jenkins. Used by permission.

The quotation from Franklin S. Haiman is from *Group Leadership and Democratic Action,* published by Houghton Mifflin in 1951. Used by permission.

Selections from *The Stress of Life* are by Hans Selye. Copyright 1956 by McGraw-Hill. Used with permission of McGraw-Hill Book Company.

Quotations from "Controlling Executive Stress" by Merrill T. Eaton are used by permission of Dr. Eaton. This lecture has been published in a slightly different form and is reprinted by permission of the publisher from "Executive Stresses Do Exist—But They Can Be Controlled," by Merrill T. Eaton, *Personnel,* March/April 1963. © 1963 by the American Management Association, Inc.

The material from Malcolm and Hulda Knowles is from *Introduction to Group Dynamics,* published by Association Press. Used by permission.

The table "Representative Theories of Learning" from *Learning Theories for Teachers* by Morris L. Bigge (Harper & Row, 1964) is used by permission of the publishers.

SET UP, PRINTED, AND BOUND BY THE
PARTHENON PRESS, AT NASHVILLE,
TENNESSEE, UNITED STATES OF AMERICA

To

Marvin Garrett and Jean
Dwight Henry and Ruth

History and Acknowledgments

In the spring of 1963 the late G. Harold Duling, Executive Director of the Religion Department of The Lilly Endowment, Inc. of Indianapolis, Indiana, was the invited speaker at a regional meeting of the Religious Research Association in Dallas, Texas. A chance conversation with Dr. Duling led to our mutual concerns and interests in the problems and effectiveness of the church staff. At Dr. Duling's invitation I presented to the Lilly Endowment a research design to study "The Appropriate Functions and Relationships of the Church Staff in the Protestant Church." A substantial grant was forthcoming that made the study possible.

Three major objectives were written into the research design: (1) To produce a major book in the field of the church staff. This book is that accomplishment. (2) To develop a course for use in theological seminaries to train persons in staff relationships. This has been done in an experimental fashion in three seminars. A syllabus and bibliography have been developed. (3) To develop short-term in-service training for church staffs. Five such seminars have been conducted in Kansas, Missouri, Ohio, and Texas. One was devoted entirely to the work of staffs in cooperative parishes in town and country areas. Material in the book has been tested in lectures and discussions in the seminars and classroom.

The research design consisted of: (1) Accumulation of data from church staffs. Questionnaires were sent to 55 city and state directors of church councils asking for names and addresses of churches that had multiple staffs in 20 denominations. A list was obtained of 1,400 churches and pastors from every section of the United States and representing 22 denominations. Letters were sent to the churches asking if the staff would participate by questionnaire and/or personal interview. The positions on the church staff were to be listed on the returned correspondence. Seven hundred senior ministers responded. Questionnaires were mailed to each of the churches. Each person on the staff was to return his questionnaire directly to me without its going through the pastor's hands, insuring freedom in preparation of the questionnaire. Members of staffs of 500 churches responded, and data were used for 306 churches, representing 1,400 persons. Questionnaires were used only when all staff members responded. The questionnaires were coded and processed on IBM cards. There were two cards for each church and two cards for each person. Information was then obtained by computer process. Comparative statistics are in Appendix A.

(2) Personal interviews with church staffs were conducted in 120 churches in 22 cities in the United States and Canada, and in 12 cooperative parishes in either town and country areas or inner cities. Interviews were with individuals on the staff and with the entire staff together. They lasted from a few minutes to several hours.

(3) I audited a course in personnel management in the Graduate School of Business Administration at Southern Methodist University.

(4) Interviews were held with such persons as the late Alex F. Osborn, Robert P. Crawford, Sidney Parnes, and Charles E. Hendry, representing related disciplines.

(5) A "Consultation on the Appropriate Functions and Relationships of the Church Staff" was held October 19-21, 1964. Seventeen persons representing seven denominations and each major position on the church staff studied and discussed papers that had been commissioned for the Consultation. Papers and their authors were: "Personnel Management and the Church Staff" by A. Q. Sartain, Dean, School of Business Administration, Southern Methodist University; "Personality in Church Administration" by Ordway Tead, author, teacher, lecturer, and past Editor of Social and Economic Books for Harper and Row; "The Pastor as Director of the Church Staff" by Andrew A. Jumper, pastor, First Presbyterian Church, Lubbock, Texas; "The Professional Christian Educator on the Church Staff" by W. Randolph Thornton, then Executive Director, Department of Administration and Leadership, National Council of Churches of Christ in America; "The Professional Musician on the Church Staff" by Carlton R. Young, Associate Professor of Church Music, Perkins School of Theology and Director of the Master of Sacred Music degree, Southern Methodist University; "The Church Business Administrator"

by Carroll B. Fitch, Church Business Administrator, Riverside Church, New York; "Historical and Theological Foundations for the Professional Church Staff" was the topic for a presentation by David C. Shipley, Professor of Theology, Methodist Seminary, Delaware, Ohio. The papers and discussions laid a foundation for the entire work.

There have been approximately 2,500 persons involved in one or more phases of the study. Corporate thanks are expressed to these people, as it is obvious by the sheer number that individual thanks are impossible.

Two persons mentioned above stand out as being especially helpful —David C. Shipley and Ordway Tead. Both men have retained a personal interest in the study since the Consultation. They have suggested numerous books and ideas. Dr. Shipley has been in close counsel on the first chapter of the book and made helpful suggestions before the final writing.

Mrs. Susie Banks, secretary, has carried the responsibility for voluminous mailings, coding and classifying the questionnaires, and the final typing of the manuscript. Sincere thanks are expressed to her.

Acknowledgment and thanks are expressed to Dean Joseph D. Quillian, Jr., Perkins School of Theology, for assisting in obtaining the grant for the study and releasing me for a time from seminary responsibilities so I could do the research and writing. Other colleagues on the faculty have been most helpful in making suggestions. Mr. J. B. Harvill and his staff in the Computing Center of Southern Methodist University provided the necessary skills for programming and producing the tabulation. Dr. Glen C. Hoskins, Professor of Education, Southern Methodist University, has been especially helpful in material on education.

Lilly Endowment, Inc., through the late G. Harold Duling and his successor Charles G. Williams, have been generous in supplying funds to finance the research and travel to make this work possible. Sincere thanks are expressed to the staff and trustees of the Endowment.

My wife, Murlene, has carried a major role in bibliographic research. Four years of intensive study have gone into her work. She has done much in exploring new fields which have added a number of related disciplines to the book. Though I have been responsible for the actual writing of the book, in every phase of the material we have been in collaboration. Heartfelt thanks and appreciation are expressed to her.

To the Reader

Three basic types of material will be found in the following pages: theoretical, analytical, and practical. Theoretical material deals with theology, sociology, psychology, and administration. Analytical material deals with statistics primarily concerning the various positions on the staff and the application of the data to human relations and self-understanding. The practical material deals with administrative procedures for good human relations within the staff.

It is advisable to read the book from beginning to end rather than to select a chapter here and there which may speak to the immediate need. Theology and theory are foundational in the work, and without an understanding of these basic tenets the reader will have difficulty interpreting practical applications.

Sociological statistical reporting is always difficult. It has been kept to a minimum. There are, however, sections within the chapters on staff positions which report facts and findings about the respective offices. Statistics are generally of interest if they relate to the reader. Family background, educational background, influences in life, and personal attitudes make a vast difference in human relations in the case of the church staff. Some readers will find the statistics interesting and helpful, others will find them boring. In the latter case, one can skim over the section, getting only the high points.

MARVIN T. JUDY
Perkins School of Theology
Southern Methodist University
Dallas, Texas

Foreword

In his remarkable little book *The Choice to Love,* the noted novelist Robert Raynolds coins a term, "the small parish of love." "Our life is at home, and in a small parish of the heart. A man's small parish of love begins at home. Our first choice is to love each one with whom we live, our wife and our child, our brother and our sister, our father and our mother. If we have not begun here at home, any claim we make about loving mankind at large, or even our neighbor over the hill, is but hollow chatter." *

Since the family is the smallest of communities, and love is the central cohesive force, the Christian message finds its greatest release and witness in this context. This book has been created in partnership. New ideas have been formed, different disciplines have been brought together, and the consultative process has gone into the entire work.

This book is sent out in the hope that each member of a church staff and each member of a church shall find a community of Christian love in his own family. It is in this spirit we have dedicated this book to our children, who are a part of our own small parish of love.

MARVIN AND MURLENE JUDY

---

* (New York: Harper, 1959), p. 125.

Contents

1

A Doctrine
of the Multiple Staff Ministry

There is scarcely an area of investigation in church and theological circles today that is receiving as much attention as a doctrine of the church, laity, and ministry. Studies and publications are clearing the air in regard to who the laity are, what the church is, and the meaning of ministerial orders.

Some Relevant Questions

The investigation of the functions and relationships of the church staff in the Protestant church soon leads into a series of questions concerning employed persons in a multiple ministry and on church staffs. Who are the ordained clergy, and to what extent are they different from the unordained? What is "ministry" for the person professionally trained in education, music, or counseling, and to what extent is his ministry different from that of the ordained? Theologically and historically who are the employed people with delegated administrative responsibilities in a church staff, such as hostesses, dietitians, church business administrators, and directors of day schools? Who are the people who look after the physical plant of a church and its use, such as engineers, custodians, and yard men? Who are the people, theologically and historically, who do the clerical work in the church staff— the secretaries, bookkeepers, and typists?

When a small congregation employs a minister he is the sole employee—unless there is a part-time custodian—and the problem concerning the theological meaning of a church staff is not present. In the one person are priest, pastor, counselor, evangelist, educator, musician, preacher, secretary, and custodian. The pastor has been "called" to the ministry, duly trained, and recognized through ordination by his denomination. He has been formally called by the congregation or appointed by the proper denominational official. He is assured of polity rights within his denomination, including the right of appointment, certain tenure conditions, and retirement plans. He enjoys the freedom of the pastorate, being able to a large degree to regulate his own work schedule. He is the sole recipient of praise and affection from the congregation, and his wife is "queen of the manse."

As the congregation grows and responsibilities of the pastor increase, additional help is employed by the congregation. Usually the order of additional help is: a secretary, assistant pastor, and director of education. Are such persons employed to help the pastor get his work done, or are they, too, ministers to the congregation?

The present-day large church, with staffs being composed of from two or three employed persons to as many as a hundred or more, poses many theological and doctrinal problems concerning the ministry. Some of the questions that must be considered are:

1. What is the church?
2. What is the role of the laity of the church?
3. What is the difference between the laity and the clergy?
4. What is the role of the unordained person on a church staff?
5. What is the relationship between unordained and ordained members of church staffs?
6. What is ministry? Lay and clerical?
7. What is the relationship between the paid church staff and the laity?
8. What are the purposes, goals, and objectives of the employed staff in a local church?

Basically each of the above questions is rooted in the more fundamental question of a theological concept of church and ministry. Without a firm understanding on the part of laity, clergy, and other employed persons on the church staff as to a basic concept of church and ministry, the work of the church will tend to become secular in nature and lose its *raison d'être*. Much confusion stems from the lack of clear understanding of the nature of the church, the nature of the ministry, and the purposes, goals, and objectives of the employed staff in a local church. The church as a secular organization taking on the pattern of "big business," developing status symbols and hierarchy of authority has developed a tension between the fundamental nature of the church and the nature of the secular world. This has been a major factor contributing to the rise of the critical and sometimes cynical literature that stands in judgment of the church and ministry.[1] At the same time, serious positive books have come from the presses that take the attitude, "Yes, we have mixed too much of the sacred and secular, we have become 'organization men,' but the church is of God and can be redeemed as an instrument of God in our confused society." Lay groups are studying the theological meaning of the church, and every major denomination has its special study commissions diligently attempting to define theologically the church, laity, and clergy, and the meaning of ministerial orders. Such works are clearing the air and assisting clergy and laity to gain new perspectives and a sense of direction. Yves Congar, Hendrik Kraemer, J. A. T. Robinson, L. Howard Grimes, H. Richard Niebuhr, Daniel Day Williams, James M. Gustafson, Browne Barr, Mark Gibbs, T. Ralph Morton, James Smart, Daniel Jenkins, and a host of other writers in various denominational and ecumenical groups are pointing, or have pointed, the way for a better understanding of the church in our day.[2] The following summary of the concept of church and laity is presented to provide a foundation on which this entire work has been developed.

The Theologizing Process

Assuming one of the traditional concepts of the theologizing process, one begins with existence and what is actually happening in time and space—and through, alongside of, and beyond—and becomes aware of another power, another dynamic, an ultimacy which can be called *Being*. One reasons from existence to essence or to Being. The understanding of God in biblical literature has stemmed from event. The continuum of the theologizing process has been: event, recognition of Divine Providence within the event, analysis of causes of the event, discernment of the workings of God in the event, statement of the nature of God as the result of his working within the event, and a final statement of a doctrine concerning God and the event. A theology for the New Testament is primarily descriptions of the "mighty acts of God"; hence, theology is chiefly an accurate description of what is, or what is happening, and the recognition of the presence or sense of the holy in the actuality of history.

Therefore, with the above presupposition we begin the theologizing

---

[1] Peter L. Berger, *The Noise of Solemn Assemblies* (Garden City, N.Y.: Doubleday, 1961). Pierre Berton, *The Comfortable Pew* (Philadelphia: Lippincott, 1965), Charles Merrill Smith, *How to Become a Bishop Without Being Religious* (Doubleday, 1965). Gregory Wilson, *The Stained Glass Jungle* (Doubleday, 1965).

[2] See Bibliography.

process concerning the church with the proposition that the large church is the result of the creative act of God. It *is* event. It is *present,* now and in being. The large church has made it necessary to develop a multiple ministry with specialized fields of work. As church staffs have grown in size, responsibilities have become specialized. Additional help, other than the ordained ministry, has been employed until the concept of ministry has become confused. Too much emphasis has come to focus upon the importance of the church staff in "running the church," and a minimum of emphasis upon the fact that the church is the "people of God." To illustrate: A study a few years ago in one major denomination revealed that 40 percent of the laymen questioned concerning the nature of church and ministry reported their concept of the laity was "to help the minister run the church."

The question must be asked, where has such a concept originated? Is it a concept of the church in harmony with the basic teaching of the New Testament and spirit of the Christian faith? By examining the history of the church it is possible to trace developments which cast light upon the confusion surrounding the present-day roles of laity and clergy, and the meaning of ordination.

Historical Developments for a Doctrine of the Ministry, Laity, and Church

George Huntston Williams[3] gives to Clement of Rome the credit for using the term *layman* for the first time in a written document. In a letter written about A.D. 95 Clement states, "The lay man (*ho laïkos anthrōpos*) is bound by the lay (*laïkos*) ordinances" (I Clement 40. 5). Clement implies in his writing that the layman was a full participant in the life and work of the church, including the liturgy, and not a mere observer.

Quite early in the life of the church, baptism came to mean ordination to the royal priesthood in which every person so baptized was set apart with the people of God (*laos theou*) to be a witness to the Christian faith. It was not considered out of order for any professing baptized Christian to perform the liturgical rites of the Christian community. It was a brotherhood in the faith.

To sum up, the laic in the ancient church had an indelible "ordination" as priest, prophet and king, no longer in bondage to the world, but freed

---

[3] "The Ancient Church A.D. 30-313," *The Layman in Christian History,* ed. by Stephen Charles Neill and Hans-Ruedi Weber (Philadelphia: The Westminster Press, 1963), p. 30.

through Christ to know the truth in the illumination of the Spirit, to exercise sovereignty over the inner temple of self, to join in the corporate thanksgiving of the redeemed, and to forgive the brethren in Christ's name. The laity was a true order (taxis) with its own often distinctive liturgical, constitutional, eleemosynary and witnessing role in the gradual differentiation of the People of the Mission into laity and clergy.[4]

There is considerable evidence in first- and second-century literature that the Christian considered himself a part of a body of people who were set apart from the world through faith in God's act in Christ to live in faith and to express such faith in daily structured conduct. The sacraments of the church were means of grace to be shared by the whole church. Certain persons were set aside as leaders of the congregation to perform leadership roles, but in their absence, or in assistance to such leaders, all Christians had the right of participation. Tertullian (A.D. 160?–230?) stated:

> Are not even we laics priests? It is written in Revelation 1:6: "A kingdom also and a priest to his God and Father, hath he made us." It is the authority of the Church and the honor through the sessions of the *ordo* sanctified to God which has established the difference between the *ordo* and the *plebs*. Accordingly, where there is no session of the ecclesiastical *ordo*, thou offerest the eucharist, and baptizest (*tingues*) and art a *sacerdos* (priest) for thyself; for where three are there is the Church, albeit they be laics.[5]

In the first-century church Christians did not claim that the followers of the Nazarene replaced Judaism, but rather they claimed that they were the fulfillment of it. The sacrifices of the old dispensation and the function of the priest as an offerer of sacrifices were good until the old dispensation was fulfilled and made perfect in the new. The priest and priesthood of the old dispensation were necessary until they were replaced with the perfect Priesthood of Christ, and the old sacrifices were consummated in the one perfect sacrifice of Christ—a sacrifice so complete and perfect for all time and for the sins of all mankind, past, present, and future, that it need never, and could never be repeated. Christ was the perfect Priest offering the one perfect sacrifice of himself to the Eternal Father so that there would never be another priest to offer sacrifices for the forgiveness of sins.

In the early church there is a noticeable absence of any analogy between the priesthood of the Old Testament and the ministry of the

---

[4] *Ibid.*, p. 32.
[5] *De exhort. Cast* 7.

New Testament. Instead the church is thought of as a priestly people with a ministry authoritatively appointed to give expression to worship. (See I Peter 2:5 and Revelation 1:6, 5:10, 20:6). Therefore the ministry of the early church was selected by the congregation according to: (1) the particular ability of the individual, (2) the desire of the individual. Paul suggests in I Corinthians 12:28, "And God hath set some in the church, first apostles, secondarily prophets, thirdly teachers, after that miracles, then gifts of healing, helps, governments, diversities of tongues." The two aspects of the ministry arose very early in the church when one was endowed with "gifts" and was "prepared." The congregation selected for ministerial office those persons from their own number whom they felt were qualified to fill the office. Thomas M. Lindsay points out, "The people were taught to recognize that God was with them while they selected their pastor. When they had made the choice known and had clearly intimated the man whom they had elected, they were enjoined to say, 'O, God, strengthen him whom *Thou* has prepared for us.' " [6]

Such persons were set apart by the "laying on of hands" in a simple service of ordination. It was felt that God was in the act of selecting and ordaining, but not in a sense any greater than he was in the life of the true believer.

With the expansion of the church and the development of a paid clergy there arose the necessity for an overall supervision of the work of the church. This gave rise to the expansion of the clergy into various ministerial offices and eventually into an ecclesiastical hierarchy. The terms deacon, elder, and bishop, which originally referred to local congregational leaders, soon took on hierarchical significance.

A concept of the ministry and the work of a minister cannot be separated from a doctrine of the church. In the *Didache* the Eucharist is referred to as the "pure offering," to be offered in every place.[7] Clement of Rome attempted to exhort congregations to a deeper reverence when he spoke of worship as "offerings and sacrifices," and he goes so far as to draw the analogy of the Jewish ministry of high priests, priests, and Levites to illustrate the orderly differentiation in the church between the order of the ministry and the laity in general.[8]

---

[6] *The Church and the Ministry in the Early Centuries.* (London: Hodder & Stoughton, 1902), p. 246.

[7] "The Didache," Chap. XIV, *The Fathers of the Church, the Apostolic Fathers,* trans. Francis X. Glinn *et al.* (New York: Cima Publishing Co., 1947), p. 182.

[8] "Saint Clement of Rome, the Letter to the Corinthians, 1:40," in *ibid.,* p. 41.

Ignatius is still more definitely technical in that, for him, membership in the church meant the privilege of communion in the Eucharist, and the bishop, who for Ignatius was the normal person to celebrate the Eucharist, represented Christ.[9]

The church literature and liturgies—*in the West*—that followed these early writings, led to the establishing of the dogma of the Mass as a reenactment of the sacrifice of Christ and the priest as the offerer of sacrifices. Tertullian agreed with Cyprian (A.D. 200?–258), who explicitly asserted the threefold Christian ministry as the successor of the three orders of the Jewish Priesthood. The bishop is the high priest;[10] the priesthood ordained by God among the Jews passed to the church of Christ when Jews crucified the Savior.[11] Tertullian had been clear and explicit that, while the Christian community generally is a royal priesthood having access to God, there is in that community a separate ministry and a priestly discipline (*sacerdotalis disciplina*) that is to exercise the priestly function of the church.

Probably no single person affected the concept of the church and ministry in the first four or five centuries as did Cyprian. Cyprian was a lawyer by profession. He interpreted the church in the light of civil government and the clergy in the light of civil authority. He saw the bishop as head of the congregation and authority over the lesser clergy. He saw that through ordination, the bishop is endowed with power to absolve sins and exact penance. He felt the bishop had the right to select the lesser clergy. Cyprian conceived of the clergyman as a priest who was an offerer of sacrifices and a mediator between God and man. Penance was initiated by Cyprian as evidence of true repentance, hence a means to God's forgiveness of sins. With Cyprian, the idea of Apostolic succession became a fixed doctrine of the Western church. It was not a succession *from* the apostles, as was found in Tertullian, but a succession *of* apostles. For Cyprian, bishops were apostles in the same sense as the first-century apostles—they represented Christ. The bishop became the authority over the church, and wherever the bishop was there was the church. The lesser clergy—deacons and elders—became assistants to the bishop, his "eyes and ears."

Cyprian set off the clergy from the laity with authority of office, and adopted the dress of the government officials to signify the office

---

[9] "Saint Ignatius of Antioch, I to the Ephesians, 5," p. 89, and "V, to the Philadelphians, 4," p. 114. In *ibid.*

[10] Tertullian, "On Baptism," *Ante-Nicene Fathers*, Vol. III, Alexander Roberts and James Donaldson, eds. (New York: Scribner's, 1899), p. 677.

[11] Saint Cyprian, *The Fathers of the Church*, Vol. 51, Letter 66, pp. 223-30.

of the clergy. From this has developed the elaborate vestments of the clergy, not only of the Roman Catholic Church but in other churches.

A summary of the state of the church in regard to clergy and laity at the end of the third century is stated by Lindsay:

It was no longer—people worshipping and some of them leading the common devotions, saints believing and some among them instructing and admonishing; it became—teachers who imparted and pupils who received, priests who interceded and sinners who were pardoned through the intercession, rulers who commanded and subjects who were bound to obey.[12]

It is one of the basic theses of this writing that *the doctrine of the ministry which developed into a doctrine of the priesthood, coupled with a doctrine of the Eucharist as a sacerdotal sacrifice, was the first wedge to be driven between the clergy and laity in the Christian church.* This movement led to the eventual concept of the clergy as a group of persons set apart through ordination in whom *special powers* had been implanted by God's grace. This led to an establishing of a clerical hierarchy that became the ruling body of the Christian church.

By the middle of the third century the monarchical episcopate had become the universally recognized system of church government. Ordination was a permanent step setting the clergy apart from the world and "above" the laity. "Minor orders" later emerged, consisting of sub-deacons, acolytes, doorkeepers, exorcists, and readers, which were to become a regular hierarchy of ecclesiastical grades. With each development within the system of the clergy the work of the laity in the life and direction of the church was minimized. For instance, the deacon was becoming more of an administrator, taking that function out of the hands of the laity. The "arch diaconate" came into being with its functioning responsibility to be an assistant to the bishop. The office developed through the centuries until it carried with it the responsibility of selecting, testing, and electing the clergy, and also the disciplining of the clergy.

Little literature is available on the laity in the church during the Dark Ages. However, with the turn of the eleventh century or the beginning of the Middle Ages, the Renaissance within the church began. On the one hand was a very firm belief among the clergy that all authority rested in the clerical offices. Government of the church was within the clergy, especially the episcopacy, and by and large the

---

[12] *The Church and the Ministry in the Early Centuries,* p. 266.

laity was to keep quiet. The sacramental doctrinal refinements in the period continued to widen the gap. Specific functional roles were assigned to the clergy and laity. The church authority quickly adapted to the feudal society and assumed that the role of the laity was to protect the church. The layman became the "crusading warrior" protecting the church from evil persons by the use of military force. The papal banner was carried into military conquest with the promise of Divine protection. The First Crusade in 1095 was for the protection of Constantinople and, in reality, to recover Jerusalem from the infidels.

As in all ages the Holy Spirit was at work, and in the person of Francis of Assisi, born in 1209, a movement was launched that had as its basis an attempt to release the layman in Christian witness and service to the neighbor. Francis conceived of the idea of laymen going forth two by two without purse or security to witness to and aid the poor and needy. Although Francis, through papal insistence, was ordained a deacon and many of his friars were likewise ordained, the historic Third Order of Franciscans decisively remained laymen. Francis emphasized that the prayer of simple laymen might witness to more souls than the sermons of the learned. It did not take long, however, after the death of Francis for the order to become monastic in nature with a predominance of ordained friars; yet the Third Order of Franciscans maintained their status as laymen.

Another movement in the later Middle Ages was the Brethren of the Common Life. The lay order was founded by Gerard Groot, who died in 1384. Groot was a popular lay preacher in the Low Countries and a follower of Jan van Ruysbroek, who in turn was a disciple of Eckhart. Like the mendicant friars they were dedicated to preaching and charitable work among the poor and downtrodden. The majority of the Brethren were laymen, and even though they lived a common life they took no monastic vows. By and large they were educators. Among the intellectual leaders of northern Europe who went to their schools were Nicholas of Cusa, Thomas à Kempis, Erasmus of Rotterdam, and Martin Luther.[13]

The Reformation ushered in the recognition and elevation of the laity as the church. E. Gordon Rupp[14] states that there were three distinct groups of laymen who emerged during the Reformation, helping to bring it into being and keeping it alive. These were the law-

---

[13] For further detail see Robert S. Hoyt, *Europe in the Middle Ages* (New York: Harcourt, Brace & World, 1957), p. 602.

[14] "The Age of the Reformation, 1500-1648," *The Layman in Christian History.*

yers, the merchants, and the scholars. Among the latter it is difficult at times to distinguish which ones were "in orders" and which ones were not, but orders were incidental. Some were formerly in orders, and had given up their clerical positions to declare the truth as they saw it.

Out of the Reformation came Luther's basic concepts of the church and laity.

1. Before God all Christians have the same standing, a priesthood in which we enter by baptism and through faith.
2. As a comrade and brother of Christ, each Christian is a priest and needs no mediator save Christ. He has access to the Word.
3. Each Christian is a priest and has an office of sacrifice, not the Mass, but the dedication of himself to the praise and obedience of God, and to bearing the cross.
4. Each Christian has a duty to hand on the gospel which he himself has received.[15]

Another clear statement of Luther concerning all believers as priests is:

It is faith that makes men priests, faith that unites them to Christ, and gives them the indwelling of the Holy Spirit, whereby they become filled with all holy grace and heavenly power. The inward anointing—this oil, better than any that ever came from the horn of bishop or pope—gives them not the name only, but the nature, the purity, the power of priests; and this anointing have all they received who are believers in Christ.[16]

In substance John Calvin held to the same concepts in regard to the laity as did Luther.

One section of the Christian church often overlooked is that body sometimes called the Radical Reformers. Throughout Christendom there have been groups that have stood apart from the predominant organized church and have held to the belief in lay witness, usually mediated through adult baptism, and the body of believers as a mutually responsible fellowship.

Franklin H. Littell states:

Such offices as are reconstituted in their congregations in imitation of the Early Church are, like those of the primitive congregations, strictly functional in character. The Hutterites had only the *"Diener am Wort"* (the servant of

---

[15] *Ibid.*, p. 139. Originally compiled by Rupp from *The Institution of the Christian Religion*, Bk. 3. 3. 42; Bk. 2. 15. 6; Bk. 4. 18. 17.

[16] Philip Schaff, *History of the Christian Church*, Vol. VI (New York: Scribner's 1892), p. 25.

the Word) and *"Diener de Notdurft"* (the servant of those that are in need) (Acts 6:1-6). Every Christian man, by the ordination of baptism, is called to witness. On him, and not solely on "the religious," the *consilia perfectionis* are binding. This led, in the four branches of the Anabaptist movement (Swiss Brethren, South German Brethren, Hutterites, Mennonites), to the enforcement of rules for the whole membership which previously had been applied only to "the religious": e.g., non-resistance, apostolic simplicity of life, avoidance of evil, avoidance of the oath, avoidance of the magistrate's office. In addition, separation from the "spirit of the times" (*kosmos*) showed itself in enlargement of the "peace testimony," adoption of the "hat testimony" (Quakers), plain clothes and other peculiar customs. The entire community was put under the disciplines of discipleship, and not just a small minority admired and obeyed by the rest. It has sometimes wrongly been said that the Anabaptists, Baptists, Quakers, Mennonites, Brethren and like groups have no true doctrine of ordination and frequently no clergy at all. A more perceptive over-simplification would be to say *not that they have no clergy but that they have no laity.*[17]

One of the largest sections of lay workers in the church is composed of that body broadly referred to as the deaconesses. As early as the fourth century deaconesses were a part of the Eastern Church. The movement seemed to die, however, in the sixth century due to the fact that asylums or hospitals were established for the care of the needy, decreasing the need for the services of the deaconess; infant baptism was almost universally accepted, doing away with catechetical training for baptism; monasticism discouraged women in the service of the church to the secular world; and sacerdotalism did not permit the ordaining of women.

In the seventeenth century, Vincent de Paul in France conceived the idea of women serving to distribute charity. In 1633 Madam Louise le Grass, working with Vincent de Paul, organized the Sisters of Charity in Paris. It was primarily for unmarried women. This society was declared a distinct monastic order of sisters by the Archbishop of Paris and was later recognized by Pope Clement IX. The women took the vows of poverty, chastity, obedience, and service to the poor one year at a time with a five year probation period. They adopted the simple dress of the peasant for their formal habit. A simple knit hat was used. Numerous groups have emerged through the centuries since Vincent de Paul. For instance, in the United States alone there are 269 sisterhoods in the Roman Catholic Church, each being developed around one primary type of service.

---

[17] Franklin H. Littell, "The Radical Reformation," *The Layman in Christian History*, p. 263.

In 1845 the Anglican Church started a similar type of sisterhood.

The modern deaconess movement in the Protestant church is different from the sisterhoods, however, in that women perform more duties similar to those of a pastor.

Wesley, in 1736–38, when a missionary in Savannah, Georgia, revived the ancient order of deaconesses to provide administrators of the work of the church. It was a hundred years later, however, when the deaconess movement got under way in the Protestant church through the influence of Theodore Fliedner in Germany. Fliedner in 1836 became concerned over the poverty in his Lutheran parish brought on by the closing of the silk mills in his city. He toured Europe to raise funds for the relief of the poor. While on the tour he became aware of how institutions that were sponsored by the church worked for the relief of the poor. He felt also a deep need for prison reform and the assisting of women who had been confined to prison to be integrated back into normal life. As the result of his insights and ability to meet immediate needs the Mother House of the German Lutheran Deaconess Movement came into existence. By the time of Fliedner's death in 1865 there were 30 Mother Houses and 1,500 deaconesses. One of the more prominent of his students, known for her part in the Crimean War, was Florence Nightingale.

The modern deaconess movement in evangelical churches is characterized by: (1) usually a home where the sisters live together, (2) the admitting of only unmarried women, (3) a prescribed course in training, (4) usually the pledging of a five year period in which time the candidate will not marry, though no vow of perpetual service is made, (5) usually a simple, distinctive costume, (6) support from the order or denomination, and provision for a suitable retirement plan, (7) service consisting of care for the poor and sick, teaching, and other pastoral services.

The Methodist movement, under the leadership of the Wesleys in England and later in America, revived the importance of the lay leadership of the church. Though John Wesley, due to his Anglican concepts of the ministry, rebelled at first against the thought of lay preachers, he came to accept them as God's plan for the saving of souls. The lay preacher and class leader soon became effective instruments in the church.

In the United States the work of the layman and clergy have taken on numerous forms. New denominations have come into being generally as the result of a doctrinal emphasis or an emphasis on some form of church polity. An interesting "life cycle" in such groups has been, in many cases, an unordained clergy, or ordination that was quite simple and even administered by the laymen, to the development of a trained clergy with formal requirements and an increasing emphasis upon ordination.

In the past twenty years lay movements of various kinds have spontaneously arisen. The ecumenical movement has given rise to new forms of lay service and lay ministry. Hans-Ruedi Weber points to the fact that *Laici in Ecclesia: An Ecumenical Bibliography on the Role of the Laity in the Life and Mission of the Church* (published by the Department of the Laity, World Council of Churches in 1961) refers to more than 1,400 articles, pamphlets, and books published on the subject, mainly since 1948, in Protestant and Orthodox churches. A Roman Catholic bibliography in 1957 listed 2,200 entries.[18]

Contemporary lay movements—such as the evangelical academies in Europe and their counterparts in America—and the large number of books on a theology of the laity are so well known that there is no need to review these aspects.

At this point in our discussion we return to the more crucial question before us, namely, the employed lay worker in the contemporary Protestant church. The series of questions asked earlier continue to emerge in discussions concerning church staffs: (1) What is the church? (2) What is the role of the laity of the church? (3) What is the difference between the laity and clergy? (4) What is the role of the unordained person on a church staff? (5) What is the relationship between unordained and ordained members of the church staff? (6) What is ministry, lay and clerical? (7) What is the relationship between the paid church staff and the laity? (8) What are the purposes, goals, and objectives of the employed staff in a local church?

Some Definitions

This brief discussion leads to the necessity of defining the distinctive categories designated laity and clergy, as well as the unordained, full-time church employee. Much emphasis in literature has been placed upon the basic doctrine of the church as "a People of God" rather than upon ecclesiastical organization. The church is "assembled" or "gathered" for renewal, worship, receiving the sacraments,

---

[18] Hans-Ruedi Weber, "The Rediscovery of the Laity in the Ecumenical Movement," *The Layman in Christian History*, p. 391.

learning, fellowship; and it is "scattered" or "dispersed" to witness, serve, and to fulfill the mission of God in the world.[19]

To the ministry of the local congregation is delegated the responsibility of giving direction to the congregation in worship, nurture, and work. Each of these areas of ministry is thoroughly rooted in theological and historical tradition. *Worship* is rooted in a theology reflected in faith and order, liturgy, hymnody, ritual, and preaching which reveal the nature of man, the nature of God, and assists man in adoration, praise, confession, thanksgiving, and dedication. *Nurture* is rooted in catechetical theology, which is based on an adaptation of dogmatics for faith and communication. Nurture involves learning the fundamental teachings of the Christian faith stemming from the Bible and Christian teachings. It implies the process by which the believer is brought to a consciousness of the Christian faith and the application of the principles of Christianity in every phase of human existence and encounter. *Work* implies a moral theology, or the extension of one's beliefs and faith into everyday life through personal witness, support of enterprises of the church, politics, social reform, and any phase of answering human need. This involves a doctrine of vocation, including the priesthood of all believers.

Ministry is to give direction to the laity for worship, nurture, and work. As such, ministry is united in effort and objective, but divided in responsibility. As a church grows in size, persons are added to the staff to fulfill functional roles. For want of a better term we may call the multiple staff an "organismic" ministry. By organismic I mean each person on the staff is an entity unto himself, but a part of a total organism. He cannot fulfill a total ministry alone, but is united with and dependent upon the other members of the staff. Altogether they make up one organism with separate duties and responsibilities. As such, all are "theologians" in the broad application of the term. They are theologians in that they are attempting to assist the laity to a fuller understanding of biblical and historical theology as it is applied in worship, nurture, and work.

To labor the point a little further, one may liken a church staff to the fingers of the hand. There are the "preacher," the educator, the musician, the counselor, the administrator, the receptionist, the secretary, the custodian—all are bound together as a working organism.

---

[19] See L. Howard Grimes, *The Rebirth of the Laity* (Nashville: Abingdon Press, 1962), and Browne Barr, *Parish Back Talk* (Abingdon Press, 1964). Both of these works are based upon this theory and use the terms "assembled" or "gathered," and "dispersed" or "scattered."

Special talents and professional training make for different positions in the church staff. The word "professional" is the key to differences of positions in the church staff. A study of the word "profession" reveals that the word comes from "professed," which originally described one "that has taken the vow of the religious order." By 1675 the word had been secularized to mean: "The occupation which one professed to be skilled in and to follow . . . a vocation in which professed knowledge of some branch of learning is used in its application to the affairs of others, or in the practice of an art based upon it. Applied specifically to the three learned professions of divinity, law, and medicine; also the military profession." [20]

The professionals *profess*. They profess to know better than others the nature of certain matters, and to know better than their clients what ails them in their affairs. This is the essence of the professional idea and the professional claim. From it flow many consequences. The professionals claim the executive right to practice, as a vocation, the arts, which they profess to know, and to give the kind of advice derived from their special lines of knowledge. This is the basis of the license, both in the narrow sense of legal permission and in the broader sense that the public allows those in a profession a certain leeway in their practice and perhaps in their very way of living and thinking. The professional is expected to think objectively and inquiringly about matters which may be, for laymen, subject to orthodoxy and sentiment which limit intellectual exploration. Further, a person, in his professional capacity, may be expected and required to think objectively about matters which he himself would find it painful to approach in that way when they affect him personally.[21]

The professional expects to be trusted by his client. He expects to be his own judge and to be protected in his judgment by his colleagues in his profession. He is aware that his colleagues will judge him as to his integrity in upholding the basic principles of the profession.

Each profession also establishes a basic philosophy regarding its vocational demands. Fundamental principles are established, organizations are founded, standards for admission into the professional organization are written into a constitution and by-laws. Standards for practicing the profession are articulated, and the complete body of

---

[20] *The Oxford Shorter Dictionary*. For a fuller discussion of the word and professions see *Daedalus*, Journal of the American Academy of Arts and Science, Fall, 1963. See esp. "Professions" by Everett C. Hughes, pp. 655-68. A full discussion of the ministry as a profession can be found in James D. Glass, *Profession: Minister* (Nashville: Abingdon Press, 1968).

[21] Reprinted with the permission of *Daedalus*, Journal of the American Academy of Arts and Sciences, Boston, Mass., Fall, 1963, "The Professions." P. 656.

the profession stands in judgment of the individual—professional or lay—who abuses the standards.

Within the general body of professionals, there is a continual rise of vocational standards due to increasing demands for specialization within the profession. In the medical profession this is very evident as the body of knowledge is increased, new diseases and their causes and cures discovered, and the demand is made for an ever-widening application of the science of medicine to the human body and mind. This, in turn, leads to new academic disciplines, new types of internships, and new forms of residencies before the doctor is fully qualified to perform in his chosen field of medicine.

In like manner, the rise of specialized professions in the ministry has been quite evident. For centuries there have been standardizing agencies within the church which have, by and large, been established by the clergy and which have laid down the requisites for a person to become a part of the body of clergy. Three basic criteria usually underlie the preparation for becoming a recognized minister in a given denomination: (1) A genuine sense of calling on the part of the candidate and a feeling of purpose and ambition in the ministry. (2) Academic training. This is usually formal education ranging from a few courses by correspondence in some denominations to the usual pattern of a liberal arts degree with a minimum of three years additional graduate-professional training in an academically accredited seminary. (3) Some type of in-service training or internship in which the candidate may demonstrate his gifts, graces, and usefulness as a responsible person in his chosen profession.

So much for the pastoral ministry. We are now witnessing the rise of a number of ministries of specialization which are following the normal pattern of establishing professional recognition. I mention only some of the more common professional ministries: ministry of music, ministry of education, ministry of pastoral care, ministry of visitation, ministry of evangelism, and church business administration, which could be called the ministry of administration. Denominationally and interdenominationally, some of the special ministries have been organized into professions. For example, one of the latest is the National Association of Church Business Administrators. The NACBA was organized in 1956 and is composed of dues-paying persons who are business administrators in local churches. After a decade of organization the NACBA professional group had a charter and by-laws and had established an examination for persons who wished to be certified as competent church business administrators. All the marks of a profession are in the organization: definition of purpose, formal constitution, regulation of membership, recognition of qualifications for the profession, rights of the individual which are protected by the organization, and obligations of the individual toward the organization.

In some cases, new ministerial organizations have come into existence to protect the rights of the individual in the fulfillment of his ministry. In other words, the professional organization weeds out the person unfit to practice the profession, and protects the person in the organization from encroachment upon his rights and privileges. A case in point is the organizing of the National Association of Pastoral Counselors during the mid-1960's. Hundreds of persons across America had set up pastoral counseling services, either in a church or independently. Persons involved in such services assembled to establish a constitution regulating membership in the organization through rigid educational and internship qualifications. A member of the association has the right of practice—the right to hang out his shingle, so to speak—and the organization will support this right as long as the individual complies with the standards of the organized body.

Thus, it can be seen, *the church staff is composed of a group of professional persons, presumably competent in their respective fields, who blend their services together to perform a ministry as a whole to the congregation.* This leads to definite functional roles for persons on the church staff as the entire staff working together attempt to help the individual Christian fulfill his responsibility in worship, nurture, and work.

Much of the confusion in the contemporary church as to purpose and roles of clergy and laity has stemmed from the institutional developments which have occurred through the centuries. Mark Gibbs and T. Ralph Morton analyze the movement from a ministry of the laity, or the whole church, to the development of a professional clergy and its many side issues, including the gradual development of the concept of the clergy performing the work for the church.[22] Gibbs and Morton point out that in the first-century church the congregation assembled in homes for worship, learning, and fellowship. There was no formal clergy—all persons were ministers to one another. There were, however, special talents and abilities, as is reflected in I Corinthians 12 when Paul refers to persons who were given the "words of

---

[22] Gibbs and Morton, *God's Frozen People* (Philadelphia: Westminster Press, 1965).

wisdom," "words of knowledge," of "faith," "healing," "miracles," "prophecy," "discerning of spirits," "tongues," or "the interpretation of tongues," but all persons were one with the spirit of ministry. Such functional roles did crystallize into offices, such as apostles, prophets, teachers, workers of miracles, directors of government, and administration. Persons, however, were not "professional" as yet, in that they did make their own living in a secular business and witnessed in the church on the side. The community of the family and small body of believers was the church. It was not a building or a formal congregation, but a body of believers. Gibbs and Morton hold to the belief that the professional clergy arose with the erection of a church building to house the congregation. This took the church out of the home and identified it with a building, and in due time the elected full-time clergy became identified with a building and became the pastor of the congregation which met in that building. As time has passed, more and more responsibility has been delegated to the professional clergy and the employed staff to "do the work of the church." The laity has come to look upon its roles as supporting financially the clergy and keeping the various organizations within the church operating. Connectional programs on a denominational level have demanded more time of the local church clergy and the employment of more clergy to direct such programs. All this has led to what Gibbs and Morton call "the frustrated layman and the bewildered parson." [23]

Lyle Schaller in *Planning for Protestantism in Urban America*[24] holds that the most determinative factor in shaping the work of the minister is the church building itself! With massive church buildings and even larger denominational programs which involve many days of the minister's time, the contemporary pastor feels completely "other-directed," or literally pushed around by outside forces rather than free to follow his inner direction as a shepherd of a congregation.

In his work, *Church Membership in the Methodist Tradition,* Frederick Norwood [25] related that it was the rise of the "station" church which led to the delegation, by the laity, of authority in the ministry to act *for* the congregation. As long as there was a circuit ministry in which the pastor was nonresident in the community and met the congregation only periodically—sometimes once a month or less often—

---

[23] *Ibid.,* p. 40.
[24] (Nashville: Abingdon Press, 1965.)
[25] (Nashville: The Methodist Publishing House, 1958.)

the major work of the local church was fulfilled through the class meeting. In such meetings there was one elected leader—presumably a "spiritual giant"—and eight to ten persons. They met weekly to "help each other work out their salvation." But as station ministries emerged —that is, as resident pastors were employed by a local congregation, and church services became an every Sunday routine—more and more responsibility for spiritual nurture was abandoned by the family. Volunteer church school teachers were assigned the responsibility of teaching Christian education, and a small group of officials were elected to carry the administrative load of the church, while the larger part of the congregation "paid the bills" and attended church with some degree of regularity.

With specialization of the ministry of the church the dilemma of the large church, the roles of the clergy and the laity have become even more confused. We are finally driven to the fundamental question, as has been stated before, *what is the church, and who are the clergy?*

This writing is based upon some firm doctrinal positions, which are, I trust, clearly articulated. If these basic principles are understood, I feel there is a basis for establishing a doctrine of the ministry in relationship with the multiple staff in the Protestant church.

Presuppositions for a Doctrine of the Multiple Ministry in the Protestant Church

1. A local Protestant congregation is composed of a group of Christian believers at worship, in nurture, and at work in the world.
2. The individual in the congregation, ordained to the Christian ministry through his baptism or confirmation, fulfills his ministry in worship, evangelism, missions, education, Christian social concerns, and stewardship. This is done through the assembled congregation in the designated place of meeting, and the dispersed congregation with individual and corporate witness in the world.
3. The congregation selects a professional leadership to assist it in performing its functions and to give direction to the congregation as it attempts to minister in worship, nurture, and work. Such professional leadership also serves as minister to the individual members of the congregation in pastoral roles.
4. The professional selected leadership of the congregation performs a direct ministry *to* the congregation in the following ways:
    a. Leadership in worship

b. Scholarly preparation for communicatively relevant preaching

c. Administration of the sacraments

d. Performance of functional roles, such as officiating at marriages and funerals

e. Pastoral services, such as ministry to the ill, aged, and indigent

f. Counseling the distressed, disturbed, and needy; advising about vocations, marriage problems, and so forth

g. Interpretation of the life of the congregation as part of a historical continuum of the People of God, who live responsibly in the light of that past in order to effect a significant future

h. Student and teacher of the fundamental doctrines of the Christian faith and their relationship with life in all its aspects

i. Spiritual counselor and guide, a hearer of confessions, a director of moral and spiritual life

j. A leader of evangelism in being, and assisting the congregation in being, a mediator of the reconciling grace of God to those who have not made a firm commitment to the Christian faith

k. A coordinator of program organization within the congregation

5. The professional leader performs *for* or *in behalf of* the congregation the following roles:

a. A spokesman for God's way with man and for moral justice on major issues in the community

b. A representative of the congregation in civic and community activities and organizations

c. A representative of the congregation in denominational meetings on regional, national, and world levels

d. Representative of the congregation in ecumenical meetings, organizations, and movements

e. On occasion the leader in certain congregational enterprises, such as special programs of evangelism, building and so forth.

6. The professional leader *is in himself:*

a. A professed Christian. As such he is a part of the universal church, his denomination, and a fellow Christian in the local congregation—"a sinner saved by grace." He expresses his faith in his conduct with his family, in his community, and in every phase of his existence. He is a part of the local congregation of Christian believers in worship, nurture, and at work in the world.

b. He is one who attempts to find fulfillment for his own talents in the fields of disciplined study, writing, lecturing, teaching, participation in various civic enterprises, church programs in his denomination and the ecumenical movement.

The discussion to this point has been primarily in consideration of the professional ministerial staff. A word must be said with regard to persons who are not professional ministers, but who are "lay workers" in the sense that they are fulfilling positions in the church that are little different from similar positions in the business world. Such persons are secretaries, hostesses, dietitians, bookkeepers, building engineers, cooks, custodians, yardmen, and others in similar positions. Persons in the above classifications are added to the church staff as needs arise for functional roles to get certain jobs done. They may or may not be members of the local church. It is conceivable, in some cases, that the person may not be a professed Christian. He is performing a task that has to be done. One must hasten to say, however, that many persons filling such functional roles become very devoted to the local church and grow to possess a sense of mission and calling in as deep a proportion as the professional staff. Many persons in such positions are the permanent members of a church staff, continuing in the position through the tenure of several senior ministers, educators, and musicians.

In summary, there are several categories of persons on the church staff. First are those whom we may call the *doctrinally ordered professionals*. These are the professional clergy who by nature of their training and their own inner direction have been recognized by the denomination to fulfill the traditional roles as administrators of the Sacraments and declarers of the Word. Ordination is essential to the office.

Second are those who are professionally trained to perform specialized ministerial roles, such as educators, musicians, counselors, administrators, and deaconesses. They may be ordained, or they may not be ordained. Ordination is incidental to the office. This group we are calling the *commissioned professionals*.

Third, those who perform functional roles are called *functionaries* and can be divided into three main groups: (1) those who perform functional roles for the congregation, such as hostesses and dietitians, (2) those who assist the professionals in fulfilling their responsibilities, such as secretaries, (3) those who perform functional roles in the upkeep and maintenance of the physical plant, such as custodians, engineers, and yard workers.

In the business world it is said, "If you can't chart it, you don't understand it." An effort is made below to illustrate the various roles and relationships of the church staff and the congregation.

The Universal Christian Church

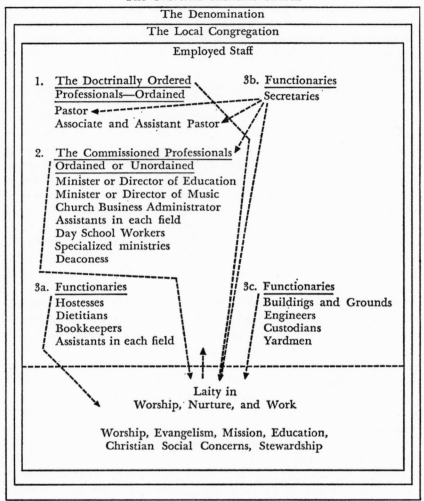

Figure 1. The outer line represents the universal Christian church. All who profess faith in God through Christ immediately become a part of the universal Christian church, sometimes called the invisible church.

The second rectangle represents an individual denomination, a visible church within the invisible church.

The third rectangle represents a local congregation within the denomination. It is divided into two sections, employed staff and the laity.

The employed staff is composed of (1) the doctrinally ordered professionals, (2) the commissioned professionals, and (3) the functionaries. All

We are now at the place where we may attempt a statement of a doctrine of the multiple ministry. Obviously, the statement is inadequate to express a concept of such dimension. It is hoped, however, that a statement can summarize the basic ideas presented above and point in a direction and lay a foundation for the basic premise of this work.

The multiple ministry is composed of persons under the call of God in the universal Christian church who are selected by a congregation or appointed by a denominational official to be its chosen leaders. It is constituted of ordained and unordained persons, both men and women. It has its mission in sharing of responsibility, of mutual concern and support of one another as it assists, directs, and participates in a local congregation of Christian believers as they assemble for worship and nurture and are dispersed for work and service in the world.[26]

---

are centered toward the one objective of assisting the laity to be the church in worship, nurture, and work through worship, evangelism, mission, education, Christian social concerns, and stewardship.

The dashed lines indicate the major thrust or direction of work.

I am indebted to James F. Gustafson for assisting in the preparation of this chart.

---

[26] Recognition is here given David A. Shipley for his careful review and insights into the formulation of this doctrinal statement.

2

Principles of Leadership

"We haven't been able to have a staff meeting for six months," a senior minister in a church of three thousand members told me. "There is so much bickering between the director of education and our minister of music that we can't get any work done in a meeting." The dilemma expressed by this honest pastor is only one of many problems of human relations faced by a multiple staff in a group, large or small. Such dilemmas demand the skill and patience of a leader in resolving basic problems. Who is responsible for problem-solving? How best is it to be done? What principles of administrative leadership must be known and applied?

In the modern church staff responsibility is placed upon the senior minister. A young minister just six years out of seminary is pastor of a church of twelve hundred members with twelve employees on the church staff. While interpersonal problems were mounting, a layman approached the senior minister, took hold of the lapel of his coat, and stated, "John, you are the administrator of this church staff. Now we expect you to perform this function well!" John was frightened by this approach. He had been called to the ministry, which for him meant preaching and conduct of worship, visiting the sick, comforting the mourning, and winning people to a loyalty to Christ. He was suddenly faced with the fact that he was a business executive, a personnel manager with a congregation and employed staff forcing him into the role. To many ministers John's dilemma is a reality, as studies on the ministry such as those done by Samuel Blizzard and Margaretta K. Bowers have revealed.[1] Ministers many times rebel, either outwardly or inwardly, against this role, resulting in frustration for themselves, their staff, and eventually poor leadership to the congregation. I am convinced there are two major reasons for such frustra-

---

[1] Blizzard, "The Parish Minister's Self-Image of His Master Role," *Pastoral Psychology*, Dec. 1958. Bowers, *Conflicts of the Clergy* (New York: Thomas Nelson, 1964.)

tion: (1) a feeling on the part of the minister that administration is *apart from,* not a *part of,* the ministry, and (2) a sense of inadequacy as to administrative procedures in performing one's work. The first reason has some validity, but as one examines the doctrine of the church and ministry and recognizes the minister is the servant of the congregation, a part of the minister's task must be to give administrative guidance to both staff and laity. Alvin J. Lindgren, in *Foundations for Purposeful Church Administration,*[2] has done a remarkable service of attempting to undergird the administrative responsibilities of the minister with theological foundations.

The second dilemma is a sense of inadequacy as to administrative procedures in performing one's work. Much of the frustration due to a lack of know-how can be overcome through study, reading, short-term courses, and listening to the laymen in the church. Laymen can teach a pastor much about personnel management and administrative procedures. A real estate agent and manager of a sizable business became one of my best teachers in an urban pastorate when I was just out of seminary. This chapter is aimed at articulating some of the basic principles of personnel management and administration as have been established in the literature aimed at the business world. There are hundreds of books and articles in the field, and all authors are not agreed. I am attempting to bring into focus basic principles of effective leadership and personnel management that I feel are applicable to the church staff. Obviously, the material is only an outline, but it is designed to give the reader basic principles on which to pursue more study and on which to develop a philosophy of leadership.

What is leadership?

In the broadest sense, leadership refers to that process whereby an individual directs, guides, influences, or controls the thoughts, feelings, or behavior of other human beings. This influence may be exerted through the medium of his works—his books, his paintings, his inventions—or it may be exerted through personal face-to-face contact. The former type is known as indirect, intellectual, or creative leadership and includes the scientists, artists, and writers whose significant products and ideas profoundly influence other men.

Direct, face-to-face leadership operates most frequently through the medium of speech.[3]

In an early work by Ordway Tead leadership is defined as "the

[2] (Nashville: Abingdon Press, 1965.)
[3] Franklin S. Haiman, *Group Leadership and Democratic Action* (Boston: Houghton Mifflin, 1951) , p. 4.

activity of influencing people to cooperate toward some goal which they come to find desirable." [4]

The same author, twenty-four years later, stated: "It is easy to say that leadership is the effort to bring others into the orbit of one's organized purposes in such a way that they are eager to share them." [5] In the same work Tead states, "Administration, primarily, is the direction of people in association to achieve some goal temporarily shared. It is the inclusive process of integrating human effort so that a desired result is obtained." [6]

One could continue with many definitions of leadership. However, basic concepts emerge in the above: (1) leadership is in a person, (2) the leader is in a group of persons who have a common interest or goal, (3) the leader's task is to bring all persons into cooperation so that the common goal may be attained.

The task of this writing is to assist members of a church staff to more clearly understand themselves as persons with a common goal and objective and how they can work together to achieve their common purpose. A staff looks to the leader. In the present day Protestant church this leader is the senior minister. How he conceives of himself as leader and how the other members of the staff accept his leadership determines to a large degree how well goals and objectives will be reached. Therefore, the leader is brought under examination.

The literature in the field of leadership is fairly well agreed that leaders may be classified into one of three categories: (1) authoritarian or autocratic leaders, sometimes called direct, (2) democratic or cooperative leaders, (3) and laissez faire leaders.[7]

The three terms—autocratic, democratic, and laissez faire—need further definition. The Oxford Dictionary definitions cast interesting light on the origin of each word. "Autocratic" comes from the root word *auto*, which means self, one's own, by oneself, independently. Autocratic means ruling by oneself "a monarch of uncontrolled authority; an absolute, irresponsible governor; one who rules with undisputed sway."

"Democracy" originates in the Greek word *demos* meaning the commons, plus *kratia* meaning rule, sway, or authority. Hence, democracy

---

[4] *The Art of Leadership* (New York: McGraw-Hill, 1935), p. 20.

[5] Ordway Tead, *Administration: Its Purpose and Performance* (New York: Harper, 1959), p. 14.

[6] *Ibid.*, p. 2.

[7] Kenneth R. Mitchell, *Psychological and Theological Relationships in the Multiple Staff Ministry* (Philadelphia: Westminster Press, 1966). See pp. 73-82 for a description of the three types of leadership.

means the common people in authority, or self-rule. The combination of words has developed to mean government by the people or "the class of people which has no hereditary or special rank or privilege; the common people." Autocracy has been linked through the centuries with a ruling class, an inherited monarchy, a privileged few who had the knowledge and right of decision with authority of office to enforce the decision. Democracy has the connotation of equality of people, hence the right of self-government.

Laissez faire is a combination of two French words: *laissez,* which is the imperative of *laisser,* meaning "to let," plus *faire,* meaning "to do." Hence, the combination of the two words literally means let do, or permit to do, or permit to be. When expanded to a society of people it means "let the people do as they please." It means, in reality, that no authority is invested in a person. No laissez faire government can survive too long. Disintegration will set in. It becomes the object for the self-appointed dictator, or will eventually emerge as a democracy with an elected leader in whom authority is vested. It must be recognized, however, that in some situations the laissez faire system seems to work. Among a group of highly trained specialists, for instance, there may be a maximum degree of self-government. Each person does his work independently. Behind such an operation it can be said there has been good democratic leadership as goals and objectives have been defined, and all persons involved are moving toward common goals.

There are some church staffs that seemingly operate on the laissez faire principle. In such cases there are no staff meetings. There is little contact of each member of the staff with other members. All are specialists doing a specialized job. It does not take much imagination to see how such an operation has been motivated by some common goal or objective. There most likely is behind the group a strong figure, usually the senior minister, who has done thorough planning, setting of goals, and has helped each person on the staff understand his own position. All types of problems may emerge in such a group. In one situation in a very large church where this type of government is in operation, one member of the staff related, "It is amazing how many informal staff meetings go on in the corridors." The senior minister is a strong authoritarian figure who is actually directing the group by one-to-one relationship. Seeds of discontent are present.

In current literature the tendency is to abandon the terms "autocratic" and "democratic." They are filled with political overtones which leave a wrong impression. The term "direct" is being substituted for autocratic or authoritarian, and the term "cooperative" is being substituted for democratic. These seem to be better terms, without misleading associations which have been developed over the centuries. In this writing the terms are being used interchangeably.

Types of Leadership

In the history of mankind the authoritarian or direct leader has served in many capacities: as parent in the home, lord of the feudal state, tribal chieftain, charismatic religious or political leader, king and emperor, military officer, and gang leader in all age groups. In the authoritarian society (using the word society to mean any social group, large or small), the power of decision is placed in the hands of one person. It is presumed that the one person knows better than anyone else in the group what is best for the group. Once the leader has made the decision, direction is then given by the leader to all persons in the group for their action to facilitate bringing the desired goal into reality. The leader may use many ways to attain this end, including physical force. The important factor is that the leader has been the *author* of the idea and decision, and the persons in the group must accept this decision without question. Presumably the leader is thought of as superior to the other persons in the group, and on the basis of his superiority the group accepts his decisions.

The democratic or cooperative leader attempts to discover through various means the desires of the group being led and to bring into focus a consensus of opinion. In other words, democracy is a process in which a group is self-governed, in which all members of the group voice their opinion in regard to final decisions. The leader of such a group becomes a coordinator, a presiding officer, a keeper of the ground rules for discussion. Theoretically, the leader is no better qualified to make decisions than the other members of the group. This makes it possible for the leadership role to be changed from time to time within the group, such as a committee which may have a revolving chairmanship. The above definition is obviously quite narrow and is stated so that a philosophy of democratic or cooperative leadership in its purest form may be seen.

With laissez faire leadership each member of the group in a society is left to make his own decision regardless of the other members of the group. Obviously, such a group can have little cohesion or common goals or objectives. Disintegration is the result. Little will be said in this writing about the laissez faire group, for such does not exist too long, and likely will not be found in the church staff. Unfortunately, however, there are senior ministers who for one reason or another fail to exercise their leadership position, and they leave members of the church staff without guidance or coordination in their common goals. No staff can hold up over a sustained period of time with this type of leadership. Common goals must be defined, group decisions must be made, individual responsibilities must be clarified if there is to be any sense of harmony as a church staff works together.[8]

Authority

One of the most confusing aspects of leadership, especially in cooperative leadership, is the matter of authority. Senior ministers attempting to practice good cooperative leadership principles often are at a loss as to how far their authority goes. Conscientiously they attempt to keep decision-making in the staff as a whole, and are frustrated over knowing when they must act as presiding officers to make executive decisions.

The problem of a sense of divine leadership is always present with the leader. The religious and sometimes the political leader often has a sense of charismatic leadership. This is Abraham feeling he must go out even though he may not know where he is going; or Moses receiving his command from God beside the burning bush; or Luther with the impulse to nail the ninety-five theses on the church door. Most ministers consciously or unconsciously feel the divine compulsion within their lives, and a sense of authority ensues. This is what H. Wheeler Robinson calls "the Authority of Revelation."

It has been sufficient to appeal to the general facts of human experience, the general testimony to a fellowship between the human spirit and the divine, however mediated. The evidence that God has so given Himself to man has been found in the fact that men have recognized Him under whatever apparent disguise, and have fully responded to the offered fellowship. In other words, the authority of the revelation has been found in its intrinsic character; the presence of God is provided by the quality of the experience. In every question of religious authority, this must always be the final court of appeal. All authority that is real is ultimately intrinsic, and all authority that is intrinsic is ultimately divine authority.[9]

---

[8] For a brief history of authoritarian and democratic leadership and a further elaboration on the subject see Haiman, *Group Leadership and Democratic Action*, chap. 2, "Authoritarianism and Democracy."

[9] Robinson, *The Christian Experience of the Holy Spirit* (New York: Harper, 1928), p. 104.

This authority must be reckoned with, and the members of church staffs are in good tradition when divine impulse leads. One must be cautious, however, to not confuse personal will with divine will as one leads fellow workers.

The traditional definition in executive authority holds to the concept of the power or right to act, and to lead others. "In management, authority can be thought of as the power to exact others to take actions considered appropriate for the achievement of a predetermined objective by the possessor of the authority. Implied authority is the power of making decisions and seeing that they are carried out." [10]

Terry defines authority in two basic categories: institutional approach and subordinate-acceptance approach.[11] Institutional authority carries with it the idea that one is supported by property and has the right to put property behind decision-making. The manager may own property, or he may have been assigned by a board of directors to handle corporate property. In either case property with its value or worth is the basis of authority. Institutional authority has been recognized for centuries in kings, government leaders, and in many sections of the church. There remains a strong tendency for institutional authority to be reflected in the hierarchy of the church, especially in episcopal or papal forms of church polity. A bishop does not own property, but he has behind him the property of congregations, buildings, and institutions. It is quite easy for such institutional value to be translated into institutional authority. Once the leader who has relied upon institutions for authority is stripped of the institution behind him, authority vanishes. A case in point is a comment made by a retired bishop when he said, "All a retired bishop is called on to do is pronounce the benediction!"

It is quite easy for a senior minister who has behind him hundreds of thousands of dollars of church property, a sizable budget, and several hundred or several thousand church members to rely upon institutions for authority.

It is true that when a minister is called or appointed to a church he is automatically granted institutional authority. How he uses this authority determines his effectiveness as a leader and how well he will be accepted by his colleagues in the staff.

Subordinate-acceptance authority (or peer-acceptance authority—a term I prefer), as thought of in personnel management literature,

---

[10] George R. Terry, *Principles of Management* (Homewood, Illinois: Richard D. Irwin, 1964), p. 357.

[11] *Ibid.*, pp. 358-59.

means that authority which is conferred upon an executive by those with whom he works. In other words, the executive has no authority until it is conferred upon him by his associates. There are moral and ethical aspects of authority involved. Peer-acceptance authority conveys the idea of the dignity of man—the sense that peers are persons skilled in their professions and have creative contributions to make to the central goals and objectives of an enterprise. Leadership, in this case, becomes highly significant, for it is dependent upon the ability of the leader to *earn* support from his peers through good personnel management practices, a respect for peers, and communicative ability.

A leader gains the confidence of peers through skill in his profession, integrity, sincerity, and genuine loyalty to the goals and objectives of the organization. This sort of authority causes each person in the staff to release his fullest potential.

The word "authority" has a number of accepted meanings ranging from autocratic or direct authority, which means the power to enforce obedience, to an influential authority, meaning the power to influence action, opinion, or belief. Authority in the latter instance means, among other things, that one's opinion is accepted because one is qualified through knowledge and experience. The term "computer authority" has been coined since 1950 and conveys the idea of the authority which is based upon massed knowledge that has been classified and tested. For our purposes the term is symbolic of the age in which we live, signifying authority gained by one who is knowledgeable in his field. The word "authority" has its root in the word author, which means an agent, that which causes growth, or to originate, to promote, or to increase. In this sense, authority is a releasing agent. It is that ability lying within a person which enables his peers to be released for greatest potential productivity.

Decision-making

Another major problem in the area of leadership is the matter of decision-making. A leadership role automatically carries with it the idea that decisions must be made. At some point discussion has to stop, a decision must be made, and action begun. Leaders, in attempting cooperative procedures, frequently are confused as to how much authority they have in making decisions. The leader may err in his responsibility by not making decisions, as well as by making too many decisions. A leadership position is a decision-making position. How

47

the leader makes decisions, or comes by his decisions, and how well he makes decisions will determine, to a large degree, how well he retains his earned leadership position.

Terry defines decision-making:

Decision making can be defined as the selection based on some criteria of one behavior alternative from two or more possible alternatives. To decide means to "cut off" or, in practical content, to come to a conclusion. As stated in Webster's, it is "the act of determining in one's own mind upon an opinion or course of action." [12]

The good leader has the skill to define the alternatives for a decision, to project the results of choosing one alternative over another, and to choose that which is best in the light of the basic objectives of the group. It is essential within the church staff that the basic goals and objectives of the staff be kept clearly in mind as decisions are made. Every decision, for instance, needs to be made in the light of the fact that the church staff is to assist the congregation in worship, nurture, and at work in the world.

In the business world it has been found that many decisions made are based upon what other businesses are doing. Competition is high. One business firm adopts a practice, other businesses soon follow with similar or "better" practices. Symbols of success are everywhere— stately buildings, neon lights, office furniture, expensive automobiles, and so on. Churches are composed of people—people who are a part of the business world—and there is much of the competitive spirit of business carried into the church. There is a tendency to adopt the same symbols of success in the church as are manifest in business— massive buildings, expensive furnishings, expensive automobiles, and so on. It takes little imagination to recognize how much congregations are other-directed rather than inner-directed. Decision-making is greatly influenced by societal pressures, and congregations, including employed staff, are constantly forced to make decisions in the light of the basic objectives of the church.

Decisions are made by individuals and groups. The skillful leader attempts to take a group through the process of decision-making whereby all persons involved have a voice. All are sincerely heard and opinions are carefully evaluated. Though there may not be universal agreement, the decision is made. Seldom is a vote taken in a small group when good cooperative leadership procedures are followed.

---

[12] *Ibid.,* p. 107.

There are times when a leader is forced to make a decision without the consultative process. Time may be a factor. Involvement in situations where secrecy is necessary may be the case. When such decisions are made, however, the leader should make clear to his peers why it was necessary to make the decision without consultation.

It may be said that *not* to make decisions at the proper time is poor leadership. Cooperative leadership does not mean that the leader does not make decisions. It means the leader attempts to gain, as far as possible, the opinions of peers, sound information, all the alternatives, and makes decisions in the light of the best alternative.

Terry lists twelve "things to remember in decision making." Without comment these are listed below.

1. *Tangibles as Well as Intangibles and Emotions as Well as Reasons are Involved in Decision Making.*
2. *Every Decision Should Result in a Contribution Toward the Goal Achievement.*
3. *You Cannot Please Everyone.*
4. *Usually There Are Several Satisfactory Choices.*
5. *Use Creative Thinking in Decision Making.*
6. *Decision Making is Mental Action: It Must Be Transferred into Physical Action.*
7. *Effective Decision Making Requires Sufficient Time.*
8. *Make the Decision—Never Default.*
9. *Realize That Change is Inevitable.*
10. *Institute Follow-up to Each Decision.*
11. *Recognize that a Decision Will Start a Chain of Action.*
12. *Practice Decision Making to Acquire Proficiency in it.*[13]

An old Danish saying summarizes a sound philosophy of decision-making: "Hear one man before you answer, several before you decide."

The Senior Minister as Leader

It is quite obvious from the limited discussion above that there is scarcely any "pure" direct or cooperative leadership. In our frame of reference—the church staff—authority is assigned by the congregation to the senior minister as the leader. His authority rests in the belief that he has been professionally trained to be the pastor of the congregation and also the director of the church staff. Some senior ministers, upon reading the above paragraph, may wince under the impact of the statement. They may take issue, holding that there is a

---

[13] *Ibid.*, pp. 122-24.

"partnership of authority" in the church staff which takes the senior minister out of the professional-director role. In the hundreds of churches that have been studied in preparation for this writing, the only situations discovered where authority was not assigned to the senior minister were in team ministries or where there was an administrator-pastor. A team ministry is a situation in which two or more pastors are elected by the congregation or appointed by the denominational official to equal positions in a local church. There are equal salaries, usually equal pupit time, and equal administrative responsibilities. After examining several team ministries by questionnaire, literature, and personal interviews, I have discovered a pure team ministry is hard to find. Age differences, salary discrepancies, and areas of responsibility emerge, causing, almost without exception, one of the ministers to be looked upon by the congregation and other members of the staff as senior in action, if not in name.

In the few churches in the study where there is an administrative pastor, or a person who fills a similar position, the senior minister is looked to for policy formulation and final decisions. He may be somewhat remote from the members of the staff, and immediate contacts for direction may be received from the administrative pastor, but the senior minister is still at the controls. If the senior minister is not looked upon as being the director of the staff, most likely the seeds of dissent have been sown which will eventually result in disharmony and breakdown of the staff. I have elaborated on the role of the senior minister to illustrate what I have discovered to be almost universally true—namely, *the congregation and church staff assign to the senior minister the leadership responsibility to be the director of the staff and congregation.* How the minister accepts the leadership role and how he performs as leader is determined by his concepts of leadership and his personality.

Cooperative Leadership

It is commonly agreed in American culture that cooperative leadership is superior to direct leadership. Confusion arises, however, as a pure democracy is hardly possible. Final decision rests in a leader or a group of leaders. Certain rights of the individual are surrendered in order that the total good can be accomplished. Basically, however, a democracy is founded upon the principle that authority rests in the members of the group. The group can delegate responsibility to persons or a person. The group can authorize a committee to function for the group and make decisions for the group. Presumably the committee will be responsible in adhering to the basic principles established by the group. If the committee fails to fulfill its responsibility in accordance with group principles, the group will then refuse to abide by the decision of the committee or send the committee back to do its work again.

One of the most important aspects of cooperative leadership that has emerged in recent years is the discovery that one of the most effective ways to achieve good relations within a small work group is to *assist the group to discover its own potentials,* individual and corporate, and to become a self-directing group. The attitude of a group leader in supporting this concept is that the solution to a problem can be found, and the potential for finding the answer lies within the group with which he works. To be more specific, there lies within the church staff the potential creative power to define problems and to solve problems. The task of the leader is to provide a climate in which the group can function for the discovery of its basic ideas and the devising of plans and procedures for putting into practice new ideas or methods of solving problems. It is not the leader providing the answer, but the group discovering the answer.

Accompanying the above concept, and to a certain degree prerequisite to its fulfillment, is the task of the leader to provide a situation in which there is a warm atmosphere of permissive freedom. Each member of the group needs to sense security and support from other members of the group so that there may be complete freedom of expression, whether the idea be good or bad. There needs to be an acceptance, on the part of all persons present, of each person in the group. The democratic leader will work toward the end of providing a climate in which this freedom is expressed. This concept is based upon the fundamental principle in a democratic society that each individual has the right of full expression. It is further based upon the idea that each individual is *valuable,* that there lies within the individual potentials which, when released and given freedom for expression, will make a contribution to the group as a whole.

The cooperative administrator will attempt to provide a situation in which each person in the group has: (1) freedom of expression, (2) opportunity for full development of talent and ability, (3) the opportunity to make a worthwhile contribution to the goals and objectives of the group, (4) and, as far as possible, complete freedom of action for the fulfillment of his own personal goals and aims in life. In the light of the above, the leader of a group becomes the director of a situation in which all participating members of the group are valuable components.

Ordway Tead has summarized the basic concepts in the following statement:

> In sum, the good leader will be known by the personalities he enriches and helps to grow. He knows, respects, and has affection for the led while aiming to enlarge their personal competence for achievement and responsibility. He will show generosity of fellow-feelings, compassion, enthusiasm, patience and persistence toward the realizing of shared purposes through the labors of others.[14]

I must pause at this juncture to make an observation in regard to two differing points of view held by senior ministers in church staffs. The first position is one which believes the senior minister is employed by the congregation to direct the total activities of the congregation. He holds, in turn, that all employed members of the staff are to help him get the work done. Several pastors in our present study stated openly and frankly in substance: "When I employ a person to serve on the staff, that person understands he is my assistant. He is to help me get my work done. If he does not want to serve on the church staff under this condition, I will not employ him. If he ceases to hold this attitude, I will let him go." This attitude sounds quite autocratic.

The second general attitude held by senior ministers is, "I am employed by the congregation to give direction to a group of co-workers who are specialists in their fields so we can work together to achieve the basic goals of the church." This attitude is more in keeping with the concepts of cooperative leadership I have attempted to outline above. This does not mean that one can categorically say Denomination One has an autocratic ministry, and Denomination Two has a democratic ministry. This is too simple. There are autocratic and democratic *persons* in every denomination, and how one performs in his leadership role is determined by how one looks upon himself, conceives of his assigned role, and his own security in that role.

A further observation from questionnaires and interviews is: The personal integrity of the senior minister is one of the most decisive factors in staff relationships. A Lutheran pastor said to me quite frankly, "I operate in our church staff with a gloved iron fist." How else could this be interpreted than as genuine autocracy? Yet, upon inter-

---

[14] Ordway Tead, "Personality in Church Administration," *The Appropriate Functions and Relationships of the Church Staff in the Protestant Church.* Copyright, Marvin T. Judy, 1964.

viewing the assistant pastor, student assistant, director of education, the business administrator who had been in the church for some thirty years and worked with three pastors, the receptionist, and two secretaries, I found without exception a sense of fulfillment, loyalty to the church, and complete support for the work of the staff in the church. I sensed an *earned* role of authority assigned to the senior minister by the other members of the staff. His authority rested in the qualities of leadership he possessed that were reflected in his preaching ability, personal integrity, supreme devotion to this task, respect which he seemed to hold for all members of the staff, his personal devotional life, his loyalty to his own family, and an almost untiring energy put into the work of the church. I came away from my interview feeling the senior minister actually overrated his "iron fist" concept of himself, and I would state instead that he possessed a sterling integrity within his whole being. This integrity was recognized by the staff and respected. In turn, the senior minister's confidence in himself, coupled with his own devotion to his work, stimulated personal confidence in each member of the staff as each one attempted to fulfill his own specific role as a part of the team.

A further observation of staff performance is that each individual in the staff needs to have freedom for his own creative work. In a cooperative society there is a degree of tension that will always exist between individual freedom and initiative and group loyalty. The skillful leader, however, will take into account the individual talents of persons in the group. In a church staff a group of people have been assembled presumably because of individual talents and professional training. The leader's task is to create a climate in which the most creative work can be done by each individual. He will see to it that time is made available and material and human resources are provided for each member of the church staff to do his work. Each member of the staff, however, will keep in mind the central purpose of the work of the staff and the basic framework in which he operates, and in turn, will not go beyond the limits of his position. In other words, each member of the staff will respect the staff objectives and stay within the bounds of the objectives with creative ideas.

Only as members of the staff sense the support of the senior minister and other members of the staff can full freedom be felt. In substance, the democratic process involves the concept of leadership, which means the leader supports the individual in the group and is able to coordinate the efforts of all persons toward the objective of the group. As is stated by the Treckers in *How to Work with Groups:*

53

"In recent years the democratic group leader has come to be thought of as helper more than doer. . . . The democratic leader must be an artist in the realm of human relationships." [15] To put it another way, "First, the democratic leader gets back of persons rather than back at persons; second, the democratic leader is always on top but never on top of persons; and third, the democratic leader exercises power with rather than power over people." [16]

Defining Objectives

Repeatedly in the above writing it has been mentioned that it is essential to have stated goals, purposes, and objectives for the church staff. In literature on public and business administration one reads only a little until one is impressed with the emphasis placed upon the central purpose of the organization. Writers on leadership constantly state that there must be a clearly defined purpose, goal, and objective of the firm which is understood by everyone in the firm, from the president to the man on the assembly line.

In interviewing members of church staffs I have found a very fuzzy concept of the central goal of the staff. In most cases the subject had not been discussed among the staff. Probably there was no felt need for articulating the purpose of the church, since presumably everyone knows what it is. But too much is taken for granted, for I have found wide discrepancy of opinion among various members of the staff. One must move into the realm of the ideal when articulating the central goal of the church, but it is good to make an effort at definition. I believe I am safe in ascribing to Ordway Tead the title of dean of administrative, democratic leadership studies. Lecturer, author, teacher, and statesman, Tead, since his first publication in 1918, has been an ardent promoter of democratic principles of leadership.

In a paper prepared for a Consultation on the Church Staff, Tead wrote concerning the basic purpose of the church and church staff. It would do an injustice to the work to attempt an abridgement or a summary. Therefore, I am quoting the entire section of his paper on purpose and goals of the church staff.

"The role of *purpose* both in the individual life and in associate efforts is a determinative one. For a worthy purpose is to be under-

---

[15] Harleigh B. Trecker and Audrey R. Trecker (New York: Association Press, 1958) , p. 6.
[16] *Ibid.,* p. 8.

stood as a unified focus upon some body of activity and attitude held to be desirable, valuable, life-fulfilling, growth-assuring. Good purposes can truly elevate and transfigure life itself out from meaninglessness into a resonance of meaning and goal which can become the essence of spirituality. The character of the person and the quality of the association of persons are largely to be judged by the purposes cherished and labored for.

"In the associated efforts of a church it may be assumed that the realizing of the personality of its communicants is a cherished purpose both because this is agreed to be humanly valuable and also because individuals are deemed to be (as we symbolically express it) children of the Most High God, who are to be summoned into action worthy of the Divine Intention and caught up into an experience of self-transcendence which has been historically phrased as "the practice of the Presence of God." Personality in this context thus means the individual's total inner resources with their resulting outer expressions which are the embodiment of a worthy and noble selfhood.

"The purpose of a church becomes, therefore, the most exalted, holy and glorious that aspiring man has sought to pursue. For it has to do, in short, with inspiring, guiding, heartening, reconciling, supporting our humankind to the summons of its own best and loftiest hopes for each self toward Godlike values, conduct, and loyalties. And these values and loyalties look always in two directions at once. They look to the growing fulfillment of a loving, wise, and responsive individual personality, and they look to the full sharing which each person gladly takes upon himself for his relations to a composite of all other persons—namely mankind—of material objects and of a transcendent All-Embracing Reality, which relations are to be instrumental in advancing a world of love and righteousness, of truth and of beauty.

"The purpose of the corporate church body, therefore, and of its employed staff associates is the cherishing of the human personality of its members toward fuller disclosure and realization of some divine mandate about the elevated quality of human living, and uniquely characterizing each and every individual.

"This means, of course, that every relation of leader and staff to the body of members has to share in an elevating, heartening, clarifying quality of mutual helpfulness. As every associated worker helps toward personality growth and fulfillment in its truest and deepest sense, the churchly purpose is being furthered. In current parlance the efficiency of the entire staff is to be measured by its quickening spark of divine purpose and hope and faith in the mind and soul of everyone touched by such relationships.

"The growth of individuals in loving helpfulness advances not only what we may call the Kingdom of God, but also those persons who give and those who receive in the realm of goodness, righteousness, and heightened awareness by each of the glory and practical efficacy of his own devoted living.

"The touchstone of good purpose on the part of the servant of the church, paid or volunteer, is some advancing of the constant conjunction of spiritual, institutional and personal ends. A church fair, for example, may be a worthwhile (albeit time-consuming) effort if the individuals involved experience it as of spiritual significance and not merely as a jolly get-together to compete with the local supermarket.

"In sum, the foundational approach to church administration is: *get right with your purposes and stay right with them in lifelong loyalty and growing insight as to how you do justice, love mercy and walk humbly with your God.* This implies and requires depth of spiritual awareness and feeling, breadth of tolerance in fraternal regard and constant penetration of thought toward strategies of effective personal and social action in the realm of the spirit." [17]

Tead clearly states that the church staff must have an objective and central purpose, that the central purpose is a noble ideal, for it has to do with the vital elements of human life, and that the central purpose needs to be at the heart of the work of the staff. He holds to the theory, *"Get right with your purposes and stay right with them in lifelong loyalties and growing insight as to how you do justice, love mercy and walk humbly with your God."* This is simply an elaboration on the exhortation of Jesus to "let your eye be single that the whole body may be full of light."

Basically Tead is saying that the individual member of the church is the important focus of the work of the church staff. All the work of the church is to come to focus on the central purpose of tapping within the individual that which is his highest potential in the light of the divine mandate about the elevated quality of human living. For the Christian the ideals established by Christ in his emphasis upon the value of persons, the love of God, the atonement for redemption, all come to focus in the work of the staff of a local church. Once a staff has come to a consensus about its task, individual members can lose themselves in their work to attempt to fulfill their service as a part

---

[17] Tead, "Personality in Church Administration."

of the corporate body. Robert Cooley Angell states, "The most basic—though not the most tangible aspect of the moral order is the set of common values that motivate the members of a society." [18]

Angell points out the human relations element of staff associations:

> Every group that is to any degree self-governing has something in the nature of a moral order. People cannot work together without overt or tacit standards of conduct corresponding to their common values. Even so intimate a group as a family, which one might suppose was unified solely by interdependence and mutual affection, has to have some moral integration. There must be concern for the family unit as an ongoing system, a willingness to take responsibility for the welfare of the whole, an understanding of what is proper conduct for family members and what is not. Without these, the unit soon ceases to be a group at all. [19]

A church staff is a primary group intimately associated in work with a common goal and objective with each member of the staff making a contribution to the total task.

At this point we can return to the doctrinal statement at the end of Chapter I to assist us in establishing the basis for the central goal and objective of the church staff. It is around such a goal and objective that the group action of staff and congregation may be developed, bringing together the basic principles of cooperative leadership.

The multiple ministry is composed of persons under the call of God in the universal Christian church who are selected by a congregation or appointed by a denominational official to be its leaders. It is constituted of ordained and unordained persons, both men and women. It has its mission in sharing of responsibility, of mutual concern and support as its members assist, direct, and participate in a local congregation of Christian believers assembled for worship and nurture, and are dispersed for work and service in the world.

---

[18] Robert Cooley Angell, *Free Society and Moral Crisis* (Ann Arbor: University of Michigan Press, 1965), p. 16.

[19] *Ibid.*, p. 9.

3

Personnel Management: Policies and Methods and the Lay Committee on Personnel

Introduction

Personnel management has become a major discipline for training in schools of business administration and a major responsibility of the business world. George R. Terry states: "Succinctly stated, *personnel management is concerned with the obtaining and the maintaining of a satisfactory and satisfied work force.*" [1] Terry goes on to say that there are three major aspects of personnel management: " (1) acquisition of competent employees, (2) holding competent employees, and (3) increasing individual productivity." [2]

In reality sound principles of personnel management are for the purpose of meeting human needs. Personal goals and beliefs of the individual members of the church staff need to be taken into consideration. The psychological needs of individuals must be recognized—security, recognition, affection, and new experiences. Personal needs need to be geared to group needs and group relationships as one considers status-role, rank, power, sanctions, and facility. (For a fuller description see page 83 of this text.) Each of these aspects of human relations is directly related to employment policies, salary arrangements, fringe benefits, personal improvements through study, a clear job description, equipment with which one does one's work, and dismissal policies.

This chapter describes, in the framework of the church staff, some of the tested methods of sound personnel management that have been developed by specialists in that field. Human needs and expectations are a part of human nature. Members of church staffs are human and

---

[1] *Principles of Management*, p. 742.
[2] *Ibid.*, p. 743.

affected by the same emotional pressures, though motivated by different self-fulfillment goals, as persons in the business and professional world. Much confusion can be avoided in church staffs if committees on personnel in local churches and senior ministers will apprise themselves of personnel management policies and rigidly apply them in employment practices with church staffs.

Employment Procedures

One of the crucial areas of personnel management is that of employment policies. The ability and type of leadership are reflected in how a congregation goes about its task of securing employees in the church. Most denominations have stated policies in regard to employment of the senior minister. In an episcopal type of government the minister is appointed by the bishop after due consultation with a representative body of laymen from the church and consultation with the minister involved. In a presbyterial type of church government responsibility rests in the local church session after proper consultation with denominational regional officials. In a congregational type of government a lay committee in the local church is responsible for finding candidates and screening and testing persons who are prospects for the pastorate. The congregation has the final vote.

Such policies are, generally speaking, not so clearly defined for the employment of other members of the church staff. Usually there is a personnel committee responsible for discovering prospective candidates for positions and submitting names, credentials, and recommendations to the proper authorized board in the local church for approval.

In many churches the senior minister has a decided influence in selecting and employing other persons for the staff. He often becomes virtually the sole voice in the process, and a local committee leaves the responsibility in his hands. Regardless of who has the responsibility for selecting and employing, democratic procedures need to be followed.

A vitally important factor in staff selection is the involvement of other employed staff members. When persons are to work together as church staff people are expected to do, they should all have a voice in selecting colleagues. This can be done with a procedure that seeks genuine participation of the existing staff.

Staff members should be consulted in regard to what kind of help is needed. A pastor or a lay committee may feel there is a need in the staff for a certain kind of office. Other staff members may feel differently. An example could be that the pastor feels a minister of youth should be added to the staff. Other members of the staff may feel that responsibility could be assumed by the existing associate pastor or the director of education, provided they could be relieved of the administrative responsibilities they are carrying. A discussion in the staff meeting could reveal that all members feel they could do more effective work in their own fields if there was a church business administrator on the staff. By mutual agreement the staff would recommend to the personnel committee that the salary they were planning to spend on a minister of youth be spent for a church business administrator.

A second consideration in employment policy is to consult existing staff for prospects to fill vacancies. Frequently persons on the staff know personally individuals who may be well qualified for an opening. Personality conflicts sometimes can be avoided if proper selection is made in this manner. Obviously the personnel committee and the senior minister must seek the best talent available regardless of names submitted by members of the staff.

Third, prospects need to be discussed openly in staff meetings. If a consensus is reached by all persons on the staff that the person being considered is a good prospect, an invitation is extended to the prospect to visit the church. This is not an invitation to become a member of the staff. It is for two purposes: (1) so the members of the staff may have the opportunity to know the candidate personally prior to employment, assuring a broader basis of judgment, and (2) so the candidate may have a chance to size up the situation by seeing the church facilities, discussing the work of the church with the persons with whom he must cast his lot should he become a member of the staff, and to talk more fully with the senior minister and personnel committee about the position and conditions of employment. Expenses for a visit to the church by the candidate (and wife or husband, as the case may be) need to be borne by the church. Expensive? Yes, but not nearly so expensive as employing the wrong person. Say a trip will cost the church $200 to $500. If they employ a person satisfactory to the staff, and if the employee is satisfied, it is money well spent. If a person is employed with little investigation and proves to be unacceptable to the members of the staff and is unhappy in his position, it may take from two to five years to make proper adjustments. If the salary is set at $5,000 per year, this means an investment of $10,000 to $25,000 in the unhappy situation.

Fourth, after the candidate has made his visit and had the opportunity to be oriented to the prospective post, the staff should then come to a consensus concerning employment. If they decide to issue an invitation, this needs to go from the entire staff to the proper personnel committee in the church. The candidate should be apprised of the fact that the invitation has been issued jointly by the personnel committee and the staff.

Such a procedure as outlined above does not guarantee complete satisfaction, for there are always hidden areas of personality problems in the individual, and hidden problems in the staff and congregation that will come to the surface only after a person has been on the staff for some time. All things being equal, however, the above procedure will reduce to a minimum the chances for a misfit coming into the staff. A climate for receptivity is established in the staff. A sense of being wanted and accepted is felt by the new person coming in. Churches and pastors willing to adopt such a policy as outlined above will maximize the possibility for a greater harmony within the employed body of the church.

When secretaries are employed, the person with whom the secretary is to work needs to have a major voice in the selecting process.

The above procedure has been handled in detail because it is one of the most important aspects of personnel management. Pastors, in their enthusiasm to fill a position, frequently will not take the time for such consultation. A good decision may be made and a person brought to the staff who fits well and performs his task efficiently. However, it will at best take time for him to win his way in the group. If he is not accepted, which is frequently the case, serious difficulties may result. It takes just one poor move on the part of the senior minister to send a tremor of uncertainty throughout the staff.

Salary Administration

It is folly to be naïve in ignoring salary as a basic factor in employment satisfaction. Service within the church is the dominant motivation in the lives of staff personel, but bills must be paid and children educated.

Literature in the field of personnel management emphasizes *fair* pay rather than *good* pay. Employee satisfaction is dependent upon whether or not one feels one has been treated fairly in the light of peers in the same general age bracket, years of service, and demands made by the job. A typical complaint is that of an assistant pastor who stated, "The janitor makes more money per hour than I do." He further stated that another assistant pastor had been added to the staff at the same salary he had been raised to. He stated he was glad the new assistant was getting this type of salary, but he felt like the chap in Matthew 20:12: "And when they had received it, they murmured against the goodman of the house, saying, These last have wrought but one hour, and thou hast made them equal unto us, which have borne the burden and heat of the day." He felt there should be a careful annual review of salaries with commensurate adjustments for service and responsibility. Incidentally, the senior minister in the same church apparently sensed no dissatisfaction on the part of the assistant. Such dissatisfaction, however, can be a "hidden agenda" eating away in the life of an employee and can be the beginning of staff disintegration.

Personnel committees and official boards of local congregations need to establish some norms for salaries commensurate with responsibility placed upon the person, time required to get the work done, educational background necessary to fill requirements of the position, and necessary skills for the work to be done. This is not an easy task. Denominations vary in the evaluation of the worth of employees. There are some differences in regional standards of living that must be considered. Inquiry into salary scales from churches of similar size and budget may give some indication of the norms for the area.

Salary is important for two reasons: what the money will actually buy, and what the money signifies or represents. Salary levels carry status symbols. This can never be overlooked if equitable adjustments are to be made.

It is helpful in the long run, though discouraging in the short run of things, to realize that salary administration is seldom done to the satisfaction of all concerned. Disappointment and frustration about one's salary is highly likely. It helps, however, if the parties involved know salaries have been discussed in a committee taking into consideration all budgetary items of the church. A periodic review of salaries is essential, and there needs to be annually a consultation with all staff persons individually in regard to salary and other remunerations.

All administrators must help members of the church staff derive other remunerations than pay from their positions. A strong sense of identification with the goals of the church staff often goes far to cause one to overlook what he considers to be an injustice in pay, and leave the individual a more efficient employee and basically a better person. Many church staffs feel this loyalty and central objective so strongly that it is unfashionable for them to discuss salaries among themselves. Staff members, especially church secretaries, have indicated repeatedly that they feel decidedly underpaid but fully compensated in satisfaction because of the nature of their work, satisfaction with their staff arrangements, loyalty to the church and its central purpose, or congenialty of the person to whom they are immediately amenable.

In our study it has been discovered that churches of 700 to 2,000 members with budgets ranging from $60,000 to $200,000 will spend 28 percent to 33 percent of the total operating budget on staff salaries. Table 1 lists the percent of the amount paid to the senior minister that is paid for other positions on the staff. Actual salaries are not given because of the constant change due to the fluctuation of the economy.

Table 1. Percent of senior minister's salary that is paid to persons on the church staff in congregations of 700 to 2,000 members, with budgets of $60,000 to $200,000.

Position on the church staff	Percent of senior minister's salary
Senior Minister	100.0
1st Associate Minister	66.3
2nd Associate Minister	45.9
3rd Associate Minister	40.8
Director of Education	59.1
2nd Educator	41.8
3rd Educator	30.6
Director of Day School	34.6
Day School Teacher	30.6
Musician	37.7
2nd Musician	21.4
3rd Musician	23.9
Business Administrator	55.9
Financial Secretary	25.5
1st Secretary	35.7
2nd Secretary	30.6
3rd Secretary	28.5
4th Secretary	27.5
1st Buildings and Grounds Employee	36.2
2nd Buildings and Grounds Employee	29.5
3rd Buildings and Grounds Employee	27.5
1st Food Service Employee	26.5
2nd Food Service Employee	24.4
Hostess	27.5

Travel Expense

One of the largest items in a family budget is automobile and travel expenses. The purchase of a car, insurance, and normal upkeep of an automobile can take a large sum from routine living expenses, education, personal insurance, and retirement security.

Good personnel management provides for all the travel expenses of all members of the church staff who are required to travel on church business. Church business includes pastoral calling in homes, hospitals, and other institutions; funerals, regional and national meetings; professional meetings; short-term schooling; and any other church business.

It has been found in our study that generally the senior minister and the associate minister receive adequate travel allowances; but other members of the staff do not, in many cases, receive proper consideration. A review of the situation by the proper church officials could lead to the correction of inequities. A careful record of travel needs to be kept by each party for church records and for personal income tax purposes.

Office

An adequate office is essential for good work. Offices for staff personnel need to be well lighted, ventilated, heated in winter and cooled in the summer. Each member of the staff needs to be consulted as to his personal desires for equipment, shelving, cabinet space, filing cabinets, and other needs.

Office arrangement is important. There is a flow of work to be done and a movement of persons through offices. In the first place, a person going to a church for any type of business or personal need should be provided with directions to the church offices. Well constructed and attractive signs giving directions to the church offices need to be in numerous conspicuous places outside and inside the church buildings. This item cannot be emphasized too strongly. In my interviewing in more than one hundred churches across the country I was plagued in more than one-half of the situations by difficulty in finding the church offices. In some cases I tried as many as six locked doors before finding an open door leading to church offices! The timid soul seeking religious nurture would have given up in despair.

A directory for church offices needs to be in a conspicuous, well-lighted, and attractive space. The directory should have the name of the person, the office title, building, and room number. In a large building, an attractive well lighted diagram of the buildings and floor plan should be placed by the directory.

In the reception room there needs to be a desk marked "Information." One of the church secretaries should be at the desk during regular office hours. Her work can be coupled with answering the telephone, typing, and keeping records. She needs to be well-informed regarding the work of the church and the various persons on the staff so that she can answer questions without hesitation, accurately, and pleasantly. We can learn from the business world in regard to the importance of the reception room and office arrangements.

The reception room serves not only to promote efficiency in office operation but also as an advertising medium of the firm and its products or services. It is therefore important that this room be well arranged and kept orderly, for the visitor gets his first impression of the business when he steps into the reception room. The room should express honesty, reliability, and efficiency. It is the introductory chapter to the biography of the business.[3]

Each member of the professional staff needs to be provided with a private office. One of the chief objections to physical arrangements of offices by church staffs is that they are too far apart or too far from their place of normal operation. Secretaries need to have their space arranged so that there is a normal flow of work to them from professional staff, and on to duplicating room, mail room, or equipment rooms. The problem of adequate office space and arrangement is a major factor in old church buildings. Remodeling, however, or the erecting of new buildings can provide the facilities for more adequate office space and arrangements. Architects are generally able to assist with office arrangements. Neuner and Keeling in *Administrative Office Managmeent* devote considerable space to the various aspects of office arrangements, sizes, furniture, and equipment.[4]

Equipment

Adequate personnel management provides for adequate equipment for staff to do their work. Many church secretaries, for instance, report they are required to use antiquated typewriters, dictating machines, and duplicating equipment. Financial secretaries report, in some cases,

---

[3] John J. W. Neuner and B. Lewis Keeling, *Administrative Office Management*, 5th ed. (Cincinnati: South-Western Publishing Co., 1966), p. 173.
[4] *Ibid.*, chap. 7, "Office Planning and Layout."

inadequate or outdated filing systems, adding machines, and ledger systems. Maintenance of office equipment is essential if valuable time is not to be lost or poor work produced.

Church musicians state in numerous cases that they have inadequate practice rooms, choir robes, lack of funds to purchase new music, and poor musical instruments. Frequent tuning of pianos and pipe organs, as well as proper upkeep of such instruments, will assist the total music program of the church.[5]

Visual aid equipment, film library, book library, classroom fixtures, and other equipment are essential for an adequate educational program in the church.

Committees on personnel need to make periodic inquiries of the church staff surveying the equipment needs in the light of new equipment on the market and efficient operation of the church staff. The size of the congregation and specialized positions on the church staff vary so much that no specific directive can be given in this writing.

Housing

Housing arrangements for members of the church staff vary greatly by denominations and regions. As a general rule the senior minister is provided with a church-owned residence free of rent. Other members of the professional staff may be provided with a church-owned house, have a rent allowance, or be expected to provide their own housing out of their salary.

No argument is made at this point for one method or another. Some denominations have serious studies underway, at least regionally, to examine what is the most suitable policy. The point that needs to be made clear is: Whatever plan a church has, the plan needs to provide for all professional staff on an equitable basis. By this is meant, a fair practice needs to be considered which will not discriminate against one or more members of the staff. Serious internal problems in the staff can result from too wide a margin in kind of housing—that is, the quality of the housing—between members of the staff.

There seems to be a feeling on the part of many ministers and other professional church staff persons that they prefer to provide their own housing and receive a rent allowance or consideration in the cash salary. Such an arrangement has the advantage of making it possible for

---

[5] A rule of thumb is to set aside annually an amount of money equal to 1 percent of the value of the musical instrument for maintenance and tuning.

staff personnel to have the type of housing that is to their own liking, and at the same time to develop an equity in property as a personal investment. Many professional church workers come to retirement without a real estate equity and find it a decided hardship.

Ordained clergy are granted by law a housing allowance which is income-tax free, or a parsonage or manse. Non-ordained church staff do not have this consideration. Ordained clergy do not have to report their house, if a parsonage or manse is furnished, as income. It is not necessary to report a cash allowance for housing as income, but careful records need to be kept showing cost of housing in the event it is called for by tax investigators. If one owns his own home he may consider the cost of housing—payments, interest, insurance, taxes, utilities, telephone, and upkeep.

Retirement Benefits

Some form of retirement benefit is essential in our modern workaday world. Social Security has become a national responsibility. Most denominations have some form of retirement plan for the ordained clergy. Such plans vary greatly, but usually consist of investments made by the local congregation, or the pastor, or both. An equity is established, based upon years of service. In many congregations the retirement benefits are extended to other members of the staff, but too often persons other than ministerial members of the staff are not included. Social Security benefits for employees of churches are optional with the church. Ordained clergy must be classified as "self-employed," but all other employees have the right to come under Social Security and share the expense.

A number of denominations have provision in their pension plans for persons other than ordained clergy to enter into the retirement plan. Senior ministers and personnel committees in the local church should investigate the plans available in their denominations. It is necessary for a church to apply for participation in denominational plans for non-ordained personnel.

The Job Description

Debate is constantly going on between personnel specialists in regard to job descriptions. Some executives feel they are too binding and hamper the employee, while others feel if they define work areas they insure more efficient operation. In personal interviews with senior ministers and in examining hundreds of questionnaires prepared by church staff persons I have come to the following firm opinions:

1. A job description is necessary for clarifying the role of an individual on the staff.
2. A job description needs to be reviewed annually and revised in the light of a person's abilities, talents, desires, changing situations, and needs of the staff and congregation.
3. A job description should never be so rigid that it becomes a binding rather than releasing instrument.
4. All members of the staff need to understand the position of other members of the staff.
5. The congregation ought to have in printed form a brief statement of positions and functional responsibilities of each member of the staff. This is not a detailed job description, but a forthright statement of responsibilities. Many times church members are not aware of responsibilities of specialists in the staff and put an undue burden upon the senior minister.

In some cases the job description becomes a formal contract. In other cases it is a working agreement. Some senior ministers will outline with staff members orally their responsibilities. This may be sufficient. However, I am convinced that many problems would be avoided if more definite understandings were stated and agreed upon. Communications is one of the major problems in staff relations, and verbal agreements are frequently not understood to be the same thing by two parties who hear identical words.

A job description should include:

1. Statement of title of the position
2. Lines of responsibility, i.e., to whom the party is responsible for reporting, advice, guidance, complaints, or requests
3. A statement of duties or areas of responsibility
4. Schedule of work time
5. Vacation periods, days off, and holidays observed
6. Salary, retirement benefits, expense account, and other considerations
7. Opportunities for self-improvement
8. Advancements

A description may be drawn up in formal fashion and signed by employer and employee. It may be in the form of a letter from the senior minister or the secretary of the personnel committee. If there is no such agreement, the member of the staff may save considerable trouble and embarrassment if he will, after verbal agreement, write a letter addressed to the proper authority in which he states: "This is the conversation I understood. . . ." Then he prepares a job description closing with a statement: "If I am not correct, please advise me on any point."

Positive understandings by both employee, including the senior minister, and the personnel committee is of vital importance. Congregations are, as a general rule, quite trusting of church staffs to use their time wisely. There is generally a feeling on the part of the congregation that staffs are overworked and deserve much latitude in planning work schedules. Night meetings make for long hours. All-day Sunday activities should be compensated for by a day free from church responsibilities during the week. Members of church staffs, especially ministerial members, may abuse the privilege of freedom causing internal dissension in the staff and eventually within the church membership. Pastors need to be careful not to take too many liberties.

Samples of job descriptions for each major position on the church staff can be found in Appendix B.

If no job descriptions have been made by members of the church staff, a good beginning is to have each member of the staff draw up his own job analysis. This should be reviewed by the senior minister and personnel committee, and revised in the light of other positions on the staff. In no case should arbitrary, hard and fast lines be drawn. Flexibility should always exist. The work of a church must get done—and if one person fails to carry his load, others must pick it up. Clarity of position and responsibility will assist in minimizing many problems.

Some brief statement needs to be circulated to the congregation which will state to the congregation who the members of the staff are and their various positions. Such a statement can clarify responsibilities and assist in distributing work load of the staff and make for a more efficient use of the staff.

In Appendix B there will be found a reproduction of a brochure used by one church for the purpose of informing the congregation of staff personnel and responsibilities.

Compensations and Personnel Policies

Sabbaticals and Study Leaves

The fields of investigation and knowledge in relationship with the church and ministry are moving at such a pace that it is impossible for a person to keep abreast of literature in his field. The busy pastor, educator, and counselor on the church staff has to be extraordinarily disciplined to simply read the periodicals from his denomination and professional field and a few current books. Everyone in the professions must have time off from responsibilities for refreshing his mind and catching up with current thought in his field.

The congregation is the ultimate recipient of the benefits of study and in-service training schools for professional members of the church staff. Most denominations periodically have regional or national training schools or lectureships for professional churchmen. There needs to be a provision for persons to attend such schools with their expenses paid.

Seminaries of all major denominations across America are providing continuing education for ministers. The format for such work may be (1) prescribed reading under the direction of a member of the faculty of the seminary, (2) extension schools where a seminary professor will conduct a class or seminar for a group of pastors in a region, with the professor traveling out to meet the class over a stated period of time, (3) short-term courses, usually one to three weeks, conducted on the campus of the seminary.

Pastors and educators ought to have the privilege of an extended leave after serving in a church for three to six years. The sabbatical leave is a part of most college and university programs designed for professors to have time off for study and travel. The usual pattern is for a professor to have a one-semester leave after three years of service, or a full year's leave after six years of service. Usually full salary is granted for the leave, or a stated proportional share of salary. It is more difficult for a congregation to arrange such leaves for the professional people on the staff, but some equitable program should be designed for study leaves.

Vacations

The annual vacation in the workaday world is a part of American culture. All members of the church staff should receive annually some stated time free for vacation with pay. Amount of time must be agreed upon, and the length of time one has served in the church should receive some recognition by lengthening the vacation time.

Advancements

Few congregations provide a specific schedule of advancements for members of the church staff. Committees on personnel need to study advancement schedules in the business and professional fields and provide similar compensations for persons employed in the church.

On the average, pastor's salaries have been advancing at the rate of approximately 5 percent per year. Salaries of other members of the staff have not been in quite the same proportion. Salaries of persons in comparable fields in business have advanced 8 percent per year.

Questionnaires from members of church staffs reveal there are very few congregations that have any plan for salary advancement. All positions in the employed personnel in the church need to be reviewed annually with compensation advances in accordance with years of service, responsibilities of the position, and comparable positions in businesses within the community.

Tenure

Tenure is a subject that is almost wholly ignored by local congregations. Tenure, in the legal sense, means "the right of holding." In regard to positions tenure means the right of retaining a position. Tenure in academic faculties of colleges and universities has been established for many years. It is, as a general rule, granted to a professor after he has served on a faculty for three years and has demonstrated his competence in his chosen discipline, has performed well as a teacher, has shown scholarly potentials, and has been an edifying member of the faculty community. Tenure for a faculty member means that once granted, the appointment is permanent if the person continues to be competent and moral in character.

In the church staff the senior minister usually enjoys a certain degree of security in his position. Denominations differ in policy, but the fact that senior ministers in multi-staff churches have a record of long pastorates is an indication of security if not tenure.

Other members of the staff do not fare so well. Short terms in office and rapid turnover are an indication of unsettledness. More stability in the staff would be established if some type of assurance were given to the members that they could remain in their position for an indefinite time. Original contracts could be written for a two- or three-year period with an understanding that there would be a review of the position at the end of the stated time.

One of the vexing problems of church staffs comes at the time of a change of senior ministers. Some denominations have a stated policy that when a senior minister resigns, all professional staff members must submit resignations. The theory is that the incoming senior

71

minister should have the privilege of selecting, or having a major voice in selecting, his co-workers. There is merit in the policy, though a complete change in the staff may be quite disruptive to the church. Also, this policy causes uncertainty among staff. Obviously this is the easy way out, and makes for the least amount of trouble for committees on personnel.

Experimentation needs to be done with some form of tenure for the church staff. A model is suggested for consideration and experimentation:

1. Original contracts will be written for a three-year period with a review at the end of three years, at which time the party employed and the employer can terminate the contract or rewrite the contract.

2. After three years, if both parties are satisfied, a contract will be written for an indefinite period terminated on the basis of: desire of the employee, desire of the employer on the basis of incompetence or immorality of the employee.

3. Upon the changing of the senior minister the other staff will have the privilege of remaining in the employment of the church for a period of one year. At the end of that year the contract will be reviewed with the privilege of not renewing by the church, or rewriting the contract on the same basis as Number 2 above, i.e., for an indefinite period.

Dismissal Policies

One of the most difficult phases of staff relationships is dismissing a person from the staff. Many ministers and lay committee members have stated how disagreeable it is, and how inadequate they feel in dismissing a person from the church staff. There is no way to make this task easy. Literature in personnel management states simply that a personal confrontation by employer with the employed is essential with the facts brought out that the employees' services are no longer needed.

In church circles there are two factors that are not in the business world. In the first place the employee may be a member of the local congregation. The matter of dismissal may become a matter of congregational involvement in which members take sides, and can even lead to a major disruption in the church. In the second place, the church as a redeeming institution has built into it the idea of another chance and grace. When these elements go out of the church it has lost its *raison d'être*. The work of the church, however, does need to go on in the most efficient manner possible, and when effectiveness of the work of the church is curtailed by ineffective leadership the good of the whole must be placed uppermost. It is not right for a congregation to be hampered in work due to an ineffective leader.

In the written statement of employment policies of a local church, there needs to be a section on termination of employment. The statement can include a time factor which states a period of time for notice to be given before termination of employment. The time will vary from two weeks to three months depending upon the position in the church. Back vacation time should be considered in terminating compensation.

I have attempted to set out the basic considerations concerning employment policies, salaries, compensations, and other considerations that must be considered by personnel committees in a local church. Much confusion can be avoided if the local church committee responsible for employment will think through policies and write them out in full. Such policies become a guide for the committee and will assist the employee in an understanding of his position as he becomes a part of the staff.

In Appendix B will be found an example of a statement of personnel policies for one church.

The Lay Committee on Personnel in the Local Church

In a chance encounter with a minister approaching middle age, I discovered he was enrolled in seminary. Graduation from seminary had been fifteen years ago. He was in the first year of his pastorate in a young congregation that had been organized for twelve years and under the ministry of an aggressive, capable pastor. There was probably more realism in his statement to me than may have appeared on the surface, "I'm back taking systematics [systematic theology]. My congregation says my theology needs toning up." There was a spirit of adventure in the minister's eye. There was no sense of resentment on his part that the congregation was encouraging him to take a fresh look at systematic theology. What a healthy situation! The theme of this book is that the laity is the church, and the employed staff is to assist the laity to be the church in worship, nurture, and at work in the world. Lay responsibility is toward the needs of the staff as much as staff responsibility is toward the needs of the congregation.

To formalize lay responsibilities to the staff, specific committees need to be selected to facilitate a process for development of good relationships between the staff and congregation.

Within the local church there usually will be some design for a lay committee on personnel. Many titles are given to the committee, and the duties and responsibilities of the committee will be defined in different ways from denomination to denomination and church to church. Generally speaking, the committee has the responsibility for assisting in the selection of the staff of the local church and a general responsibility for maintenance of the staff as persons come and go.

In our research on the multiple church staff it has been discovered that there is a wide discrepancy as to the use of lay persons for selecting the staff, and the relationship of the lay committee and the employed staff. As a rule denominations with a congregational or presbyterial form of church government will have more active lay participation and lay committees than denominations with an episcopal form of church polity. There is no attempt in this chapter to write a denominational policy on the lay personnel committee. That responsibility rests with the denominational legislative bodies. This writing is for the purpose of lifting up the areas of lay responsibility that may be of greatest benefit to the local church through increasing good staff relationships within the staff, and good relationships between the staff and congregation.

Employment Policies

It is important that the lay committee have a voice in the selecting of all members of the church staff. Generally, even in the episcopal type churches, lay committees do have a voice in the selecting of the senior minister. In many cases, the selecting of the other members of the staff is left almost entirely to the senior minister. He does need to have a major place in selecting staff, but the lay committee on personnel should not put the entire responsibility upon him.

Periodically the committee, along with the staff, needs to survey the needs of the church in regard to leadership needs. The needs of a congregation change from time to time with the aging of the congregation, a shifting of age groups within the congregation, population changes in the community in which the church is located, and moving patterns of members of the congregation. A church may, for instance, need at one stage in its history a strong youth program requiring the full-time services of a minister of youth. At another stage in history the same church may require a minister of visitation to the aging membership.

As a church grows in size there may be the need to add a full-time church business administrator to the staff. A rule of thumb is to add such a person when the congregation reaches 1,000 members or a budget of $100,000.

More secretaries may be needed. A survey of the secretarial workload, and how much secretarial work the professional staff members have to do may reveal it would be a wise expenditure of funds to employ a typist, bookkeeper, membership secretary, or general secretary.

The burden of this writing is that the lay committee on personnel has a major responsibility to discover and keep abreast of the needs of the congregation for staff personnel in the various categories of positions. The committee should also assist in the selecting of such persons.

The committee can provide the staff with a detailed directive of employment policies within the church. Such policies should include: employment practices, salary arrangements, fringe benefits including pensions, health insurance and vacation time, sick leave, office and travel expense, housing arrangements, lines of authority, and dismissal policies. (See Appendix B for a sample of a church policy for staff employment.) A policy can be developed by a committee in consultation with the church staff. In most urban congregations there will be one or more persons who are in the field of personnel in some secular business. Professionally trained persons are acquainted with standard procedures in the business world and can be of value to a committee as they work through policy formulation.

One thing that remains to be developed is a method or process by which the work of a staff is evaluated. Standards are set in the business and industrial world with specific ways of measuring a worker's effectiveness. If the worker falls below the expectations a personnel manager soon investigates to discover the reason. Within the church staff it is much more difficult to evaluate one's work. The work of ministry is diverse and varied. There is always the intangible, which cannot be measured as one can measure the number and volume of sales of automobiles or insurance or the number of pieces of an article produced on the assembly line.

A lay committee can, however, be sensitive to the needs of a congregation and be aware of how well the staff is meeting the needs. There will always be some persons in the congregation who feel their needs are neglected, and a committee can be sensitive to the difference between a perpetual complaint and a genuine need. From time to time the lay committee needs to meet with the various members of the church staff to share mutual needs of congregation and staff. Much difficulty may be avoided if the lay committee will take seriously its task of evaluating the work of the staff and apprise members of the staff on how well they are fulfilling their particular ministry in the congregation.

The primary aim of the personnel committee is to assist in making the work of the employed staff more effective in the life and work of the congregation.

Salary Arrangements

Few members of the employed church staff will make an aggressive effort to seek an increase in salary even though there may be actual need. One of the major functions of a personnel committee is to review periodically the financial structure of staff salaries and other remunerations.

In our study on the multiple ministry, salary arrangements were one of the chief complaints of members of the employed staff. In most cases the senior minister's salary was felt to be about right, but other staff persons, in numerous cases, were quite unhappy with their salary. As has been stated earlier, staff morale will be maintained on the basis of *fair* pay more than on the basis of just *good* pay. Fair pay is measured in two ways: (1) by a standard of salaries by positions in comparable fields in the business and professional world, and (2) by comparing salaries within the local church staff itself.

It is generally recognized that with responsibility there should be financial remuneration in direct proportion. In the church staff this means that as there is added responsibility to one's position there should be compensation to match the responsibility. A second area of recognized discrepancy in salary scales is in regard to training. The more academic preparation, the more one needs to be compensated. A third factor is years of service and experience. The longer one is in his position, the more efficient he will become. The amount of time one puts into his working day is a fourth factor to consider in salary scales. Personnel committees need to review periodically the salaries of all employees of the church.

Staff Study and Personal Enrichment

An annual inventory needs to be made by the lay committee on personnel in regard to staff in-service training. The professional staff members, especially, need to be encouraged to enter into some type of continuing education in their respective fields annually. Ministers need to be in pastor's schools, engage in a continuing education program from one of the seminaries, participate in lectureships, or do meaningful travel. Christian educators and musicians need to attend schools in their disciplines. Church business administrators need the association of persons in their own field. Secretaries need refresher courses and specialized training, such as in the use of office machines and the telephone.

Schooling and travel are expensive. Time spent in such activities should not be charged against regular vacation time. The lay committee on personnel needs to make provision for such training with proper financial remuneration. From the point of view of the congregation, additional training of the staff usually insures a fresh approach by the staff to their tasks and a better working congregation.

Very few congregations provide their professional staff with sabbatical leaves for study. Lay committees on personnel need to examine the practice and take it under consideration. A sabbatical leave is a provision whereby members of the professional staff can have the privilege of an extended period of time away from church responsibilities for study, travel, and personal enrichment. The time can be arranged in personal counsel with the staff so that the least disruption to the church will ensue. In some cases it may be necessary for the church to employ on a short-term basis a person to fill the place of the absent member of the staff. Some denominations have a pool of available ministers for pulpit supply and interim ministries. A retired minister, musician, or educator may be available for help. At any rate, the lay committee on personnel needs to take into account the sabbatical leave. Sabbatical leaves need to be arranged so that the staff may have several options. For instance, the committee could offer a plan whereby a person who has been on the staff for three years may have three to six months leave, and this type of leave could be repeated after each three years. A full year could be taken after the staff person has been employed for six years, and this plan would be available each six years. Full salary should be paid during the leave, and through private contributions or an allocation from the church budget, the staff person should receive additional funds to assist with additional expenses such as housing, travel, or tuition and fees in a university.

In addition to the suggestions above for the educational and personal enrichment of persons on the professional staff, the lay committee on personnel can make an outstanding contribution to the entire congregation if they see to it that each member of the professional staff has a stated time in his work schedule for study. If we are true to the basic premise on which this book has been written, namely, that the employed professional staff in a local congregation is to direct and lead a congregation in worship, nurture, and work in the world—we need to recognize the necessity of providing time for the professional to keep abreast with new knowledge in his respective field. One of the chief complaints of laymen is that their minister is not fresh in his preaching, or when the associate pastor preaches he is dull, or the program of education in the church is poor. To illustrate what is meant by this, and to point up some of the problems, an actual experience is related below.

In the midst of a rather serious disruption in staff leadership in a local church, the chairman of the lay committee on personnel remarked to me that the pastor was not producing the kind of sermons that were best for the congregation. I said in substance to the layman, "The congregation has employed this man to be first a preacher. You expect him to be a scholar producing refined, enlightening, and inspiring sermons. But the congregation has placed upon him such heavy administrative responsibilities that he has had to neglect his study and personal enrichment practices. Now when the thing you have employed him to do does not measure up, you feel neglected and disappointed."

Laymen can be of yeoman service to the congregation and to the staff in making it possible for the congregation to understand that a part of the ministry of the professional staff is regular study each day, periodic short-term in-service training schools, workshops, lectures, travel, and less frequent prolonged periods of study, such as can be provided by a sabbatical leave.

Interpreting the Work of the Staff to the Congregation

A major task of the lay committee on personnel is in the field of interpreting the work of the employed staff to the congregation.

Unfortunately, in many instances, the members of the congregation do not think of a total staff being this *ministry*, but only of the senior minister being their *minister*. They look to him not only for leading worship, but for every type of ministry including counseling, visitation, education, and all phases of administration. The latter— administration—means decision-making in regard to every detail of the church, including building upkeep, use, organizational patterns, and hundreds of other items.

The lay committee on personnel needs to make a study of job analyses of the members of the staff and understand what the responsibilities of each member are. This information, in turn, needs to be interpreted for and to the congregation. Some suggestions as to actual procedure in getting this work done are made below.

1. Prepare a brochure for distribution to the membership of the church that has in it a description of the work of each member of the staff. The brochure need not be long, but should be concise in its statements. It can have a picture of each member of the staff. There can be a statement regarding the way the congregation can call upon each person for services. The brochure needs to contain the names of each person on the staff, including professional persons, secretaries, hostesses, dietitians, day school workers, and building and grounds persons. In the very large staff it may be necessary to make separate brochures listing professional staff members in one brochure and other staff members in another. (A sample can be found in Appendix B.)

2. Frequent articles in the church publications can be of great help. The work of each member of the staff can be featured in the article explaining in some detail the specialized ministry and how it can best be made available to the congregation.

3. On occasion the members of the staff can be asked to interpret their particular work to the official board or similar body in the local church. Board members can, in turn, be asked to help interpret the work of the staff to other members of the church.

4. It is not out of place for a few minutes to be taken in a regular Sunday morning service of worship to interpret to the congregation the work of the various members of the staff. This can be done with proper decorum without destroying the spirit of worship if properly spaced and timed. The congregation in worship is the only time in the life of the church when all persons in the membership are represented.

Summary

In summary, the work of the lay committee on personnel in the local church has a very important task to fulfill. It serves as a body to establish policies in regard to employment, effectiveness, and dismissal of the employment staff. It serves as the sounding board for the congregation and staff in regard to effective work. It is a means of providing for the physical needs of the staff, including salary arrangements, fringe benefits, travel and operational expenses, and housing considerations. It assists the congregation in providing the necessary time and means for staff members to engage in personal growth and enrichment. It is the means of interpreting the work of the staff to the congregation so that staff personnel can be of greatest service to the members of the congregation in their own fulfillment of their lives as a part of the church in worship, nurture, and work in the world.

4

The Staff Member: An Individual in a Group

A church secretary stated, "I wish the church secretary would receive a little recognition other than when she makes a mistake on the Sunday bulletin!" The statement when first read is amusing, but upon second thought it is recognized as an expression of one of the deepest of human needs—namely, the desire for recognition for work well done.

When the subject of human relatons is approached we are thinking of the individual in a group. We are attempting to discover what a group is internally and how a group can be the means of releasing the individual to do his best work, and what, on the other hand, causes some groups to be thwarting agents. Literature based upon good research is in agreement that all persons want to have a sense of personal dignity, the esteem of others, the basic necessities of life, a sense of security for survival in the declining years of life, and the feeling of being a part of a group within one or more social environments.

If, as Christians, we accept the brotherhood of man under God, there are several important conclusions: each person has an inner dignity with basic human and divine rights, but also fundamental duties and responsibilities; life has meaning and an overall purpose; conduct must be judged not just in the light of personal gain or convenience, but also as right or wrong; service becomes central; working with others offers a fuller means of service.

The struggle for individual freedom is often brought into conflict as the individual is forced to work with others. One person's freedom stops where another person's freedom begins. One often feels hemmed in, cut off, isolated, thwarted in achieving one's individual objectives in life. The rugged individual soon becomes a lost entity in the mesh of a complicated society. The church staff is composed of individuals who, in addition to a sense of divine guidance, have all the human emotions and personal drives and desires of all other persons. As a group of people work together in a staff it is inevitable that conflicts will emerge. The staff can profit greatly by understanding some of the fundamentals of human relations. A church staff is an aggregate of individuals who are brought together to achieve certain objectives in leading and being a part of a Christian congregation. How well the staff functions as a group and at the same time how well the atmosphere exists for individual fulfillment of personal needs will determine the effectiveness of staff operations. Extensive studies in human relations have clearly shown that the failure to get along with one's associates is the primary cause for losing or leaving a position, rather than a lack of knowledge of technical or professional skills. On the other hand, when creative ideas of one member of the work group are not accepted by the leader or peers frustration results. In some instances the individual must pit himself against the group for fulfillment of his felt leadership, and in other cases he will either withdraw from group participation, or at the earliest convenience accept another position.

If the individual feels one or more persons in the staff is hampering his freedom, or if the structure is such that his personal objectives are unattainable, anxiety and frustration result. All persons have experienced the deep pain of unfulfilled dreams, of frustrated ideas, of personal conflict that has resulted in loss of status, position, or personal worth. Camilla Anderson states, "Stress is experienced by people who feel required to operate either above or below their level of capacity, whether intellectually, sexually, or physically. Stress is felt by those who have figuratively to walk on tiptoe, and it is also felt by those who are not permitted to stand up straight." [1] Staff structure and relationships make possible either the release of the individual or the curtailment of the individual. Throughout this work we are attempting to speak to the problems of human relations and how, through good leadership practices and an understanding of persons working with a group structure, maximum release for each person can be attained.

In their extensive work *Group Dynamics*, Cartwright and Zander hold that the most determinant aspects of group effectiveness could be summarized under one or more of six main headings:

1. the extent to which a clear goal is present
2. the degree to which the group goal mobilizes energies of group members behind group activities

---

[1] Anderson, *Beyond Freud* (New York: Harper, 1957), p. 126.

3. the degree to which there is conflict among members concerning which one of several possible goals should control the activities of the group
4. the degree to which there is conflict among members concerning means that the group should employ in reaching its goals
5. the degree to which the activities of different members are coordinated in a manner required by the group's tasks
6. the availability to the group of needed resources, whether they be economic, material, legal, intellectual, or other.[2]

The study of human relations has achieved scientific proportions. Research, testing, retesting, and further research have resulted in uncovering fundamental aspects of human relations. The church staff may profit greatly by an understanding of some of the basic findings of studies by social scientists. Only a few of the basic principles of human relations can be discussed in this chapter, but they can serve as a beginning for further study. An extensive bibliography is given at the conclusion of this work for further investigation.

The Staff as a Social System

The term social system is used in sociology to designate a definable group of persons who are within an orbit of interpersonal relationships. Such a system may be as small as one family or as large as a nation. All persons are a part of a number of social systems. Loyalties within the various systems will vary and inevitably conflict. The church staff is a social system with all the definable characteristics of the social system. It may be of help in self-understanding to examine the social system and to apply the basic elements to the church staff.

The eminent sociologist Charles P. Loomis holds there are nine basic elements in the social system.[3] He would suggest that wherever there is a group of people who are in an orbit of interaction these elements will emerge. The nine elements are: belief; sentiment; goal, end, or objective; norm; status-role; rank; power; sanction; and facility. A brief description and further definition of each element is given below with considerable liberty taken for further explanation.

1. *Belief.* Loomis holds that belief is "any proposition about the

---

[2] Dorwin Cartwright and Alvin Zander, *Group Dynamics Research and Theory* (New York: Harper, 1960), p. 345.

[3] For a full description of Loomis' theory see Charles P. and Zona K. Loomis, *Modern Social Theories* (Princeton: Van Nostrand, 1961), pp. 3 ff.

universe which is thought to be true." [4] For members of the church staff this means a concept of the church, ministry, task of the church, and responsibility of the church in the light of one's own personal faith. This subject is discussed further with group dynamics, leadership, and a doctrine of the church and ministry.

2. *Sentiment.* Sentiment embodies the feelings a person has concerning the world, personal faith, institutions, customs, traditions, and so forth. With members of the church staff this involves the mixing of sentiments, appreciation for other person's feelings, and the creation of a climate in which sentiments will be beneficial rather than detrimental.

3. *End, goal, or objective.* All persons have consciously or unconsciously established goals and objectives for their lives. The obtaining of such goals causes satisfaction or dissatisfaction in a work situation. A church staff as a body of people need to articulate the corporate goals and objectives toward which they are working. Without such goals, personal goals will tend to separate the work group. If personal goals and corporate goals can be coordinated, maximum loyalty can be obtained.

4. *Norm.* Norms are written or unwritten rules that are accepted by the individual and group for the control of overt action. In practical application in a church staff this involves protocol, sharing of responsibilities, honesty with one's time and so forth. It may result in formulation of job analyses, schedules, and formal written rules.

5. *Status-role.* Status-role consists of certain accepted entities that imply attainment. Every person needs to sense respect from his peers that is based upon work accomplished or well done. Recognition may be associated with such factors as type of office, salary, benefits, and promotion.

6. *Rank.* Rank implies where one stands with one's peers. Rank may be attained through education, age, or achievement. In the church staff there are a number of levels of rank that are symbolized in ordination, type of ministerial office, years of training and preparation, years of service, and the nature of the work.

7. *Power.* Power is the capacity to control others. Within the church staff there is need for defined lines of authority. Investment of leadership power will be within certain persons at different levels, such as clergymen, secretaries, custodians.

8. *Sanction.* Sanction implies the rewards and punishments that are

---

[4] *Ibid.,* p. 3.

imposed to attain conformity to the central ends, objectives, and goals. In a church staff sanctions are reflected in promotions, demotions, bonuses, compensations, criticisms.

9. *Facility.* Facility is defined as the various means within the system to attain the member's ends. For the church staff facility may be interpreted by the various overt acts that assist in attaining the central goal or purpose of the group. One of the major burdens of this writing is to assist members of church staffs, personnel committees in local congregations, and the entire congregation to make it possible for a church staff to function with the greatest freedom for the fulfillment of the basic purpose of the church. Much of this writing must deal with *facility.* In a sense it is the "how to" part of this work.

As a church staff works together there are two major factors that must be kept in mind: (1) there are conscious short- and long-term goals, e.g., goals that have been set by the staff, congregation, committees or boards within the congregation, basic expectations in the traditional ministry, and denominational policies. (2) At the same time that the staff is engaged in its work it is faced with emotional characteristics of each individual which may be undefined, illogical, uncontrolled, and misunderstood by the group. There is the constant warring within one's self and a continual struggle which is reflected in inevitable personal conflicts and inward ambiguous, undefined emotions. The task of the human relations specialist is to identify the personality characteristics that exist in individuals, and to attempt to define how persons possessing varying characteristics will react in the small work group. By making such analyses it may be predicted what will happen under certain conditions, and there may also be some guidelines established to assist a small work group in maximizing its efficiency and minimizing its conflicts.

Theories of Group Dynamics

The term group dynamics is used in reference to a method of analyzing a group or a field of study, a body of basic knowledge concerning group behavior, the study of and application of methods by which persons in a group get along with one another, or a group under various conditions. The study of man in his relationships is as old as history. It has, however, been more intensive during the twentieth century, and especially in the past four decades. Many centers for the study of group behavior have emerged. These centers have been based primarily in university environments. As the result of studies, there is confusion and many points of view. Malcolm and Hulda Knowles, in their small but incisive volume *Introduction to Group Dynamics,* make a clarifying statement:

The apparent confusion in the literature is partly the result of the many different kinds of groups used for research—school classes, factory production teams, jet bomber crews, and fabricated laboratory groups are illustrative of the range. Partly the confusion stems from the diversity of social problems that have motivated research, ranging from intergroup conflict to factory production. And partly it is a product of the interdisciplinary character of the field, with its ideas, methods, and terminology consisting of a potpourri drawn from psychology, sociology, psychiatry, anthropology, industrial relations, social work, education, speech, a pinch of political science and economics, and even a frequent dash of mathematics and physical science.[5]

In the case of this work there has been added a concentration on the doctrine of the church, ministry, and, more specifically, the relationships of the staff in a local congregation.

In the years since the beginning of the studies of the late Kurt Lewin research in how to get along with people has emerged under both private and public sponsorship with major emphasis being given to group dynamics, human relations, creativity, sensitivity, democratic leadership, motivation, and altruistic love. Hundreds of long-term and short-term studies have been made, such as the ten-year study of Leadership in a Democracy at Ohio State University. Out of the mass of literature have emerged many insights that are relevant to our study of the church staff.

Cartwright and Zander, in their book *Group Dynamics,* list eight "orientations" in the field of human relations: (1) field theory, (2) interaction theory, (3) systems theory, (4) sociometric orientation, (5) psychoanalytic theory, (6) cognitive theory, (7) empiricistic-statistical orientation, and (8) formal models.[6] It is beyond the scope of this writing to go into an analysis of each of the systems. The reader may wish to pursue some of the systems on his own through further research and the use of the bibliography.

The field theory orientation is so relevant to the church staff that an additional word is said at this point.

Kurt Lewin, a German-born philosopher and psychologist, came to the United States in 1932 and taught at Stanford, Cornell, and the University of Iowa, and in 1944 became director of the Research Cen-

---

[5] (New York: Association Press, 1959), p. 23.
[6] *Group Dynamics Research and Theory,* p. 40.

ter for Group Dynamics at the Massachusetts Institute of Technology. He developed the "field theory" of psychology. Lewin's major interest was in motivational psychology and the relationship of environment that was conducive or nonconducive to motivating a person to fulfillment of one's personal goals in life. He was interested in leadership principles and practices that set the "field" for motivation. Experiments were conducted with various types of leadership—autocratic, laissez faire, and democratic—to determine how one was best released for self-fulfillment. He became an advocate of the democratic principles of leadership.

The field theory is a highly complicated system and entirely too detailed to review in this writing. Reduced to its simplest form the field theory proposes that an individual reacts in accordance with the environment in which he is at the moment. It is not a reaction that can be predetermined by the stimulus-response theories of psychology. Reaction is relative in accordance with a given set of circumstances. It is the total psychological world in which one is living at a certain time. It includes all that has gone into one's life from the past, life forces that affect the present, and anticipations of the future. Lewin used the term "valency" in speaking of negative and positive, repellent and attractive powers in a given environment that operate within a "vector." The vectors are the moving forces within a given environmental structure. The vectors may be indicative of what is likely to happen or what is in the process of happening.

Lewin's theories are difficult to understand primarily because they move from mechanistic psychology, which has a tendency to be fixed and rigid, to a relativistic psychology that places action and reaction in a large field of environmental forces.

A church staff can be considered an environmental structure in which each person in the staff is a struggling individual within his own "life space," seeking self-fulfillment and affected by other individuals in the group in the same manner.[7]

Individual behavior of a member of a church staff is often puzzling to the other members of a staff and frequently just as puzzling to the individual. All of us at times have muttered to ourselves, "Why did I act that way?" or "Why did I say what I said? I know better," or the usual, "I could have kicked myself for doing that." The more we

---

[7] See Lewin, *Field Theory in Social Science* (New York: Harper, 1951). For a detailed discussion of the cognitive-field theory of learning, see Morris L. Bigge, *Learning Theories for Teachers* (Harper, 1964), chaps. 7 and 8.

know about ourselves and those with whom we work the better the chances of getting along in our human relations.

Malcolm and Hulda Knowles have summarized the basic forces in each individual's background that consciously or unconsciously result in the type of behavior exhibited. It may be of help if we can be aware of such forces in our lives and in the lives of those with whom we work.[8]

1. *The first force in the life of the individual is "Life History Forces."* Each member of a church staff brings to the staff a framework out of which his life has been conditioned. Early family life and associations with peers at various age levels determine to a degree how one performs in the group. One may feel hostility or warmth toward other members of the staff as he felt hostility or warmth toward parents and peers in his home environment. It is in the home environment that the valency patterns are formed, being reflected in fight, pairing, dependency, or flight in the small work group under varying conditions.

2. *Forces based on psychological needs.* Physical needs—food, water, rest, and so forth—are well known and accepted. Psychological needs are just as great, but less definable and less understood. Basically psychological needs can be summarized as the need for security, recognition, affection, and new experience. How one reacts in a group may be rooted in fulfillment or lack of fulfillment of these needs. A church secretary related to the author her very unhappy working conditions in a local church. She felt unaccepted by the two other secretaries in the office. They did not, for instance, invite her to lunch with them. When the other secretaries were out of the office she was not to answer the telephone. She was not in on things. A rationalization of the reason for such action was that her husband was a military officer in a nearby base, and "miltiary people are never accepted as permanent residents, though we have lived here for twelve years." The secretary had never discussed the problems with the pastor, for she felt he was so trusting of the main secretary that she would bias his opinion. Obviously there were psychological problems that were probably deeper than a lack of want-fulfillment, but the case in point is illustrated.

3. *Associational forces or "invisible committees."* All persons have certain organizations, formal or informal, to which they belong and which, to a certain degree, demand loyalty. Families have established

---

[8] *Introduction to Group Dynamics*, chap. 2, "Understanding Individual Behavior."

standards, civic and community organizations have standards, if no more than a demand for time or attendance. Each person has a political party—Democratic, Republican, or Independent. Most persons have a church to which they belong and give token or wholehearted support. They may be Protestant, Catholic or Jew. They may be Baptist, Episcopalian, or Presbyterian. There is the P.T.A., the Dad's Club, the Garden Club, or a bridge club. To say the least, each person on the church staff has many "invisible committees" that have shaped, or helped shape, his personal standards, values, purposes, and goals. Decisions in a staff situation are always conditioned by such associational forces.

4. *Forces from goals and ideologies.* Each person on the church staff has, through the years, formulated personal goals, dreams, ambitions, and desires. Such goals are based upon many background experiences and conditioning factors in a general framework of ideologies. The Knowles have designed the following chart depicting the forces that are at work in the individual as he enters a group.[9]

Figure 2.

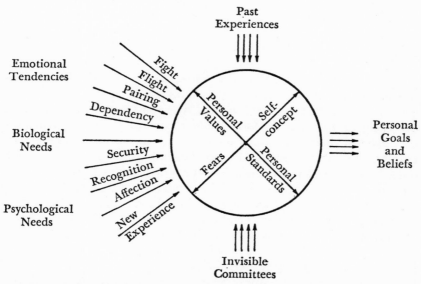

One of the fundamental tasks of a church staff is to recognize the differences of each individual on the staff and to work toward bringing

[9] *Ibid.,* p. 38.

each member of the staff into focus on the central purpose, goals, aims, and objectives of the staff as a whole. At the same time that this is done, every effort must be made to maximize the setting for freedom of the individual to have creative expression and release for his own person.

Again the Knowles have diagrammed the ideal situation in which all persons have their own personal goals, but when brought into a group, they merge their individual goals into group goals with lines of communication between all members of the group.[10]

Figure 3.

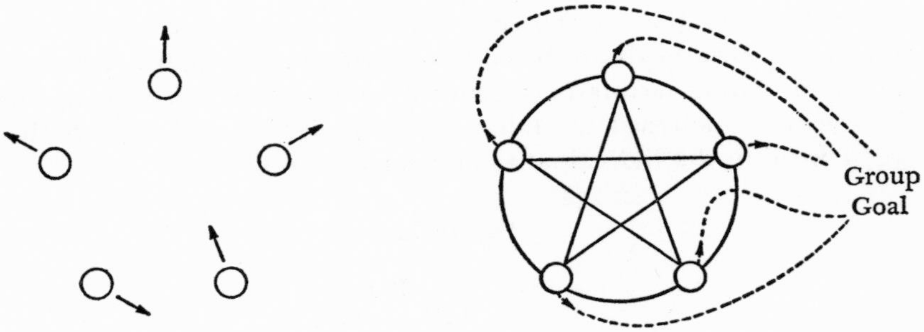

A Collection of Individuals
with personal goals

A Group
(The Church Staff)

Ultimately human relations are getting along with people. Human relations in the church staff are how the various members of the staff get along together, how they function as a group in ministry, how they get along in assisting the local congregation to be the church, how they exist in their own family environment and as citizens of a community. We are dealing with communications, common goals and objectives, sensitivity to the worth of the individual with personal goals and creative ideas, the respect for the fundamental dignity of the individual, the general welfare of each individual, and, in simple terminology, the love of one's neighbor.

I am attempting in this work to speak to the basic areas of human relations. A church staff is a small work group. All the principles of human relations, group leadership, group structure and change, human emotions and drives are present. These are the frame of reference for the book.

In addition to the basic areas of human relations within the small

[10] *Ibid.*, p. 40.

work group, there is added to the church staff the element of Christian concern and self-consciousness of the group that the group is ministry in a Christian congregation. Ethics, moral principles, theology, and heritage all take on a dimension that should be, but is not always, considered in the secular business world, and cannot be avoided in the church staff. Throughout all the efforts to establish good human relations the church staff must be conscious of the Christian interpretation of human relations. In its ultimate analysis the Judaeo-Christian tradition is one of relationships—the relationship of man and his God, and the relationship of man with man in the light of the teachings of the Holy Scriptures. The major function of Jesus the Christ was to be a reconciling agent—reconciling man with God and man with man. Good staff relationships are rooted in reconciliation.

A church staff is composed of individual persons who are human in all respects, full of human emotions, conflicts, and frustrations, but who are committed to the truth that individual and corporate redemption lies in the acceptance of the will of God revealed in Christ. The member of a church staff is first of all a committed Christian. He is, secondly, aligned with other persons with similar goals and all have a corporate goal of leading a congregation of Christian believers to fulfillment in finding and doing the will of God in worship, nurture, and work.

5

The Senior Minister

Without question the most strategic position on the church staff is
that of senior minister. I am using the term senior minister, though
I prefer some other title. My preference would be a title that would
imply a co-worker with other members of the staff, but one who has
the executive responsibility of giving direction to the staff. The term
"pastoral director" coined by Richard Niebuhr has not received a
good hearing. The term "executive minister" is more descriptive of
what the office is. A new term is difficult to define. Therefore, the
term "senior minister" is used with reservations. The title implies
seniority in executive authority, not seniority in professional abilities
in the staff.

It is difficult to establish normative data for the members of the
church staff, but comparisons can be made in various positions that
assist in understanding who the persons are who work together in the
fulfillment of church leadership. Comparisons can also be made that
help to unearth potential causes for staff frictions.

In the sample of senior ministers used in the research for this writing, 37 percent were in their early forties, and another 15 percent were
in their late thirties. One fourth were between 45 and 54 years of age,
and 8 percent were older than 55 years. More than one half of the
senior ministers (54.5 percent) were born in communities of less than
10,000 persons. This is the area commonly described as town and
country by church leaders. Seventeen percent were born in open country, and 18.8 percent were from farm families. Incidentally, the above
statistics confirm research indicating the rural areas of America have
provided a large portion of the leadership of the church. Ten percent
of the senior ministers were born in towns of less than 500 persons,
13 percent in communities of 500 to 2,500, and 14 percent in communities of 2,500 to 10,000. Twelve percent of the senior ministers
were born in cities of 500,000 or more, and 13 percent were born in
cities of 100,000 to 500,000.

Thirty-eight percent of the senior ministers came from homes where the father's occupation was one of the professions, 18 percent were from farm homes, 12 percent from homes where the father was engaged in some type of managerial work, 9 percent were in sales, 13 percent were craftsmen, 3 percent service workers, 4 percent skilled laborers, and less than 1 percent were from the homes of unskilled laborers.

Senior ministers are well trained. Ninety-seven percent hold a liberal arts degree, 94.4 percent hold a Bachelor of Divinity or its equivalent, one-fourth hold a master's degree, and one out of ten holds an earned doctorate—Ph.D. or equivalent—with most majors being philosophy or theology. (This figure is somewhat higher than samples in other studies.) Thirty-nine percent of the senior ministers have one or more honorary doctorate degrees, and one-fourth have done special work in college or university. Most ministers attended seminary in a school owned by their denomination, and 52 percent attended a liberal arts college of their denomination. Members of church staffs and laymen need to think upon the above data, and become aware of the years of preparation in the lives of senior ministers. A liberal arts degree and a divinity degree require a minimum of seven years beyond high school. A master's degree requires a minimum of one additional year (usually two), and a Ph.D. requires a minimum of three additional years. There can be no overlapping of credit for the degrees.

At the time of compiling the data concerning the senior minister, 43 percent had been in the present pastorate for more than 9 years, 22 percent from 6 to 8 years, 21 percent from 4 to 5 years, and 12 percent from 2 to 3 years. The large church provides a place for a longer ministry than the small church. While length of pastorates seems to be increasing in most denominations, it is still almost a scandal that averages for tenure in pastorates are still only 2 to 3 years for all ministers. This is a striking comparison with the longer tenure of senior ministers.

Prior to their being made senior ministers, 5 out of 100 senior ministers have served as associate or assistant ministers in the same church. One-fourth of the senior ministers had held 3 pastorates prior to their present position, 18 percent had held 4 pastorates, 10 percent had held 5, and 14 percent had held 6 or more. One-fifth of the senior ministers had held 2 pastorates prior to their present positions. Forty-four percent of the pastors had spent 4 years in each previous appointment, 26 percent had spent 6 years in each previous appointment, and 10 percent had spent 8 years in each previous appointment. It can be said the senior ministers are persons who wear well, staying with their pastorates longer than the average of their peers.

Ninety-four percent of the senior ministers were born in the United States, with 6 percent born in Canada, Europe, or South America.

Sixty percent of the senior ministers had considered the ministry as a life vocation prior to their twenty-first birthday and 30 percent had considered the ministry prior to their fifteenth birthday. Eighty-seven percent of the senior ministers had made the firm decision to be a minister by their twenty-second birthday, and one half had chosen the ministry by the time they were twenty years of age. The decision to be a minister was made through various influences, with 44 percent of the ministers registering their parents and home life as the strongest influence; 17 percent attributing the major influence to a pastor; and 15 percent feeling the "secret call" or an inner persuasion was the strongest influence. Studies in motivation bear out similar influences and a combination of the above, along with other influences.

All the senior ministers were ordained by their respective denominations and hold full clergy rights.

Fifty-two percent of the senior ministers receive between $6,000 and $10,000 cash salary, with an overall average for all senior ministers in our study of $9,800. Nineteen percent of the senior ministers receive $12,000 or more cash salary. (Since 1966 ministers' salaries have been increasing at the rate of 5 percent per year. Similar professional salaries have increased 8 percent per year.)

Fifteen percent of the senior ministers feel their salary is not adequate, and 12 percent must supplement the salary with honoraria, writing, or a working wife to meet all financial needs. However, 88.5 percent feel the salary is about right under the circumstances, with a brave 7 percent stating it is too high! Ten percent of the senior ministers feel salary differentials cause friction in the staff, with there being too large a difference between the senior minister's salary and that of other staff personnel.

Eighty percent of the senior ministers live in a rent-free parsonage or manse, and an additional 17 percent receive a housing allowance for a parsonage. Forty-two percent of the senior ministers have all housing utilities paid by the congregation, and an additional 21 percent have some utilities paid. Sixteen percent of the senior ministers have a person provided to do yard work at their residences.

Only 5.5 percent of the churches provide the senior minister with a car, but 80 percent provide a travel allowance in the following categories: $500 to $700, 25.8 percent; $700 to $900, 10.7 percent; $900 to $1,200, 24.1 percent; and $1,200 to $1,500, 25.8 percent.

Practically all senior ministers are under a pension program provided by the denomination, in which all the investment in the program is paid by the denomination or shared both by the local church and the minister. The amount of pension that senior ministers can expect to receive varies greatly by denomination and years of service. Slightly more than one-half (51.8 percent) of the senior ministers can expect to receive between $1,500 and $3,000 per year upon retirement. Twenty-one percent can expect more than $4,000 per year from pension funds. Most ministers expect to retire by virtue of their denominational policies by the age 70 with right of retirement at age 65. Only 8 percent of the senior ministers under study are not registered for Social Security as self-employed persons.

Thirty-six percent of the senior ministers will be dependent upon retirement on the pension supplied by the denomination and Social Security with little or no additional income. Twenty-one percent, however, state they will have annual incomes of $1,000 to $2,000 from additional sources; 11 percent will have $2,000 to $3,000; 6.5 percent will have incomes of $3,000 to $4,000; and 7 percent will have additional incomes of more than $4,000 annually.

Ninety-eight percent of the senior ministers are married, with 35 percent having two children; 28.6 percent, 3 children; and 22.6 percent, 4 children. One percent of the senior ministers have never been married, and one percent are widowed.

Approximately one-half of the senior ministers have hospital insurance provided by the congregation for them and their families.

Only 13 percent of the congregations provide any system for salary advancement. In regard to vacation plans, only 8 percent of the congregations make no provision for the senior minister. Sixty-eight percent of the churches provide a 4-week vacation; 5 percent, 3 weeks; 7 percent, 2 weeks; 11 percent provide from 4 to 8 weeks; and 1 percent work it out with the pastor.

Sabbatical leaves for special study are not offered by most congregations on a systematic basis. Some denominations, such as The United Methodist Church, make provision for a sabbatical which may be taken after ten years of service and each successive seven years thereafter, but there is little provision for the senior minister to finance such a leave. Only 3.5 percent of the senior ministers reported a regular system of sabbatical leave in which the congregation makes a provision for support. Another 2 percent of the pastors reported they have had leaves on an irregular basis. Local congregations would profit in the long run by granting their senior minister more time for study and travel and providing an adequate stipend for such time. Fifty-five percent of the senior ministers reported they do have funds available from the local church for short-term study periods of in-service training, and 10 percent have an allowance from the church for books and periodicals.

Many senior ministers feel inadequate in their preparation to be the administrator of a church staff. Eighteen percent of the ministers in the study stated they had had some training in staff relationships, and 76 percent felt the seminaries should provide training for the multiple ministry. To the question, "Do you feel seminaries should offer training for the multiple staff?" 6 percent stated a definite "no" and 18 percent questioned how much good seminary training would be in regard to the multiple ministry.

Forty-three percent of the senior ministers have obtained help in staff administration through experience in the business world, reading, learning from friends, workshops on the church staff, military experience, and professional people. A general consensus among senior ministers seems to be that they have not been trained for their task and feel the educational institutions of the denominations should assume a leadership role in this field of training, both as a routine part of the seminary curriculum and in continuing education for ministers.

The Senior Minister as Executive

The senior minister by virtue of his office is an executive. Crawford H. Greenwalt in his lectures in the Graduate School of Business, Columbia University, summarizes executive ability:

The best that I can say the basic requirement of executive capacity is the ability to create a harmonious whole out of what the academic world calls dissimilar discipline. This is a fancy way of saying that an executive is good when he can make a smoothly functioning team out of people with the many different skills required in the operation of a modern business.[1]

The senior minister has the responsibility of working with persons of dissimilar backgrounds and professional skills and creating a harmoni-

---

[1] *The Uncommon Man* (New York: McGraw-Hill, 1959), p. 28.

ous whole, assisting the staff to focus on the basic objectives within the church. Greenwalt holds, "His most important function is to reconcile, to coordinate, to compromise, and to appraise the various viewpoints and talents under his direction to the end that each individual contributes his full measure to the business at hand." [2] He continues by outlining the basic qualities of the executive: "judgment; initiative; integrity; foresight; energy-drive; human relations skills; decisiveness; dependability; emotional calm; fairness; ambition; dedication; objectivity; cooperation." [3] This is a large order, and each of the above characteristics applies to the senior minister. Some of the characteristics can be acquired. Most characteristics are native. All characteristics can be cultivated through disciplined study. The development of executive skills is vitally important for the senior minister as he leads and participates in the church staff and local congregation. Only basic aspects of executive skills and responsibilities can be discussed here, but it is hoped enough is said to open the doors of self-study to the senior minister and to give some direction and focus to this position.

The task of the senior minister is to help create a climate within the congregation, and more especially the employed staff, which will bring about maximum participation of each person involved.

J. D. Batten has listed what he considers to be the ten most essential elements in achieving a good work relationship:

1. Lay out clear over-all company objectives and aspirations of all the company's people toward objectives or goals in harmony with them.
2. Select the best people for appropriate jobs. . . . The ability to screen and hire good men systematically for key positions is a talent pathetically lacking in many of our present management personnel.
3. Define job duties and performance requirements. Insure that every employee knows the *what, where, when, who, how* and—above all—*why* of his job.
4. Establish accountability for results in key jobs throughout the organization and provide the necessary feedback.
5. Regularly evaluate the worth of every department, job, and person in the company in terms of contribution to company goals.
6. Establish the philosophy that good management is the develop-

---

[2] *Ibid.*, p. 64.
[3] *Ibid.*, p. 60.

ment of people, not the direction of things. Aim at developing the whole man.

7. Teach key personnel the management techniques of research, planning, organization, direction, coordination, and control.
8. Motivate people by—
   a. Fulfilling basic needs for security, opportunity, recognition, and belonging.
   b. Keeping the lines of communication open.
   c. Displaying candor and a positive mental attitude.
   d. Using action words and concepts.
9. Develop the realization that work can and should be a pleasant and rewarding part of life.
10. Establish the belief that integrity is the most important ingredient in all human activity.[4]

With minor adjustments each of the above elements for achieving good working relationships can be applied to the church staff and especially the position of senior minister as leader. It is quite evident that good executive practices need to be established upon the theory of the development of people. A church staff is composed of professional persons with individual skills and abilities. The senior minister has the responsibility of coordinating the staff so that each person is released for maximum use of his talents. Staff structure in this light is a releasing rather than a binding process. Loyalty of staff members is not to a person, but to the central goals and objectives of ministry by employed staff and the congregation. Mutual respect for and by all persons on the staff is essential for maximum release of professional abilities.

The Senior Minister as Co-worker

An area of tension in the work of the senior minister is in regard to his position as executive and administrator while he must be at the same time a co-worker with other members of the staff. It is at this point that many senior ministers have the most difficulty. On the one hand, they are expected by the congregation and employed staff to be the executive of the staff. On the other hand, the senior minister is expected to carry a full professional role as minister and pastor while working with the other members of the staff. He is expected to be one professional along with other professionals. It is not a case clearly

---

[4] *Tough-minded Management* (New York: American Management Association, 1963) , p. 25.

defined, as in secular business, of superior and subordinate. It is a case of superior persons working together, with one of the group assigned to the executive position.

The problem may be complicated by the fact that congregations select the senior minister on grounds, as a general rule, other than executive ability. He is selected first of all because of preaching ability, or pastoral ability, or counseling ability, or his reputation of success (whatever this may mean) in other pastorates. In other words, the senior minister is selected or appointed on his professional ministerial abilities rather than upon his ability as an executive. Unfortunately professional skills do not guarantee executive skills. There may be some correlation, however, between a man's professional attainment and his reasoning-learning ability to acquire good executive skills. Senior ministers need to examine carefully the above areas of responsibility. Their professional schooling has laid great emphasis upon professional discipline and a bare minimum of emphasis upon executive training. Seminaries have been very slow in placing academic approval on training in church administration, leadership, church planning, and meaningful field education. Somehow through an osmotic process the minister is supposed to absorb from his environment an understanding of human relations, personnel management, group organization and structure, and good leadership techniques. In reality an understanding of human relations and the development of executive skills are vitally important for an effective professional ministry.

To further complicate the scene, all members of the church staff possess the dignity of their position by virtue of: ecclesiastical recognition through ordination or certification; professional training, education, and experience; or development of skills in their own fields. In this sense, all are equal. Each is an authority in his own right. There is no hierarchy of professional ministries. All are contributing to a corporate ministry within the congregation. At the same time, all persons in the staff are dependent upon staff structure and an administrator to maintain coordination and to meet individual and corporate needs. It is quite easy for the one on whom executive responsibility is placed to develop unconsciously a professional authority that is inconsistent with a doctrine of the multiple staff in ministry, and that leads to a false hierarchy of levels of professionalism.

Any illustration or diagram of a complicated social system is incomplete or inadequate. An effort is made below, however, to diagram what is meant by executive or administrative responsibility and professional responsibility.

Figure 4.

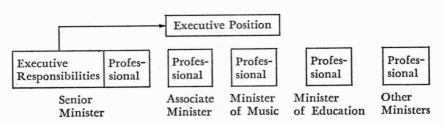

The diagram attempts to illustrate the fact that all professional staff members are equal in their ministries. The senior minister is one of the professional staff, but he has as a part of his office executive responsibilities. It is this phase of his office which is different from others. This segment of his office is drawn out and placed in a position of administration and leadership of the group. He may share the executive work with other members of the staff, such as a church business administrator or a minister of administration. He will assist each member of the staff to assume phases of the administrative load.

How well the staff members work together is dependent upon how each member carries his responsibility and how well all staff persons understand human relations, fundamentals of leadership, and administration, and how committed all are to the goals and objectives of this work. There is a basic concept behind this entire work that all members of the staff need to be apprised of all elements of the disciplines of human relations and leadership, as well as an understanding of each position in the staff, if genuine team ministry is to emerge. At the same time it is necessary to understand the uniqueness of each office. In the light of this discussion, some of the unique areas of responsibility of the senior minister are lifted up.

The Roles of the Senior Minister

Selecting the staff

Considerable space has been given in an earlier chapter to the staff selecting process. Needless to say, the senior minister has a major role in choosing the persons who are to come to the church staff. Obviously, he must work through the various channels that have been previously suggested and in direct cooperation with the committee on personnel in the local church. However, major responsibility does rest upon his shoulders in the staff selecting process. A basic assumption of this writing is that the personnel are added to a church staff as areas of responsibility emerge that cannot be fulfilled by the persons who are already on the staff. Such responsibilities are in specialization areas, and a new member can be brought in to assist someone who is already on the staff or to fulfill a role that is not being filled adequately. A pastor would do well to make a self-evaluation to discover for himself his strongest points and his weakest points. In the selecting of staff he should attempt to find persons who can supplement his weakest points, for in doing so the staff will become much stronger in its services to the congregation. Many staff frictions arise at this point. Often a pastor does not recognize his own weaknesses, and as he sees someone come to the staff who has a strong quality in a certain field and is able to fill a need in the congregation more capably than the pastor, he becomes jealous of this person. But if the pastor can assume a basic philosophy of service to the congregation, then he can admit that the more his weaknesses are supplemented and the stronger the persons who are brought to the staff, the more able the staff is to serve as they attempt to help the congregation. It has been observed that some very fine senior ministers have brought to the staff persons who are very capable in fields such as counseling or Christian education, and as these persons fulfilled their roles responsibly and found a ready response in the congregation the pastor felt that a part of his prerogative was being usurped.

To illustrate how this situation can be avoided the following account is given. Several years ago I asked Marshall Steel, who at that time was pastor of the Highland Park Methodist Church in Dallas, to be present for a field education session with a group of seminary students. With unvarnished candor one of the students asked, "Dr. Steel, how do you feel about it when members of your ministerial staff are asked by persons in the congregation to perform more weddings, funerals, and baptisms than you are?" Dr. Steel replied without hesitation, "Young man, any time that any member of our ministerial staff is asked to perform any service for any member of the congregation I feel that our staff is serving the congregation better." That kind of philosophy of pastoral administration and group participation in the ministries of the church leads to a long tenure for both the senior minister and associates. (A side issue: At the above mentioned church there are no associates. All persons who have ministerial responsibilities are called ministers, each with his own specialization, such as minister of music, minister of education, minister of visitation, min-

ister of evangelism, minister of administration.) A total staff is successful in direct proportion to the success of each of the members of the
staff. As long as team cooperation can be felt and the senior minister is
one of the team there is the making for a more efficient and larger area
of service to the total congregation.

The senior minister as enabler

In the field of group dynamics and leadership certain terms have
emerged that are helpful in our understanding of the role of the senior
minister. One of these is *enabler*. To be an enabler means to be one
who accepts innovative ideas and makes it possible for such ideas to
emerge and to come into full bloom. It is said that 98 percent of the
creative ideas that occur in the mind of the individual never come
to fruition. One of the reasons for this is that the persons who are
in a position to accept such ideas and get them into operation do not
accept them as legitimate, and the ideas die. All members of the church
staff are in a position to have creative ideas that should have a hearing
for their validity as a part of the total program of the church. In the
business world the value of such creative ideas has taken hold to such
a degree that there are "think" people employed. These are persons
who are especially skilled in their ability to think up new ideas for
the firm in the fields of experimentation, manufacturing, sales, and so
forth. Such ideas then are presented to the administrative body of the
firm where they are given a hearing, are refined, and finally are put
into practice. A number of years ago the late Alex Osborn and his colleagues at the University of New York at Buffalo developed the idea
of "brainstorming," which is a method by which a group of people are
able to explore a problem in an attempt to bring into being new crea-
tions. One of the basic principles of brainstorming is to give any idea
that is presented the opportunity for a valid hearing. Anyone has the
privilege of presenting an idea and will be honored for his idea regardless of how ridiculous it may sound. Obviously, many ideas are
lost, but new ideas are also brought into being which provide the opportunity for new innovations. The pastor stands in a strategic role to
create a climate of acceptance in the staff and congregation and to help
the individual who has ideas to get them out into group discussion for
further development. An associate pastor related to me that he had
taken ideas to the senior minister a good many times in the church
in which he was employed. The senior minister heard him and then
immediately started punching holes in the ideas to the extent that

many times an idea was completely lost. It is vitally important that the senior minister understand his position as one who does hear ideas and makes possible the release of the creative ability of every individual on the church staff. Much of the work of the church has been stifled because senior ministers have been shortsighted or have felt that an idea that may have been purely in embryonic form was not sufficiently good to have a full hearing.

The senior minister as coordinator for responsibilities

A multiple staff is for the dissemination of responsibilities that must be met by the leadership employed by a congregation. The functional role of each member of the church staff needs to be clearly understood by all the members of the staff and the local congregation. Better understanding can be attained through a consensus of opinion concerning each person's position in the staff than by the pastor's decision in this regard. There needs to be a well thought out plan of operation allocating areas of responsibility to each individual. One of the basic problems that has been discovered in staff relationships is the ambiguity with which each person works in regard to his own position in the staff. There is much overlapping of responsibilities and also areas of neglect due to this problem. Staff members are selected to fill certain roles on the basis of competence in their respective fields. Such competence needs to be respected and given the opportunity for the fullest expression. But all work on the staff needs to have some kind of coordination, and this can best be achieved through the central office of the senior minister as he works with the various members of the staff and the committees within the staff. Time is of the greatest importance, and only as persons work efficiently with one another can time be used to best advantage. A minister may feel that he is saving time by making decisions himself, but ordinarily decisions made simply on his own initiative will not find acceptance as readily as decisions made by the group. Frequent staff meetings, personal conferences with each person on the staff, informal discussions of staff roles and responsibilities, and an opportunity for complete freedom in discussion of all responsibilities and areas of work will insure a much more effective and efficient operation of a church staff in a harmonious and happy relationship. A study of various forms of denominational polity reveals that the major denominations have a similar pattern of congregational organization. Basically the areas of committee responsibilities within the local congregation will hinge around six major concerns: evangelism, education, mission, Christian social concern, worship, and stewardship. There will be subcommittees under each of these areas, and in many denominations there will be additional committees, but most of them could be coordinated into one of the six basic areas. It has been discovered that allocating certain committee responsibilities to specific members of the church staff is a wise administrative plan. This prevents the various members of the staff from spreading themselves too broadly across each of the committees, makes someone on the ministerial staff directly responsible to the various working committees, and also provides each member of the staff a working body of people within the congregation for whom he has specific responsibility. There must be constant consultation with the various members of the staff and the senior minister to coordinate all the work that has to be done.

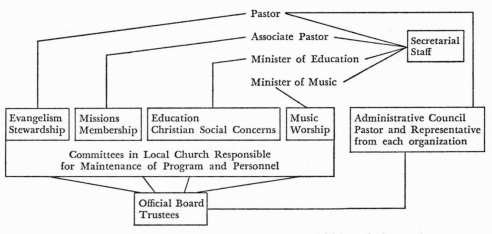

Figure 5. Diagram of administrative responsibilities of the staff with major committees in the local church.

Church calendars are of vital importance. Much confusion, antagonism, and frustration within church staffs would be avoided if there was a strict adherence to a calendar of events and each member of the staff was thoroughly apprised of the calendar. The calendar needs to be kept by one of the secretaries in the church offices and should be discussed at every staff meeting. I knew of a minister of youth who had invited a professor to speak to the youth fellowship on a Sunday evening on a very pertinent topic concerning social action. When the professor arrived for the evening service there were very few young people present, and it was discovered that the minister of music had the youth choir at another church giving a performance that night. This kind of misunderstanding is inexcusable. Another case in point is revealed in a situation in a church where there were to be an art exhibit and a religious ballet calling for special staging in the sanctuary over Palm Sunday. The minister of evangelism discovered that the receiving of the membership class into the church on Palm Sunday had not been scheduled! A discussion in the staff led to a recognition that there was an oversight and wrong seasonal emphasis. Quickly adjustments were made, and the receiving of the membership class was scheduled as it should have been. Again, such misunderstandings can be avoided if there is complete freedom of communication between members of the staff and coordination through good administrative procedures. All members of the staff must feel a genuine sense of loyalty to the church calendar and program responsibilities of each member of the staff.

The senior minister as "truster and supporter"

By *truster* is meant one who puts his complete trust in the ability of the staff to perform responsibly in their respective positions. This trust is essential if anyone on the staff is to work with freedom. The minister who is constantly checking on the individual to see if he is getting the job done adequately most likely will cause nervousness and frustration within the individual to the point where efficiency will be stymied. It is quite obvious that if a person does not perform responsibly and does not get the task done which is his to do then there has to be an accounting by that individual to persons of authority. But freedom of action comes as one feels he has the confidence of his peers and can move ahead on his own initiative to perform the task that he feels is his. By "supporter" is meant one who supports those on the staff in the work that they are trying to do. Halfhearted interest in what members of the staff are doing will soon cause them to feel that there is not much concern about their work in the church. It means in a sense that they are lackeys doing menial jobs around the church that nobody else wants to do. Everyone has to do a certain amount of that kind of work, but when people who are trained are brought to a church staff to perform some particular role and function they need to have the freedom to work and a sense that others in the staff are supporting what they are trying to do. The pastor needs to inquire on occasion about what kind of work the individual is doing and how his work is progressing. This needs to be done out of a deep sense of appreciation of what is taking place. A sincere word of appreciation for work well done will go a long way in lifting staff morale.

There are times when persons on the church staff come in conflict with members of the congregation. Anyone who attempts to have a prophetic and forward-looking ministry is going to find a certain degree of friction with certain members of the congregation who do not understand the visionary aspects of the task of the ministry. The minister should be very cautious in aligning himself too quickly with the members of the congregation before he understands thoroughly what the situation is. Staff morale can be undermined quickly if the minister does not lend his support to new and creative ideas and throw himself completely behind his colleagues who are trying to perform the work of the church. Opportunity can be afforded to each member of the staff to share with the rest of the staff the areas of work and experimentation that he is conducting. This is one way to have some interesting discussions in staff meetings and extra sessions when the staff members get together on a more informal basis. Work becomes genuine teamwork in this kind of situation, where everyone feels the interest and concern of the other persons on the staff as they all attempt to work together to fulfill the ministry for and to the congregation.

The senior minister as communicator

Communication is one of the most difficult tasks within the church staff. Open lines of communication are absolutely essential if there is to be staff harmony and efficiency of operation. Communication in many aspects of the term is dependent upon an atmosphere rather than on actual word of mouth or memorandum. Communication is a freedom in which people operate as they attempt to work in close harmony with one another to perform functional roles with a common objective. There can be little communication as long as there are hidden fears, jealousies, animosities, hatreds, misunderstandings, and blurred areas of responsibility in which individuals work. Elsewhere in this work I have described some of the areas of breaking down the barriers that exist between staff members that are elementary problems of human relations. Frequent staff meetings, frequent get-togethers over a cup of coffee, occasional parties, and informal situations make for good communications within a church staff. On the more practical side, the calendar, interoffice correspondence, a clear understanding by all of what is expected of each one, and complete freedom of expression all enter into good communications.

Terry has prepared what he calls the "Communication Equation":

Giver			Receiver		
(1)	(2)	(3)	(1)	(2)	(3)

Stimulus + Interpretation + Behavior=Perception + Interpretation=Behavior[5]

In the formula the giver is the initiator of the communication. He has in mind that which he wants to convey to another. This goes through his own behavior—through his actions, speech, gestures, tone of voice, facial expressions, or memorandum. The receiver of the communication perceives that communication is being made. It may be a "wide open" perception, or a blurred "half-received" perception. The receiver will interpret the communication in the light of his own experience. He will interpret words as he understands them. He will interpret the communication in the light of the attitude, action, speech, gestures, tone of voice, facial expression, or memorandum of the giver of the communication. He will then respond in behavior to the communication as he receives and interprets it.

Research in communication reveals that the amount of communication heard and understood by persons in a business firm diminishes appreciably between various levels of management. For instance, the Board of Directors will have unanimous agreement on a communication. The president of the firm will receive 90 percent of the communication; the vice president will receive 67 percent; department director, 50 percent; foreman, 30 percent; and nonmanagement member, 20 percent. This is an enormous loss of the original communication, and can be disastrous in a business enterprise. It can be just as disastrous in the church.

From the point of view of the receiver it has been discovered through research that the attitude and ability of the receiver to accept and understand communication is just as decisive a factor as the attitude and ability of the giver to make himself heard. Studies in business communications show only 34 percent of the persons in a work force said they understood their foreman, when 95 percent of the foremen thought they were being heard. "Of the same foreman,

---

[5] *Principles of Management*, p. 518.

fifty-one percent felt that their general foreman thought that they understood the problems of their foreman well." [6]

The ability to establish communication between two individuals is more than words. It is *rapport,* meaning a stage in communication at which point each party relaxes in understanding the other. Another term that has gained status is *empathy.* This is the ability to enter into another person's feelings, emotions, or experiences until there is a point of genuine understanding. In the earlier stages of the development of the concept of empathy it was defined as the unconscious tendency to act out that which one sees. It is, for instance, the bodily gesture of the spectator trying to help the basketball player on one's team get the ball in the goal. Later development of the term goes deeper and into the realm of understanding and emotion. "It has been defined as a state of perceiving the feelings, attitudes, understandings, and state of mind of another." [7] Empathy is vitally important as members of the church staff communicate with each other about every phase of their work.

In a cooperative or democratic form of staff procedure, communication is established through a clear understanding and agreement on the purposes, goals, and objectives of the church and the place of the staff in assisting a congregation to obtain their goals. Communication is established as each person on the staff has a clear understanding of his position and an understanding of other persons' positions in the staff.

In frequent conversations with many persons on church staffs I have asked an individual if he would like to have the opportunity to share with the rest of the members of the staff his feelings about his own job and what his work could be within the functional staff. In every case I have had a ready and enthusiastic response that the individual would love to do this kind of thing. Musicians especially have said to me over and over again, "If I could only tell the rest of the staff how I feel about music in the church and my position as a musician in the church, I believe we would all have a better understanding." The same is true with the director of youth, or the director of education, or the minister of evangelism, or the hostess in the church, or the business administrator, or the secretary. Each should have complete opportunity for expression on how he looks upon his own position and how he would like for the rest of the staff to look upon him and

---

[6] See Roger Bellows, Thomas Q. Gilson, George S. Odiorne, *Executive Skills* (Englewood Cliffs, N.J.: Prentice-Hall, 1962), p. 61.
[7] *Ibid.,* p. 63.

his work. Frequently, a secretary feels that the rest of the staff members do not understand her position, and that they have a tendency to put upon her work that should be the responsibility of someone else. Many times the secretary will see errors or she will see areas of need within the church, but she does not have freedom to express her observations to the members of the staff. If genuine teamwork characterizes the staff, areas of communication should be much freer than they generally are. Returning again to the business world, it has been discovered in a good many businesses that communication begins when management and various employees, including persons on the assembly line, sit together to talk about their common interests and work. This tends to counteract the segmentation of work and to create genuine teamwork. Teamwork is the attempt to fulfill a common aim, goal, and purpose when all the members involved in the staff attempt to fulfill their own individual roles but share the total with others.

The senior minister as pastor to the staff

Some of the most lonely people in the world are full-time church employees. This is also true for the senior minister, but is more so for the other members of the church staff and their families. The senior minister stands in a unique role to be able to minister to members of the staff in their individual problems and needs. He needs to be well enough acquainted with each member of the staff and his family that they become first-name persons to him, not only on the surface but in actual understanding. This happens as he comes to know each person intimately and is able to establish confidence, and as each person gains confidence in him. He needs to visit staff members in their homes and share their problems in personal life, assuring each that there are a ready ear and sympathetic heart that can be trusted with supreme confidence. The pastor needs to share with individual members of the staff their joys, heartaches, and sorrows. He needs to be able to pray freely with any member of the staff as the person stands in need of the ministry of the church. Too often this intimacy of understanding is not present with the members of the staff even though the pastor may be ever so good a minister to other members of the congregation in their needs. An associate pastor shared with me the delight he felt when the senior minister called upon the associate's wife at the birth of their first baby. A prayer by the senior minister at the bedside will always be remembered. This, of course is routine work to the minister with members of

109

the congregation, but so often it is forgotten with members of the church staff. Such a concern cannot be artificial, but must be out of the depths of sincerity and love in the pastor's heart. If the senior minister's wife is of such a nature that she can share this kind of intimacy with members of the staff it is all for the good.

The pastor as an example

Most ministers will shun the idea of being an example to anyone. But regardless of how he may feel about it the minister is an example to other members of the church staff. He is an example in a number of ways. He is an example in the matter of integrity. Integrity means sterling character in regard to one's own calling; a sense of mission and responsibility; the wise use of time; the honesty with which one deals with his family, staff members, and congregation. Integrity is something that one does not buy or gain through a book. Integrity is gained only through self-discipline as the individual applies himself to the principles of the Christian faith.

The staff looks upon the pastor as an example of a worshiper. How deeply does he worship when he is leading a service? Does worship mean something in his own life? Does the staff know that his ministry is developed out of his own personal attitude of private worship as well as public worship? All aspects of worship are not on display but will emerge from time to time as the basic cement that holds a minister's life together. Loyalty to the institution in which one is working is of supreme importance. Pastors expect members of the church staff to be loyal to the local congregation under the ideals of the group, but he cannot expect them to go beyond his own loyalty and integrity in this matter. Pastors would do well to search their souls daily to examine their own motives and their own spiritual well-being.

The position of senior minister is strategic. He carries in himself the professional skills of his ministerial office and the executive skills of his assigned position in the church staff. In the former he is on a par with other employed professional members of the staff. In the latter he is the executive director of the staff. Mutual respect of each member of the staff will result in good working relations and the fulfilling of the basic goal and objective of the staff to assist the congregation in worship, nurture, and work in the world.

6

The Associate or Assistant Minister

When an associate minister was asked about the most dissatisfying part of his position, he stated, "Organizing church dinners, promoting attendance, not being able to do anything on my own. No preaching, no baptisms, and few weddings, funerals, and sick calls. It is difficult for a man who has been a pastor for twenty years to adjust to staff work with a division of labor and the feeling that one is a 'hired hand' rather than a regular pastor."

The above statement is expressive of many of the problems that are in the mind of the associate minister. (I will use exclusively the word *associate* rather than using both *associate* and *assistant*. Terms will be discussed later.) Probably no position on the church staff is fraught with as many problems as is that of the associate minister. In this chapter an attempt will be made to define problems and offer some practical solutions.

At the outset the basic problem of human relations between senior minister and associate may be described, to borrow a term from biology, as symbiotic. Webster defines symbiosis as "the living together of two dissimilar organisms in close association or union, especially where this is advantageous to both." The word carries two basic concepts: independent from, but dependent upon. The classic illustration in biology is that of the relationship of animal life, plant life, and minerals. For instance, some honeybees are dependent upon clover for life; clover is dependent upon the honeybee for pollination and also is dependent upon certain minerals, such as lime, for growth. In return the clover returns to the soil nitrogen, which makes lime and other minerals available for plant consumption. Each—bee, clover, and soil—is an independent entity, yet each is dependent upon the other for existence. They compete, yet are dependent. In like manner, an associate minister and a senior minister are independent entities —persons, personalities—but are dependent upon each other for a total ministry within a congregation. In all likelihood, both men (or women) have been trained in college and seminary to do the work of the ministry. Both have been ordained. Each has a self-image of his role as minister. Yet there must be divisions of labor. Areas of individual responsibilities must be defined. Some of the self-concepts may be denied expression, and duties of office may frustrate one's personal goals. A working team with mutual professional respect can lead to a fruitful ministry.

Some Facts About the Associate Minister

In the study of associate ministers in more than three hundred Protestant churches representing each region of the nation, various size churches, and various size communities, a number of facts have been discovered.

Thirteen percent of the associate ministers in the study are under 24 years of age, and 12 percent are over 65. Twenty-one percent are 25 to 29 years of age, and 20 percent are 30 to 34 years of age. Ten percent are 35 to 39 years of age, and 15 percent are 45 to 54 years of age.

An analysis of age brackets leads to the following generalizations. There are a large number of associate ministers who are quite young. Such men, as it will be discovered later, have accepted an associateship as a means of in-service training following their seminary education. A few, probably 2 percent of the total sample, are interns doing an "intern year" between the second and third year of seminary training. There are a number of associates, probably 10 to 12 percent, who have retired from the pastorate and accepted an associateship. One-fourth of the associate pastors are career associates. This term refers to persons who have either deliberately or accidently become associate ministers and intend to remain associates during their entire ministry or for an extended period of time. Further research in the study supports the above findings. Some of the problems that arise in the office of associate minister can definitely be traced to the age factors involved.

Generally speaking, there are three distinct types of associate ministers, and the three types are used below for analysis. (1) The "intern associate." This is the young minister who may be doing an intern year while still in seminary or just out of seminary. Some denominations require such a year for ordination. Many young ministers choose to do a year or two as an associate following ordination before assuming their own full-time pastorate. They definitely look upon their associateship as an internship. (2) The "career associate." This is a group of associates who have chosen the associate ministry, or who have decided to remain in the associateship for one reason or another and make it their ministerial career. (3) The "second ministry" associate. This group is composed of persons who have been pastors, missionaries, teachers, chaplains, or carried other church positions, and who in later life accept an associateship. Many in this category have accepted early retirement and have gone into the associateship.

Seventeen percent of the associate ministers were born in the open country, and 18 percent were from homes where agriculture was the way of making a living. Twenty-one percent were born in towns of 500 to 2,500 persons, and an additional 13 percent were born in cities of 2,500 to 10,000. Thus, one-half of the associate ministers were born in communities of less than 10,000 persons, or that area commonly thought of in the church as town and country. Sixteen percent of the associates were born in cities of 100,000 to 500,000, and 10 percent were born in cities of more than 500,000. The above figures compare quite favorably with those for senior ministers. There are 54.5 percent of the senior ministers as compared with 51 percent of the associates who were born in communities of less than 10,000 people, and 12 percent of the senior ministers as compared with 10 percent of the associates who were born in centers of more than 500,000. However, there are 13 percent of the senior ministers as compared with 16 percent of the associate ministers who were born in cities of 100,000 to 500,000, or, in both cases, one-fourth of the ministers were born in urban centers of more than 100,000 population.

As was pointed out above, 18 percent of the associate ministers come from homes in which agriculture was the mode of livelihood, 26 percent from homes in which one of the professions was practiced, 19 percent had fathers in one of the managerial forms of work, 8 percent had fathers in clerical positions, 8 percent were engaged in sales, 15 percent were craftsmen, 2 percent were in service positions, 3 percent were skilled laborers, and 1 percent unskilled laborers.

Fifty-five percent of the associate ministers considered the ministry as a life vocation before they were 20 years of age. This compares with 67 percent of the senior ministers. Ten percent of the associate ministers considered the ministry as a vocation after the age of 30, while less than 1 percent of the senior ministers considered the ministry as a vocation after 30 years of age. A significant correlation between senior ministers and associate ministers can be drawn in regard to the age at which the final decision was made to enter the ministry. One half, or 50 percent of the associate ministers, made the decision to enter the ministry after they were 23 years of age, as compared with 14 percent of the senior ministers. Twenty-five percent of the senior ministers had been in secular work prior to entering the ministry, as compared with 39 percent of the associate ministers. Of those who had been in secular work prior to the ministry, 35 percent of the senior ministers had been in one of the professions compared to 50 percent of the associate ministers. Six percent of the senior ministers had been in managerial positions compared with 17 percent of the associate ministers. This leads to a supposition that a large number of associate ministers bring to their position professional and managerial skills. Senior ministers need to be aware of such skills and make it possible for the associate to find a useful release for such knowledge.

Thirty-eight percent of the associate ministers had been in their present position less than 2 years compared with none of the senior ministers. Thirty-two percent of the associate ministers had been in their present position 2 to 3 years as compared with 13 percent of the senior ministers, and 17 percent of the associates had been in their present position 4 to 5 years as compared with 21 percent of the senior ministers. Two-thirds of the senior ministers had been, at the time of the study, serving their present pastorate more than 6 years as compared with only 12 percent of the associate pastors. It is quite obvious there is a high rate of turnover of associate pastors and a low rate of turnover of senior ministers in the multiple-staff church.

Fifteen percent of the associate ministers had held another position in the local church in which they were serving prior to being associate pastor. This suggests some internal mobility within the staff.

For 23 percent of the associate ministers their present position was the first full-time church position. Fifteen percent had held one other position, and 20 percent had held two other positions. Seventeen percent had held 3 other positions. In other words, three-fourths of the associate pastors had held 3 or less positions in other congregations, and one-fourth had held from 4 to 8 or more positions. A partial analysis of the above data would indicate; first, there is a large number of quite young associates entering the associate ministry immediately following seminary. Second, there are a number of persons who have been in the associate position for a short period of time, but who may have been in other church positions prior to their present associateship. Third, there is still a third group who have held many church positions, either as associates or full pastors, who are now serving as associate ministers. Many older associate ministers will fall into the latter category, having served as a pastor or in other church positions for many years before accepting the associateship.

Ninety-two percent of the associate ministers hold a liberal arts degree, and 78 percent hold a Bachelor of Divinity degree or its equivalent. Twelve percent hold a Master's degree, and 3 percent hold a Ph.D. degree. Forty percent of the associate ministers have had special training in some field other than the ministry, such as business college, technical school, or crafts.

The most decisive factor in influencing the associate minister to choose the Christian ministry as a life vocation has been: first, parents, and second, a pastor. There is a clear indication that the younger associate minister has followed the usual vocational choice patterns while the older associate has had a strong influence from other pastors. There has been a decided trend in recent years for persons to enter the ministry at an older than normal age after being in a business or profession. Such persons have been deeply involved in church work and have seen the value of the church in modern society. They have discussed their desires for service with their pastor, and he has helped them to orient to the ministry. Strong emphasis on lay participation in local churches in evangelism, stewardship, and education have led a number of persons to feel they could invest their lives more adequately in the pastoral ministry. Faced with the necessity of an adequate income at a mature stage in life, such persons have found that the associate ministry offers an answer to the desire for the ministry, a specialization in the ministry rather than full pastoral responsibility, and a better than average starting income. In all likelihood there will be an increasing number of such persons entering the ministry. A president of an Episcopal seminary reported that 80 percent of the students in the seminary of which he was president had come from the business or professional world, not directly from college. This may prove to be one of the richest sources of manpower for the associate ministry. Many times such persons have learned from the business world how to work in groups, how to work with administrative leadership, how to be punctual, how to work with people, and how to fulfill a specialized role. All these areas are potential trouble spots for the associate minister.

Only 10 percent of the associate ministers are unordained, and 90 percent have full clergy rights. Most of the unordained associates anticipate ordination upon completion of the requirements of their denomination. Some of these are seminarians doing an intern year prior to receiving full clergy rights.

When asked why the associate ministry was chosen instead of the pastoral ministry, the following answers were given, with the percent of associates in the study who gave the answer: "the challenge of a specialized ministry," 37 percent; "there was no other opening available at the time I needed a position," 29 percent; "I felt I needed the in-service training I could get from being an associate," 30 percent; "I don't like to preach but like pastoral work," 4 percent. There were, however, approximately one-third of the associate pastors who did not answer the question. This leads one to believe there is considerable questioning on the part of many associates about the reason for being an associate. Other than the in-service training group (almost one-third of the associates), approximately 40 percent of the associates seem to have a clear-cut concept of the ministry and have deliberately chosen the associateship because it offers an opportunity for the release of their best talents. Such roles are evangelism, some phase of education, counseling, visitation, administration or other specializations.

The Intern Associate

An area of concern that may be overlooked by many senior ministers is that of the associate minister who looks upon his position as further education and anticipates the time when he will be pastor of a church or a senior minister on a church staff. The associate in this position expects the senior minister to take time to be his teacher. He is anxious to have the opportunity to be exposed to every phase of the pastoral ministry. He expects the senior minister to be a supervisor of his work and is disappointed if such supervision is not forthcoming. Few senior ministers are willing to give the time needed for supervision. Not only are few willing to give the time, but many admit they do not know how to give supervision. Some seminaries have spent vast sums of money in training pastors to be good supervisors of seminary students in their field education or internships, but in many cases it is a sad story for both student and senior minister.

A second major problem that arises with the associate who feels he is interning is his criticism of the senior minister. The young man who is just out of seminary, or who is still to complete his seminary work is frequently highly critical of the work of the senior minister, other members of the staff, the organizational structure of the church, the church program, and laymen. This leads to much friction, anxiety, and frustration. A senior minister will frequently lose patience with the "impudent young whippersnapper," rather than project his mind back to seminary days and remember when it was his place to challenge the status quo. Learning begins with an honest doubt. The seminary student lives in an environment of inquiry and serious questioning. He has heard his seminary professors refute the arguments of other scholars in theology, Bible, and ethics before the professor presents his own thesis on the subject. The student has been exposed to new forms of worship, new concepts of the church and ministry, new concepts of the laity, new forms of ministry, and new ideas on preaching. As yet these ideas are "in embyro"—theories that are not tried or experiments that have been observed.

If there is not to be a complete disruption and breakdown of communication there must be a give and take on the part of both senior minister and intern. The intern needs to be aware of the fact that he is entering into an ongoing, well-established church. He is joining a staff that has a program in operation which, in all likelihood, they feel is pretty good. Laymen have been at the job of witnessing in the church for many years. They may be conservative or liberal, or they may not be aware of some of the more recent movements in theological circles. At any rate, innovation by a young seminarian may not be as welcome as he may think. Patience, a season of orientation, listening more than talking, accepting directions for work, becoming acquainted with other persons on the staff, an open mind, an acceptance of other persons, and a genuine willingness to be a servant can go a long way in establishing good staff relationships.

The senior minister needs to assume a role as supervisor with the young associate pastor who is expecting to receive in-service training. A supervisor means exactly what the term implies—one who gives direction, oversees work, and assists in evaluating work done. Too frequently the senior minister is so involved in his own work that he does not take the necessary time to do supervision. He assumes the associate is equipped to perform his task, initiate his own work, and to perform responsibly in any assigned duty. This is usually too great an assumption. Some of the most frustrated associate ministers are those who have been given a special assignment by the senior minister, but do not know how to assume responsibility. I interviewed a young associate pastor in a prominent church located in a cluster of colleges and universities. The associate had been given the responsibility of ministering to college and university students. This task is one of the most difficult for even the most seasoned minister, but I found a man newly graduated from seminary who was at a total loss as to how to assume his responsibility. The senior minister assumed a "sink or swim" attitude, and the young man was sinking fast!

At the risk of exposing too much personal biography, I can illustrate what I mean by supervision on the part of the senior minister. Before going to my first full-time pastorate I served as an associate minister in a church in St. Louis. The senior minister, the late Rev. J. C. Montgomery, assumed his role as supervisor in an excellent manner. I had my specific responsibilities, but the senior minister exposed me to every phase of the parish ministry. He took me with him for pastoral visitation including evangelistic calls, sick calls, calls on the aged and shut-in, hospital calls, emergency calls, and calls on persons who were dying. I was with the senior minister as he took the Sacrament of the Lord's Supper to the sick and shut-in. I was with him as he arranged for a funeral service with a family, a wedding, an infant baptism, and reception of persons into the church. I was with the senior minister as he conducted funerals, weddings, baptisms, confirmations, and administered the vows of the church to older persons. He shared with me some of the personal problems he was dealing with in counseling sessions with members of the congregation.

We planned services of worship together, and he coached me on my part in the services, assisting me in making meaningful the reading of liturgy, Holy Scriptures, and leading a congregation in prayer. Each Friday morning the senior minister called me into his office for a two-hour session in preparation for the Sunday services. This was a time for study of the sermon to be preached, scriptures to be used, liturgies, prayers, and hymns to be sung. The music, including prelude, anthems, and postlude was considered. These sessions became hours of training for me as I gained an understanding of the meaning of worship, the unity of the service of worship, the structure of the sermon, and the importance of the sermon in worship.

The senior minister exposed me to the record-keeping system of the church. I was shown how to prepare church letters, the church newssheet, and financial statements, which were mailed to church members periodically. I was shown how to prepare an annual conference report. I was given experience in preparing a report for a Quarterly Conference (an official meeting of the former Methodist Church, which the District Superintendent conducted), and was a part of the Quarterly Conference. I was taught how to prepare for an official board meeting and was a part of the official board. I was given instructions in how to work with committees, commissions, and both men's and women's organizations in the church.

As I was shown my office the senior minister said to me, "I believe it is wrong for a pastor to be out of his office in the morning hours. This is your study, I hope you will take advantage of it as a *study*. Likewise, I feel it is wrong for a pastor to be in his office in the afternoon. He needs to be among his people and tending to the work of church organization during the afternoon." Here was established a habit of study, including a place and a time for study. One of the chief complaints of associate ministers is that they are not given the opportunity to study and that senior ministers do not make it possible for regular study time during the work day.

When the senior minister was on vacation I was expected to assume full responsibility for the pastoral ministry of the church. The congregation was so informed. Before the senior minister left for vacation he went through the four Sunday services with me, making sure we had orders of worship, selected hymns, and so forth, and I shared with him, as he had routinely done with me, the outline of the four sermons I was to preach in the morning services of worship. Suggestions were made for improvement of the sermons, and assurance was given to me that the sermons were of such quality that they would be helpful to the congregation.

Some of the most treasured experiences in my associateship were the periods of worship by the church staff. These were unhurried periods once a week conducted quite informally, but with deep sincerity. The senior minister shared with us the meaningful scriptures which had been guides for his own life and ministry. I received in these periods of worship dozens of sermon texts and "sermon starters"—a vitally important portfolio for the young minister starting his ministry!

I am sure many senior ministers reading the above will feel there was too much supervision, too much time given to the associate, that I should have been more on my own. Actually, it did not take as much of the senior minister's time as the account may imply. Much of what was done by the senior minister was routine. He simply invited me to share experiences with him. The senior minister confessed that the sharing in worship and in the preparation of his sermons became a refreshing experience for him. It takes a person with self-confidence and a nondefensive attitude to be so open and free with his staff. In the long run, however, the senior minister receives the greatest reward for such freedom. His preaching becomes better, the services of worship are more meaningful, and staff association becomes more dynamic.

Incidentally there are church staffs that have a weekly meeting of the ministerial staff to discuss the service of worship, including the sermon, for the succeeding Sunday. In such cases the staff members have developed a solidarity and a camaraderie of commendable nature. Associates feel they have made a contribution to the service of worship, and the senior minister is enriched by the associates. For many years the staff sharing in regard to the Sunday service and sermon has been a part of the Wednesday noon staff meetings in the East Harlem Protestant Parish in New York.

It cannot be too strongly emphasized that the intern associate looks upon his work in the church as a learning experience. The senior minister who does not see it this way is in for serious trouble. But the senior minister who proudly accepts the responsibility of being teacher and supervisor will derive much pleasure from his work, make a lastingly important contribution to the work of the ministry, and will see an enormous amount of work done by the associate minister.

Two words of warning need to be stated in conclusion: (1) To the intern associate—accept your position as a learner and a worker. Do not be openly critical to members of the congregation about how you would do things if you were at the controls. Avoid building a group of laymen about you who may be somewhat disgruntled with the senior minister. It is very easy for the young intern to become a victim of flattery by well-meaning, but unthoughtful laymen. I observed over a period of a year a young intern associate who drew about himself a group of laymen in the congregation who were somewhat unhappy with the senior minister. Cottage prayer meetings in the homes of some of the laymen, undue attention to them on the part of the intern associate, and finally direct planning resulted in the group leaving the church and organizing a new congregation with the intern associate as pastor. Needless to say, the new congregation was not authorized or accepted by the parent denomination, and the associate was forced to surrender his ministerial credentials. This meant the new congregation became affiliated with a small sectarian body, and the associate became a recognized member of that denomination. After four years the congregation dissolved, resulting in some very frustrated laymen, some of whom found their way back to the parent church, and the pastor of the abandoned church is now completely out of the ministry. This may be an extreme case, but it vividly illustrates the folly of an intern associate being prone to listen to flattery and building a small clique around himself.

The intern associate, as well as any associate, must be cautious in assuming pastoral responsibilities that are agreed shall be reserved for the senior minister. Frequently an associate has a self-image of the ministry that he desires to express. He may be immature in his ability. He may be in conflict with other persons on the staff whose responsibilities overlap some of his assignments. A case in point is an intern associate who conceived of himself as a better than average counselor. He was gifted in the ability to listen and to help people to discuss their personal problems with him. He had had enough formal training in psychology and pastoral care to understand some of the techniques of counseling. It all looked good until the intern associate began calling on persons who were under the direct counseling of the senior minister. It is entirely possible the intern associate may have done a better job of counseling than the senior minister, but until the senior minister was ready to release the parishioner to the intern associate, the latter needed to recognize his obligation to refrain from that particular responsibility. The final upshot of the matter was that the intern associate had an open conflict with the senior minister, and even carried this to the denominational executive! The associate lost his position and for some time was held in question by his denomination. Fortunately, he recognized the "error of his way," and he is now a very successful pastor. The story does illustrate the problem that arises when an associate minister attempts to move too fast, or to assume authority that is not his own.

(2) The second word is to the senior minister. If the senior minister is not willing to assume the role of teacher and supervisor with the intern associate, or if he feels ill at ease with such an associate, he had best not employ the intern associate. Some ministers are adept at being teachers and take pride in starting young men in the ministry. Other ministers feel threatened by the intern associate, and this leads to neglect and isolation, or withdrawal. Communication breaks down, and frustration on the part of both parties results.

The Career Associate

The second major group of associate ministers is what I am calling the career associate. The career associate is one who has chosen the associate ministry for one reason or another and has intentions of remaining an associate for a major part of his ministry. The career associate, as a general rule, has entered the ministry later than the senior minister or intern associate. Some have been in a position in the business or professional world. There are two major reasons the professional associate accepts his position: (1) He sees the associateship as an opportunity to release his ministerial talents and abilities without the necessity of assuming the total ministerial responsibilities; (2) the associateship offers a financial remuneration more commensurate with the economic level to which he has been accustomed in the business or professional world than does a "starting" pastorate.

There are a number of career associates who have started their ministry in an associateship or as an intern associate and have found it to be an acceptable and gratifying position. They have remained in the associateship by choice. In some cases these persons have attained an economic level that would be difficult to equal in a pastorate. This is particularly true in denominations with an episcopal form of government.

As a general rule the career associate has specific duties and responsibilities in the church staff. He goes about his work in a routine manner, quite happy and satisfied in his ministerial role. Specializations, such as calling on shut-ins, some phase of educational work, evangelism, or administrative responsibilities, are assumed by the associate. There is usually a clear understanding between the career associate and the senior minister as to areas of responsibility, and each grants complete freedom to the other to fulfill such responsibilities.

Internal mobility within the church staff may take place with the career associate. In other words, he may be shifted from one responsibility to another from time to time as needs arise within the church.

The larger the church and the larger the financial resources of the congregation, the more opportunities there are for specialization. For instance, a large church with an endowment may employ an associate minister for special language groups who may be in the vicinity of the church. They may employ a special minister of counseling, or a minister to college groups, or a minister of administration, or, as I discovered in one church, a full-time minister of drama. As the Protestant church continues to expand in size there will be greater demands for the professional associate, especially in specialized fields.

Many professional associates express a desire to remain associates all through their ministry, or at least are in doubt as to whether they will accept a pastorate. There is, however, considerable movement from associateship to pastorate by the career associate. This is brought about by dissatisfaction arising in the associate position and opportunities arising for a pastorate. Ordinarily if a career associate wants to accept a pastorate he is at an age when family and financial responsibilities are at a high point, making it necessary for him to have a pastorate with a substantial salary. Such pastorates are difficult to find, especially in a church with an episcopal form of church government. Moves in such churches are based, to a large degree, on exchanges—that is, exchanging ministers in certain salary brackets. The associate has nothing behind him to trade and must patiently wait for an opening to come through retirement or death of a minister. Even under these circumstances bishops are reluctant to place an associate in such an opening when it would afford an opportunity for advancing several ministers in their appointments. These are the hard facts of church politics that must be reckoned with. One of the chief frustrations of the career associate comes when he desires to change positions or to accept a pastorate, but is unable to find a position of comparable salary. Some career associates leave the ministry at this point and return to secular business.

This study leads to the following conclusions: (1) There is a firm need for the career associate in the Protestant ministry. (2) The need for the career associate will become greater. (3) The career associate should have a theological education and should attempt to discover his best talents and abilities and specialize in them. He needs homiletics and preaching. He will have the opportunity to preach on occasion, but not too often. Specialization can be in worship; administration; pastoral care, including parish visitation, group work, visitation evangelism, youth work, adult work, working with senior citizens; publicity; or church finance, to mention only a few areas.

The career associate needs to understand, along with all members of the staff, the executive responsibility of the senior minister. Associates are, as a general rule, quite willing and happy for the senior minister to assume the executive position. It is necessary in any organization for someone to be responsible for coordinating work. When the senior minister carries his executive responsibility with good cooperative leadership practices, and when tried and tested fundamentals of personnel management are applied by the congregation, all persons on the staff are released for greater service.

The Second Ministry Associate

The second ministry associate is described as the person who has served in some ministerial capacity and decides to accept an associateship, usually in the later years of life. Many persons feel they want to rid themselves of the heavy responsibility of the full pastorate, but want to continue in some form of ministry. Sources for such second ministry associates are retired ministers, retired college or seminary professors, retired military chaplains, returned missionaries and persons who have left one of the above ministries for various reasons. Twelve percent of the associate pastors in our basic study were 65 years of age or older, and 9 percent were 55 to 65 years of age.

The second ministry associate takes into his office years of experience and seasoned judgment. He can be an invaluable source of information for the senior pastor and an excellent help to other members on the staff. When placed in a definite responsibility role in the church staff the second ministry associate will usually function well. An example is one such minister who had been a very successful pastor, who made more than 2,000 pastoral calls per year. This was in a church of 3,500 members. He made evangelistic calls, visited new people in the community, the sick, and shut-ins. Though he had passed his three score and ten years, his health was good, his mind clear, and he possessed a tremendous "pastor's heart."

Adjustments are difficult for the second ministry associate. He must recognize that he is not in an executive position. He has to be reconciled to the fact that he is to preach no more, or only on rare occasions. Many times, however, the second ministry associate adjusts to his position more easily than the intern or career associate. Much literature in recent years has brought into the open the problems of aging and retirement. A gracious acceptance of the fact of increasing years and a ready adaptation to that fact can help the second ministry associate to be grateful for the opportunity to serve.

Conflicts of theology, administrative procedures, ideologies, and concepts of the ministry are inevitable between the second ministry associate, the senior minister, and other members of the staff. I recall visiting with a second ministry associate in a Midwestern city church. He had served for twenty-six years as a missionary in India. He, at the time of the interview, was sixty-six years of age, and was designated as minister of evangelism in the church. It was quite difficult for this associate to recognize, as a part of a meaningful phase of the church program, an exhibit of contemporary art accompanied by a week-long art festival and closing with a modern ballet in the church sanctuary! He disagreed theologically with the senior minister, twenty years younger than he, and felt out of place in many aspects of the program of the church. Yet, this highly trained and experienced associate had the ability to adapt to such a strange environment and fit into the total program of the church. He could not enthusiastically support those phases of the church's ministry which seemed foreign to him, but he went about his ministry of visitation and evangelism with zeal and dedication.

The retired military chaplain faces a serious problem of adjustment. He may be comparatively young, retiring after twenty years of service at the age of forty-five years or a little older. He is accustomed to the military command system with full expectations of having his orders obeyed. With laymen serving voluntarily and with staff personnel feeling their command is from the senior pastor, the retired chaplain may feel he has been sheared of his authority. It takes considerable time and patience to orient to a team concept in the church staff and a genuine servant attitude with laymen. Many times ministers would like to "command" laymen, but the good pastor soon learns that nurture and patience are most conducive to good ministerial leadership.

Terms or Titles

There has been much conversation among ministers as to terms or titles to be used for ordained persons on the church staff other than the senior minister. Some denominations have designated titles, such as the Episcopal Church, which uses the ancient and traditional term of curate, which means one who assists a vicar, rector, or pastor. The Presbyterian Church by constitution assigns the term associate to the pastor who has been elected by the Session as its chairman and serves as an administrator. The assistant is one who is assigned to some specialized ministry. The United Methodist Church has designated that a member of an annual conference shall be called a minister—e.g., minister of music, minister of education. If the person is not a member of an annual conference, he is to be called a director of music or a director of education. No specific direction is given for the associate or assistant pastor. Some congregations have adopted the policy of calling all ministers by the term minister. Hence, there is the minister of administration, minister of evangelism, minister of pastoral care, minister of visitation, minister of special activities, minister of music, minister of education, minister of youth work, minister of adults, and so forth. Those who are in a church that uses such terms seem to be pleased with the system. It identifies each person on the staff with a specific area of responsibility and implies teamwork rather than an association with or an assisting of the senior minister.

The term associate is used quite broadly. It implies a team situation in which senior minister and associate work together to perform the ministry to the congregation. The term assistant implies a helper or one who assists another. The term is used quite frequently in regard to the intern serving on a church staff.

A concept of the ministry is implied in the terms used. For instance, in our questionnaires several ministers emphatically stated that they were the pastors and all persons on the staff were their assistants to help them get their work done. If this is the philosophy of administration (a philosophy with which I happen not to agree) then the term assistant is appropriate and proper. If the pastor looks upon other members of the staff as associates in the total ministry of the church, with each person having an autonomous ministry to perform, then associate or minister is properly applied. Only rule of thumb direction can be given here. A number of denominational bodies have special committees at work attempting to define the specialized ministries, with all the implications in terms and job analyses.

Some Problems of the Associate Ministry

Through questionnaires, personal interviews, and special studies of the associate minister, a number of problems connected with the associate pastorate emerge. Some problems are listed here with supporting data and some suggestions for relieving the problems.

1. *There is a definite frustration on the part of many associates over the desire to have one's own pulpit.* This is particularly true of the associate who has been in the pastorate. Sixty percent of the associate pastors in our study stated they felt they were not asked to preach often enough. Only 28 percent of the associate ministers were satisfied with the arrangement in regard to preaching, and 19 percent stated it was not a serious problem, but they would like to preach more. Two percent emphatically stated the problem was irreconcilable.

Sixty-eight percent of the associate pastors stated there was a definite schedule for them to preach, and 27 percent stated there was no definite schedule. Eighty-three percent of the associates assisted with the Sunday morning service of worship by leading the ritual.

The problem of the associate being satisfied or dissatisfied with his preaching seems to vary by denominations and emphasis upon the place of preaching in worship. In the more liturgical denominations, such as Episcopal and Lutheran, the opportunity for conducting a service of worship, such as the celebration of Holy Communion or the leading of a brief service of worship in a day school, offers much satisfaction. Such services, which are conducted almost daily and at more frequent intervals on Sundays, afford many opportunities for ministerial leadership. With denominations that have made the sermon more the center for worship, the problem for the associate pastor is more acute. Sometimes the problem is solved by the associate preaching at an early service and the senior minister preaching at the traditional eleven o'clock service. Or the associate may preach at a vesper or evening service. Arguments are strong in favor of the senior minister doing all the preaching, however. A general attitude prevails, whether right or wrong, that when the senior minister does not preach the service is of secondary importance. There is also the threat that the senior minister may feel the sermon of the associate will have a better reception by the congregation than his sermon. It takes a mature senior minister to accept compliments from the congregation on the associate's preaching. If the senior minister is secure in his own preaching ability and does a creditable job of preparation, he can take pride in the fact that he has had a share in selecting an associate pastor who is a good homiletician.

There is an emerging, though not widespread, practice of ministers preaching on a rotation schedule. For instance, a congregation in Nebraska assists in maintaining two small mission congregations in the city along with the central church of several thousand members. There are three pastors. There are three services on Sunday morning in the central church and one each in the mission churches making a total of five services each Sunday morning. The three ministers move through a schedule week after week in which all share each service. This requires two ministers to conduct two services per Sunday. Each, however, moves through the routine of scheduled services with the senior minister taking his turn in the same way as the two associates.

Team ministries have been tried in various places and denominations. Little is being said in this writing because experiments, in most cases, have failed to establish the pattern as a sound working principle. There are, however, a number of situations in which two ministers share equal pulpit time.

The problem of who will preach in the absence of the senior minister is frequently a point of contention. Sixty-five percent of the senior ministers in our study stated the associate pastor preaches in the absence of the senior minister. Eighteen percent stated a visiting minister is recruited for preaching during the absence of the senior minister. It is quite clear that if the associate pastor feels capable of preaching and is bypassed in the absence of the senior minister, friction arises.

Probably there is no area with as much potential difficulty in pastor-associate pastor relationships as at the point of preaching. Here is competition at its height. The Protestant minister usually feels called to preach, not to pastor, or administrate, and when the opportunity for preaching is thwarted, frustration results and many times a sense of guilt. "Woe be unto me if I preach *not* the Gospel," was the cry of the Apostle Paul, and this remains the heartfelt center of the ministry.

The problem can be relieved, though probably never completely reconciled, by: (1) a definite understanding on the part of the pastor and associate (s) as to who will preach in the pastor's absence; (2) stated times in the church calendar when the associate will be expected to preach, such as early morning church service, Sunday evening service, or at certain seasons such as Lent; (3) preaching at a junior church service (The junior church, which is a separate worship service for children, has had its acceptance and criticism. It has never been accepted widely across the nation, but bears study for its own merit.) ; (4) conducting of brief services of worship by the associate minister in day schools or other special activities of the church.

Basically, the problem is one of clarity of roles and open communication between pastor and associate. If the truth were known, the matter of preaching is one of the major problems in pastor-associate relationships that leads to dissatisfaction and is the cause, in a number of cases, of men leaving the associateship.

An associate pastor needs to resign himself to the fact that he is not to preach often and that other phases of the ministry are equally important. True, it is at the point of preaching that the pastor receives the most praise. It may be quite galling as the associate stands beside the senior minister at the close of the Sunday morning service week after week and month after month while members of the congregation file by shaking hands and complimenting the pastor on such a fine sermon. Seldom does a layman compliment the associate on how meaningfully the liturgy was read or how helpful were the prayers. He simply speaks a word of greeting, as the congregation has come, in reality, to speak to the senior minister. I suppose the custom of greeting the minister at the close of the service will remain and be considered a part of the Protestant tradition symbolizing the fellowship of believers. Blessed, however, in the case of the multiple ministry, is that church which has two doors so the associate pastor can become an official greeter apart from the senior minister!

2. *A second major area of concern is the relationship of the senior minister and associate.* In other words, is the second minister an associate or assistant? Does the senior minister consider the associate as

one equal in ministry—that is, does the associate share all ministries with the congregation except, perhaps, preaching—or is the second minister an assistant doing what the senior minister cannot get done? As can be discerned, this is primarily a matter of attitude on the part of the senior minister. Do he and the associate form a team to fulfill a total ministry in the congregation? Do members of the congregation call with freedom on the associate for needed service, or only in the case where the pastor cannot perform the service? Does the associate have freedom to initiate his own work, or must he wait for direction from the senior minister?

To the question, How do you as senior minister look upon your associate? the following answers were received: (1) as a fellow worker on a team, 54.8 percent; (2) he does everything I do, 12.4 percent; (3) he does everything that I do, except preach, 5.6 percent; (4) he has specific responsibilities that do not conflict with those of the pastor, 23.4 percent; (5) he is definitely an assistant to me, 1.4 percent; and (6) no clear-cut concept, 2.1 percent.

The most satisfactory relationship in regard to meaningful roles is that of complete acceptance on the part of the senior minister and associate that both are ministers with equal responsibilities and rights. A clear job description which is periodically reviewed is essential if friction is to be avoided. The congregation needs to be thoroughly informed as to responsibilities of different members of the staff and how they are to look upon the associate in his work. Attitudes on the part of both senior minister and associate are determining factors in good and harmonious relationships at this point.

3. *A third question raised by associate pastors is, How creative can the associate be?* Can he move on his own initiative, or does he wait for instructions from the senior minister?

All persons have the desire for self-expression, and all members of the staff need the freedom to move on their own initiative. One senior minister stated to me that his policy is: (1) a thorough job description for each member of the staff with clearly defined responsibilities; (2) weekly staff meetings; (3) weekly periods of staff worship; (4) an annual three-day staff planning conference; (5) a complete "hands off" policy to allow the staff initiative, creativity, and freedom to act on their own; and (6) consultation with the pastor only when major policy changes are to be made. I found a happy, hard-working staff. On the other end of the continuum of staff freedom, I interviewed a minister to youth who said, "I can't be out of my office for twenty minutes without the senior minister questioning what I am doing."

This, no doubt, was an exaggeration, but it illustrates the fact of tight control by the senior minister. Needless to say the entire staff of the church was uneasy, there was a rapid turnover of personnel, and the senior minister was asked to leave after only two years.

Communication at all times and maximum freedom for each person on the staff is the only way to meet the needs for individual freedom in creativity. A senior minister needs to be open to any idea presented by any member of the staff and to serve—as has been suggested in the chapter on the senior minister—as enabler, making it possible for creativity to take place.

4. *When does the associate pastor assume the authority of the senior minister?* Is there a clear understanding of responsibilities when the senior minister is on vacation or unavailable in a given situation?

It does not take much imagination to realize how frustrating it is for an associate pastor to be left in a church in the absence of the senior minister without authority to make decisions and act upon decisions. Emergencies are a routine part of the life of every congregation—sudden illness, death, accidents, nervous collapse, and many other problems arise in the congregation that need immediate attention. In our sample study of church staffs, 79 percent of the senior ministers stated the associate pastor was in charge during his absence. Three percent stated all staff in charge, and 7 percent stated another minister was brought in. However, 43 percent of the senior ministers stated they had no policy in regard to the use of other staff persons for funerals and weddings. It can be readily observed that both staff and congregation would be confused without some understanding as to whom they could select from the church staff for special services.

Again, communications and understanding between the senior minister and associate are essential, and the congregation needs to be informed of the understanding. A statement in a newsletter or church publication can clear lines of communication quickly.

5. *How does the associate pastor accept the false concept of second-place standing with the senior minister?* Do remarks of others about his position bother him? If so, why?

There is much sensivity among associate pastors in regard to the secondary role. Again, this is the symbiotic relationship of competition and cooperation. There is a prevailing attitude among ministers and laymen that the associate pastor is strange or odd—there must be something wrong with him if he wants to be an associate. This attitude prevails primarily toward the career associate. One can look upon the intern associate and, to a certain degree, praise him for wanting to complete his training for the pastoral ministry. It is all right and even proper to serve as an intern associate—"just don't stay too long!" Or one feels it is "nice" for the older minister who has served the church well in some capacity to close out his active years as an associate. But the intern who stays more than two or three years in an associateship and seriously considers becoming a career associate, or the person who has already made the choice, faces serious problems with his colleagues and laymen.

Frankly, this is a prevailing false concept of the career associateship that needs to be changed among ministers, laymen, and denominational officials. The associates can do more to change the attitude than anyone else. Self-confidence and self-respect will go a long way to assist others to respect the position. Laymen need to orient to the fact that they have employed associates not as the senior pastor's assistant, but as ministers for and to the congregation. Many false attitudes toward the ministry have been created which put the senior minister at the receiving end of gratuities, praise, and an almost "holy admiration."

In a workshop on the church staff, after the persons present had finally molded into a group, one of the directors of education, a young lady in her mid-twenties, spoke up with the following quip, "Where do we get this pedestal bit for the senior minister anyway?" "Pedestal bit" is quite slangy, but nonetheless expressive. The senior minister is on a pedestal, and all too often the distance between the senior minister and associate is noticeably wide, especially as viewed by the associate. It takes a very mature and self-confident associate to cope with the false secondary role he is forced into fulfilling. There is a strong argument at this point for a team ministry where two ministers serve a congregation with absolutely equal status. As yet there are too few team ministries of success to have established a pattern.

We are at a stage in history where there is a need for acceptance of specialized ministries as ministry. By this I mean that ministers and laymen alike need to recognize that all staff personnel are ministers in the congregation, and as such there should be no "pedestal bit" for any minister. Denominational executives, especially in the episcopal form of government, need to orient to the fact that there is a need for the career associate to be included in the appointive system of the church. Too frequently the associate is left on his own to make arrangements with senior ministers and personnel committees without serious consideration by the bishop of the associate's needs. Bishops need to recognize that when they have ordained a minister and said to him in the service, "Take thou authority . . . ," the authority of the church is

131

responsible for all ministers regardless of their fields of specialization. Bishops are reluctant to accept the fact that associate pastors, as well as all ministers serving under appointment, are the responsibility of the conference. With the expansion of ministry to include many forms of ministry, denominational executives must reckon with the fact that ministry no longer refers only to the pastor, or to the senior minister in a multiple staff church. Some systematic plan must be devised for appointment of the associate minister, minister of music, and minister of education.

· 6. *The wife of the associate is looked upon as "number two."* Status symbols, rank, superior-subordinate roles all play into the prevailing attitudes of congregations regarding the wife of the senior minister and wife of the associate pastor as well as wives of other staff members. Traditionally in the Protestant church the senior minister's wife has been "queen of the manse," a sort of first lady of the congregation. Many minister's wives accept this role graciously with all the gratuities that go with it. It is quite natural, however, for a congregation to overlook the fact that there are other wives in the church staff family. It is also difficult for the senior minister's wife to share the attention she receives from the congregation with other staff wives. To even discuss this matter may seem out of place and out of harmony with the basic ethics of Christianity where servanthood is the essence; however, this is a very real problem in hundreds of church staffs. A dissatisfied wife, or a wife who feels second or overshadowed, can cause untold agony in the life of her husband. He is torn between loyalties and frequently will develop a strong sense of guilt because he has subjected his wife to a secondary role.

A genuine fellowship built around mutual concerns and interests can go far in breaking down resentment and jealousies. Wives of staff members need to build a fellowship through frequent association.

The wife of the senior minister holds the key to good relationships with other staff wives. If she holds herself aloof, feels superior, and fails to take the initiative for staff fellowship, cliques between other wives are inevitable, and resentment will result. Personality characteristics play a large part in staff harmony at this point. Self-analysis, honest evaluation, patience, give and take, are essential if one is not to be submerged into frustration. The staff fellowship gatherings have been discussed elsewhere. At the point of fellowship of the families lies the secret to much of the avoidance of staff wife problems.

Wives of staff members need to be apprised of the central objectives and goals of the staff. They need to feel the spiritual fellowship of the staff. They need to be accepted by the entire staff and, as far as they desire, they should have a voice in staff decisions. I am sure this raises all kinds of problems for many senior ministers, but there are hundreds of hidden motives in members of church staffs because of unhappy wives. It is common knowledge that in the business and professional world the counsel of a good wife is highly prized by her husband. Many major business decisions must wait for family counsel. Much joking about this fact goes on in the business world, but it remains true. With women as well trained academically as men, and minister's wives frequently sensing a calling to the profession, their judgment in decision-making can be a valuable asset to staff planning. Some staffs include wives in their planning sessions, especially in the annual retreat where long-range planning is done. No wife should be forced into a position in which she is expected to participate in staff planning, but on like account, no wife should be left out if she desires to be a part of the staff planning. In interviewing church staffs, I found one of the most harmonious groups in a Colorado city. I discovered that the staff was to be in their annual summer retreat and planning session in a resort near our family summer cottage. After we had enjoyed a noon luncheon together I suggested the wives could go to the front porch and talk while the staff had a business session. The pastor said in substance, "We don't make any distinction. Wives remain in our business session if they want to." They did, and made some excellent suggestions for staff planning. There is no doubt in my mind that openness, fellowship, and self-confidence on the part of the pastor, who incidentally had excellent managerial ability, all contributed to the harmony and fine work of the staff.

7. *When the senior minister of a staff is moved and a new senior-minister comes into the church, the associate minister is put into an uneasy position.* The matter of changing staff at the time of a change of senior ministers, tenure, employment and dismissal policies are discussed elsewhere. Sufficient is it to say at this point that the associate pastor needs to be aware of the policies of the congregation and denomination and abide by them.

8. *Loyalty to the senior minister is essential, and the associate should be careful to not become a prima donna.* This point needs no elaboration, but expresses a major area of staff problems.

9. *There should be no surprises for the associate.* In a large church with several ministers on the staff, all associates should be a part of all major planning. Communication is central in good staff relationships.

In addition to the problems raised above by associate pastors, eighteen areas that they felt would make for more efficient staff operations are listed. It must be remembered that the following is the expression of what I have termed the career associates.

1. There should be a clear job analysis. Who is responsible for what, and to what extent? What are church policies concerning office hours, vacations, days off, and so forth?

2. There should be a good relationship with the pastor—a give-and-take process that goes beyond the boss and worker experience. There must be an open line of communication.

3. Regular, structured staff meetings in which plans are projected and problems are discussed are necessary, so that programs can be coordinated and information can be exchanged.

4. There is a need for worship, study, and sharing experiences for the staff as a whole.

5. Fellowship time for staff members to get to know each other as persons is helpful to offset knowing these same people as only representatives of certain church programs. If some opportunity of this kind is not provided, staff meetings will be hampered by misunderstandings.

6. There should be some definition of the staff and lay responsibility for church programs. Some idea needs to be given of this church's understanding of the laity, the role of the staff members, and so on.

7. An associate pastor must acknowledge the head pastor as head pastor. This involves acknowledging the head pastor to be the pacesetter and director of the total staff atmosphere.

8. One must learn to maintain something of a oneness of attitude and effort, while at the same time honoring differences.

9. It should be noted that better relationships and work will be the mark of a staff that has been assembled from among persons with similar philosophies and theologies.

10. Criticisms should be made first within the staff family, second (if needed) to the personnel committee, but never openly to the "public."

11. Honesty and frankness must prevail between staff members.

12. The pastor should make, from time to time, public statements to the congregation with regard to the responsibilities and status of the associate pastor.

13. Each staff meeting should feature a devotional period. This helps a staff to remember that, though they are in a sense a "business,"

ultimately the "business is the work of Christ's Kingdom." The devotional period helps the staff to keep this perspective and helps them avoid losing a good sense of values.

14. Each staff member needs to be autonomous, insofar as this is possible. (They should be like chief petty officers in the Navy. The captain of the ship issues general instructions but virtually never interferes with the chief's job or tells him how to do it.) This should apply all the way to the custodians.

15. Staff members, especially associate ministers, education directors, and music directors, need to keep the pastor advised constantly on how projects assigned to them are developing. This is also true of the pastor. Communication is a two-way street!

16. An associate should have frequent conferences with the senior minister.

17. There should be a constant theological sharing between ministerial staff members.

18. The senior minister must have a willingness to support the staff person in his difficult decisions.

7

The Church Educator

Introduction

The term "the church educator" is used as the title of Chapter 7 in a broad and inclusive manner. There are a number of types of professional educators on the church staff with different titles and responsibilities. The major portion of the chapter treats the work of the office of director or minister of education, which includes administrators of education and divisional personnel, such as children, youth, and adult workers.

In addition to the more traditional positions there are directors of recreation, drama, art, specialists in the field of older adults, writers and educators of church publications, college and university campus ministry directors (who in many instances are members of a church staff), counselors, Boy Scout and Girl Scout directors, day school directors and teachers, and so forth. Each person has a field of specialty that requires a specific type of training. Some denominations designate the title of the position on the basis of professional education. For instance, The United Methodist Church designates as Director of Religious Education one who has a professional graduate degree in religious education; an Educational Assistant is one who does not have a professional religious education degree; and a Minister of Education is one who qualifies for the ordained ministry with special studies in religious education. The Southern Baptist Church does not have any official ordination except to the pastoral ministry. Thus many ordained ministers serve in specialized ministries and are generally listed as associate or assistant pastors.

Though there have been specialists on the church staff in religious education for almost fifty years, there is considerable confusion as to the work of the educator, the central goals and purposes of Christian education in the local church, and the relationships between the Christian educator and other members of the church staff. James D.

Smart states, "So confused is the educational situation in the Church that we may easily be guilty of harsh and uncharitable judgments unless we understand something of the interplay of forces and ideas during the past two centuries." [1]

To speak more intelligently to the office and work of the Christian educator on the church staff this chapter is divided into three major sections. "Christian and Public Education in History" will trace briefly the relationship of public and religious education, their interdependence, their separation, and their influence upon each other and the Christian education movement in particular. This material may cast some light upon the difficulties that seem to be present in defining the basic aims and objectives of Christian education in the local church.

"The Office and Person of the Director of Christian Education" presents basic statistical data concerning the persons in the office of Director of Christian Education as gleaned from research, some of the basic problems the Christian educator faces in his position on the church staff, and some suggested solutions.

"The Day School Workers, Directors and Teachers" is a brief statement concerning the day school staff and their relationship with other members of the church staff.

Christian and Public Education in History

The teaching aspects of the Judaeo-Christian faith tie back historically into the teaching of the faith by parents and primarily by the father in the Jewish family. Tradition placed the responsibility upon the father. "And these words which I command you this day shall be upon your heart; and you shall teach them diligently to your children, and shall talk of them when you sit in your house, and when you walk by the way, and when you lie down, and when you rise." (Deuteronomy 6:6-8 RSV)

Smart has summarized in a few sentences the development of the educational task of the church:

Little is known concerning the provisions for education in the Biblical period, perhaps because it had its locus so largely in the home. In Israel the parents were charged with the responsibility of educating their family in the true faith, and there were religious festivals in the home which gave oppor-

---

[1] *The Teaching Ministry of the Church* (Philadelphia: Westminster Press, 1954), p. 46.

tunity regularly for calling attention to essentials of that faith. In the time of Jesus there were synagogue schools, elementary and advanced, in which boys first learned to read and memorize the Scriptures and then went on to problems of interpretation. In the Early Christian Church, new emphasis was placed upon teaching because of the necessity that converts should be thoroughly instructed in their faith. . . .

The medieval period represents an all-time low for education in the Church, and the general neglect was reflected in the ignorance of many of the clergy. The emphasis upon the sacraments as the essential means of grace led to a decline and even to an abandonment of preaching, so that the people, uninstructed in the Scriptures in worship, became incapable of teaching their own children in the home. Schools attached to monasteries reached a few youths, but rarely any except those destined for a special vocation in the Church.

The Reformation Churches, therefore, with their restoration of the preaching of the Word of God to the center of worship, with their reinstitution of catechetical instruction before confirmation, and with their insistence upon the duty of every parent to instruct the members of his family in the Bible and doctrine, were actually returning to the order that existed in the churches of the first three centuries. But, like all such returns, it picked up the lines of development and carried them farther than they had been carried before. A church reformed according to the Word of God in Scripture depended for its health upon the ability of its members to read and understand the Scriptures for themselves. The Bible, therefore, was translated into the language of the common man by Tyndale, Luther, and others. But that was not sufficient unless the common man was trained to read. So the Reformers were propelled into new developments in education. In Geneva, Calvin founded schools to provide an elementary education for all, and in that education the religious and the cultural elements were united. John Knox, under Calvin's influence, initiated similar educational reforms in Scotland. His aim, which was not always realized, was a school in every parish, and a *schoolmaster* [italics mine] alongside the parish minister, in close co-operation with him.[2]

The insistence by the reformers on each person reading the Bible stimulated a new interest in education as "each man is his own High Priest."

The modern Sunday school movement had its start in England in 1780 by Robert Raikes. It was a movement to teach illiterate children to read. The movement grew until it emphasized the need for all children to have instruction in reading, writing, arithmetic, and Bible lessons. Thus it became a school for all children instead of just the poor. In the establishment of the colonies on American shores, the educational pattern was that of joining both secular and religious teachings. "Thus, when the Puritans came to New England, one of their primary concerns was to establish their own religious orthodoxy as the law of the land in Massachusetts, Connecticut, and New Hamp-

---

[2] *Ibid.,* pp. 46-48.

shire. In many ways they showed their intent that the state should support the Congregational Church in accordance with Calvin's outlook." [3]

Butts and Cremin continue to describe the religious education movement:

Denominational schools. As the colonial period progressed, the most active promotion of schools was undertaken by religious groups. This took the form of schools established by an individual congregation or minister, by neighboring churches as a cooperative undertaking, or by religious societies organized on a wider basis. The most characteristic educational pattern of the middle colonies was the development in the eighteenth century of denominational schools sponsored by a local church or by denominational effort.

In Pennsylvania, after the first efforts at state promotion of schools, the several denominations promoted their own schools. The Quakers established schools in Philadelphia and eastern Pennsylvania; such sectarian groups as Lutherans, German Reformed, Moravians, and Mennonites established their elementary schools in the middle counties of Pennsylvania; the Scots-Irish Presbyterians were especially enterprising in setting up schools in the western counties; and the Puritans who settled in the Wyoming Valley in northern Pennsylvania brought their New England type of school with them. As noted earlier, the Pennsylvania legislature passed acts in the early eighteenth century making it possible for the various religious groups to own property for educational purposes. [4]

The joining together of church and state and later the struggle for separation of church and state are all a part of the history of the United States. Since denominations were the most active agents in the promotion and establishing of schools it is plain to see how the religious influenced the secular teaching, and how the secular teaching influenced the religious.

With the separation of the church and state in the educational movement, there eventually arose problems between the two as to what should be taught and how it should be taught. As long as the key persons in the learning and teaching process were such men as John Calvin and Jonathan Edwards, the main emphasis was placed upon the Hebraic-Christian traditions as being fundamental to all that was taught. When the teaching was moved from church control to state control, with exponents in the teaching field holding some or few basic Christian beliefs, then no longer was the main goal the complete incorporation of the Hebraic-Christian faith in all teaching.

---

[3] R. Freeman Butts and Lawrence A. Cremin, *A History of Education in American Culture* (New York: Holt, Rinehart & Winston, 1964), p. 17.

[4] *Ibid.,* p. 111.

Learning originally was natural and easy when it was carried on in an informal way. The natural way was at the knee of the parent, and no matter whether the knowledge was religious, biblical, or cultural, no great problem was posed. In the primary group little resistance to learning was encountered.

Learning was less effective, however, when education, either religious or public, was transferred to the formal classroom. Barriers between teachers and pupils were more in evidence. To surmount these obstacles various theories of learning have been developed through many hundreds of years.

Morris L. Bigge in *Learning Theories for Teachers* gives an excellent chart outline of ten representative theories of learning with key persons representing these theories, spanning the time from Plato and Aristotle to the present late Kurt Lewin and J. S. Bruner.[5] (See Appendix C.)

The influence of Johann Pestalozzi (1745-1827), Jean Jacques Rousseau (1712-1778), Friedrich Froebel (1782-1852), Horace Bushnell (1802-1876), William James (1842-1910), John Dewey (1859-1952), and many others shaped not only the theories and focal point of the educational systems of both Europe and the United States, but also provided the backdrop for Western religious educational thought into the 1950's. The influence is still felt at this time.

In 1847 Horace Bushnell published his first draft of *Christian Nurture*. He held that the child born and reared in a Christian home becomes a part of the Christian experience early in life and participates in the church from birth. This teaching led to a concept of the church school as being a nurturing agent rather than an evangelistic agent.

The influence of Bushnell, the advances of form criticism in biblical scholarship, the rise of child psychology, the psychology of religion, and educational psychology produced educational theories that have resulted in the permissive church, the permissive home, and permissive education. This brought an era in which goodness of the individual was emphasized without parental, church, or teacher discipline being applied in principle or content. John Dewey was the chief proponent of the progressive movement in the educational field. Randolph Crump Miller states, "The theories of John Dewey, especially his idea of 'education as a social process,' were taken into the

---

[5] Bigge, *Learning Theories for Teachers*, pp. 12-13.

thinking of all competent religious educators." [6] "Dewey was primarily concerned with how things were taught rather than with what was taught." [7]

Since the Second World War there has been the population explosion, the educational explosion, the rapid rise of technology, and the space race. In the midst of confusing speed there has been a deterioration of moral standards and confidence in basic institutions that have maintained the stability of American culture: the home, the school, and the church. With more wars and rumors of wars and major conflicts in political and governmental ideologies, the Christian educator is having to regain his *raison d'être*. "The death of the Progressive Educational Association in 1955 and the passing of its journal, *Progressive Education*, two years later marked the end of an era in American pedagogy." [8]

The above quotation that the progressive education movement under the tutelage of the late John Dewey has faced a collapse in academic circles, raises the question, What then happens to a religious education movement that was based upon Dewey's principles?

The question here is the *source* of educational theory. If Christianity adopts secular theories without questioning them, it will be working for secular ends. Teaching based on an uncritical acceptance of Dewey's educational theory and view of the universe will point students toward a Dewey world-view rather than toward a Christian view of life.

Christian educational theory must not be a footnote to secular discoveries. The goals and values of Christian education are derived from Christian theology and not from secular methodology. From a theological perspective, educational theories and methods are to be evaluated and used within the framework of Christian faith. [9]

The cognitive-field theory of learning, the goal insight, and insight theories have emerged in recent years, influencing to a great degree contemporary education.

Contemporary Christian educators are making a noble effort to redefine the purposes and goals of Christian education in the local church. Rachel Henderlite in her opening statement in *The Holy*

---

[6] *Education for Christian Living* (Englewood Cliffs, N. J.: Prentice-Hall, 1956), p. 33.

[7] Richard LaPiere, *The Freudian Ethic* (New York: Duell, Sloan & Pearce, 1959), p. 115.

[8] Lawrence A. Cremin, *The Transformation of the School Progressivism in American Education* (New York: Knopf, 1962), p. vii.

[9] *Education for Christian Living*, p. 45.

Spirit in Christian Education points to the problem and recognizes the basic difference between Christian and secular education.

> Christian education is basically different from general education. Our failure to recognize this fact has cost the church incalculable waste in effort, if not in lives. It has been the church's great mistake over the years, and without deliberate intent, to set up general education as its model, and then copy it in objectives, in methods, and even in psychological theory. As a consequence, Christian education has been more educational than Christian, and in failing to be both, has led the church into a blind alley which the church can now extricate itself only with great effort.[10]

The vast revisions of church curricula in most major denominations with a new emphasis on biblical and historical theolgy is evidence of the contemporary effort to establish a church school movement and Christian education movement based upon sound Christian principles. New curricula are based upon new definitions of Christian education Henderlite states:

> The goal of Christian education is the life of faith that we see first in the New Testament church. It cannot be otherwise. Christian education is the work of the church for the nurture of its members in faith. Its goal is that men may respond to the call of God in Jesus Christ and may live in all life's relationships and responsibilities as children of God.
>
> But because such faith in God is a gift from God himself and is called forth by the work of his Spirit, the church is able only to provide a context and means that the Holy Spirit may use. To this end the church must develop a program of education that takes full account of the nature of man and the nature of God and that leaves itself in readiness to be used of him.[11]

An effort is being made to recapture the basic concepts of nurture in the faith and personal commitment by the individual as well as continued growth in Christian knowledge and practice. Howard Grimes has summarized the contemporary thought:

> Thus, the ministry of teaching, as it grows out of the nature of church, is at least threefold, as Roger Shinn has made clear. First, it is responsible for introducing persons, young and old, to Christian community, and this includes the hope that a faith relationship with God will be the result. Second, it is responsible for transmitting the heritage of the community, of making known a systematic formulation of the faith. And third, it must also equip its members to be the church in the world so that they may not only live Christianly in the world but also witness to their faith in deed and word. A fourth respon-

---

[10] (Philadelphia: Westminster Press, 1964), p. 15.
[11] *Ibid.*, p. 36.

sibility, which we have already noted, grows out of this latter, namely, the work of witness and teaching in the world by those who have been taught within the structure of the church.[12]

In closing this phase of this chapter I call attention again to the need for a clear statement of goals and objectives. Goals and objectives must be established for individuals as well as for the staff as a whole. When the basic goals of the church staff are placed alongside the basic goals of Christian education as stated by Howard Grimes, it is clear the two are in complete agreement. It must be repeated that for good staff relationships it is essential that corporate goals of the church staff be established, and as far as possible individual goals of persons on the staff be brought into accord with corporate goals.

The Office and Person of Director of Christian Education

After the separation of church and state in the United States, the Sunday school movement found a ready acceptance. Local churches of most denominations organized Sunday schools with the primary purpose of teaching the Bible and bringing people to grips with the relevance of the gospel to personal commitment and Christian living. Sunday school unions were formed in America in the early nineteenth century, and in 1824 the American Sunday School Union was formed as a means of coordinating the work of the unions. It had a profound influence on the Sunday school movement, with one of its major accomplishments being the establishment of the Uniform Lessons in 1872. In 1908 graded lessons were formed, developing further the refining of the teaching-learning process. The Religious Education Association was formed in 1903, and two decades later the International Council of Religious Education was formed.

Churches with large memberships in the beginning of the twentieth century were feeling the need for a ministry of education, and by 1909 several churches in the eastern United States had employed directors of Christian education. As early as 1902 educators were seeing the need for special training in the field, and Vanderbilt University established a department of religious education. In 1903 the Hartford School of Religious Pedagogy was established. Other universities soon followed, and formal graduate degrees in religious education were established.

---

[12] "Theological Foundations for Christian Education," *An Introduction to Christian Education*, Marvin J. Taylor, ed. (Nashville: Abingdon Press, 1966), p. 35.

By 1915 there were more than one hundred employed directors of Christian education. This number had grown to three hundred by 1929. After the depression in the 1930's, there was a new emphasis upon the position. At this time, the demand is greater than the supply. It is estimated that there are approximately eleven thousand persons currently employed as Christian educators in local churches in the United States.[13]

There is no other position on the church staff, except the pastoral ministry, that has received so much attention. Volumes have been written in the field of Christian education. Journals produced by Christian or religious education societies, national and international, have carried hundreds of articles in the field, many of which have been written specifically about the office of the professional educator on the church staff. Annual meetings, denominationally and inter-denominationally, have brought together religious educators to hear lectures, formal papers, and to discuss the various phases of religious education.

The next section is a description of the persons in the position of DRE and some of the attributes of the office.

From data obtained from directors of religious education (referred to as the DRE) some statistics have been compiled giving insights into the characteristics of the DRE and the office in the local church.

Table 2. Age distribution of DRE's

Age	Percent of DRE's
65 or older	6
55 to 64	14
45 to 54	20
40 to 44	12
35 to 39	10
30 to 34	24
25 to 29	13
24 or younger	1

Fifty-eight percent of the DRE's in our study are women, and 42 percent are men. Thirty percent are ordained and have full clergy rights, with 70 percent not ordained. For persons with full clergy rights their position is in some cases a combination of associate pastor with

---

[13] Gentry A. Shelton, "The Director of Christian Education," *An Introduction to Christian Education*, p. 117.

special emphasis on the educational ministry. As far as the work of the professional educator on the church staff is concerned, however, ordination is incidental and not essential to the office, as is described in Chapter 1.

The age distribution of the DRE's in the study is shown in Table 2.

The largest number of DRE's is in the age bracket of 30 to 34, with the second largest number 45 to 55 years of age.

Thirty percent of the DRE's were in their first church position, with 25 percent having had one other position in a church. Table 3 lists the length of time persons were in their present position.

Table 3. Percent of DRE's who had been in present position by years

Years in present position	Percent of DRE's
Under 2 years	41.7
2 to 3	26.6
4 to 5	14.3
6 to 8	10.7
9 to 12	4.3
13 to 15	1.0
16 to 20	1.4

Table 4. Number of positions DRE's have held in other churches

Number of positions	Percent of DRE's
No other position	30.3
1	25.0
2	16.6
3	12.2
4	6.0
5	4.6
6	3.7
7	1.5

Of the DRE's who have served in more than one church, 44 percent had served from 1 to 2 years, and 37 percent had served 3 to 4 years.

It is obvious that, as a general rule, the tenure of the DRE in a local church position is comparatively short.

Forty-two percent of the DRE's have served in another business or profession prior to their selecting a religious vocation. Of the persons in secular work prior to church work, 48 percent had been in a profession, and 27 percent had been in clerical work.

Education for the work of the DRE varies considerably. Table 5 lists the percent of the DRE's and type of education. It will be observed that 4 out of 5 hold a liberal arts degree, and 1 out of 3 holds a Master of Religious Education Degree. One out of 4 holds the professional ministerial degree of Bachelor of Divinity or its equivalent.

Table 5. Educational background of DRE's

Educational Level	Percent of DRE's Completing
High School	96.3
Liberal Arts Degree	82.7
Bachelor of Divinity	26.3
Master of Religious Education	30.2
Master of Sacred Music	1.0
Master of Sacred Theology	2.0
Master of Arts	9.3

The place of birth and occupation of fathers of the DRE's compares favorably with that of the senior ministers.

Table 6. Size of community of family residence at time of birth of DRE's

Size of Community	Percent of DRE's
Open country	15.8
Under 500	5.7
500–2,499	13.6
2,500–9,999	13.6
10,000–24,999	12.9
25,000–99,999	10.7
100,000–499,999	16.5
500,000 or more	10.7

Table 7. Occupation of fathers of DRE's

Father's occupation	Percent of DRE's
Professional	32.8
Agricultural	23.8
Managerial	18.6
Clerical	5.9
Sales	5.9
Craftsman	1.4
Skilled labor	.7
Laborer	1.4

More than half of the DRE's were reared in homes of professionals or agriculturists. Agricultural homes provided 1 out of 4 of the DRE's.

Three out of 4 DRE's considered a church vocation as a life profession prior to their twenty-fifth birthday, with more than half of the DRE's considering a church vocation before they were 20 years of age. A few, however, delayed the definite decision to enter a church-related vocation until they were a little older. Table 8 lists by percentage the number of DRE's in different age brackets, giving the age when they considered a church vocation and age when the definite decision was made.

Table 8. Age when DRE's first considered
a church-related vocation,
and age when decision was made

Age	Percent who considered a church-related vocation	Percent who made decision to enter church-related vocation
10 or younger	3.2	
11–13	4.8	7.5
14–15	17.8	16.6
16–17	20.3	16.6
18–19	13.0	16.6
20–21	11.3	11.6
22–24	5.6	4.1
25–29	3.2	10.8
30–39	20.3	26.5

Sixteen percent of the DRE's made the decision to go into a church vocation after the age of 40 years. Some of these were widows.

Motivating factors that entered into making the decision to go into a church vocation were parents, a pastor, the secret call to a religious vocation, and a variety of other reasons, such as being widowed and interested in a church position.

Table 9. Influential factors in the decision to choose
a church vocation and percent of DRE's who
consider the factor a major influence

Factor	Percent of DRE's
Parents	23.8
Pastor	14.2
Friends	2.3
Secret call	15.0
Church school teacher	11.1
Youth camp experience	6.3
College professor	1.5
Other	25.3

The above is an indication of the major factors entering into the decision. It is quite obvious that there are in many cases a combination of factors that have influenced persons to choose a church-related vocation.

One-fourth of the DRE's receive between $5,000 and $6,000 annually, and an additional one-fourth receive between $6,000 and $8,000.

Forty-three percent of the DRE's receive less than $5,000 annually. Of that number approximately one-half are part-time employees.

Thirteen percent of the DRE's have a parsonage or manse supplied by the church, and an additional 24 percent receive a housing allowance. Twenty percent receive part or all of their utilities. Sixty percent of the DRE's receive an allowance for travel on church business, with the largest number receiving between $300 and $500 annually.

One-half of the DRE's have provided by the church some type of retirement plan other than Social Security. Eighty-seven percent participate in Social Security.

One out of three DRE's feels the salary is too small, with the same number required to supplement their income from another source.

At the time of the gathering of data, 62 percent of the DRE's were married, 22 percent were not married, and 16 percent were widowed or divorced. Twenty-six percent of the DRE's had no children. Eighteen percent had one child, 26 percent had two children, and 17 percent had three.

Forty-two percent of the DRE's are provided four weeks of vacation annually, 30 percent have two weeks vacation, 11 percent have no vacation plan, with the remaining 17 percent varying from one week to the "entire summer off." Two percent of the DRE's have a stated sabbatical year, and 30 percent receive some funds from the church for travel and study outside the parish on an annual basis.

One out of two DRE's has a job description or job analysis.

In the churches employing DRE's, 74 percent have regular staff meetings with 71 percent of those having staff meetings holding them once per week.

Eighty-seven percent of the DRE's feel the staff meeting creates harmony in the staff, with the same number feeling it adds to the efficiency of the work of the staff. Of the DRE's who are in churches where staff meetings are not held, 77 percent feel they should have staff meetings, 10 percent feel they should not, and 13 percent are unsure.

DRE's were asked a series of questions concerning areas of conflict within the staff. Table 10 lists some of the common problems with the percent of DRE's in the study who felt each was or was not a problem.

Table 10. Problem areas in the church staff
and percent of DRE's who felt each was or was not a problem

Problem Area	Percent of DRE's feeling a problem	
	Yes	No
Theological differences	20.0	80.0
Difference in age	17.2	82.8
Length of time on the staff	30.8	69.2
Salary differences	12.0	82.0
Pastor shows favorites	12.3	87.7
One person on staff too dominant	38.3	61.7

One person being too dominant in the staff and tenure on the staff are major areas of staff conflict. Theological differences and age differences are the other areas of major conflict. These are probably in rather close coordination since theological positions vary greatly according to the period in theological education when one was in formal training. There is a tendency for one to retain throughout life the basic theological position received in seminary. As younger persons come on the church staff they bring with them the theological position of their day. This can result in serious conflict. An open-minded-ness on the part of all staff members and a willingness to engage in mutually respected discussion on theological issues will assist in the growth of all persons in theological knowledge. It has been discovered that theological differences are not as divisive in the church staff as an unwillingness to engage in theological discussion with an open mind and respect.

One-fourth of the DRE's in the study were unhappy with their office space, with "too small" and "not enough privacy" being the major complaints. Sixteen percent felt their equipment was inadequate.

Approximately one-half of the DRE's felt they had adequate help. Eleven percent have no help at all, and the remaining 39 percent had to share secretarial help and did not receive enough time from the secretary.

Eighty-six percent of the DRE's are members of the local congregation in which they work, with an additional 6 percent members of the denominational body or an organization of the denomination, such as an annual conference.

Sixty-five percent of the DRE's stated they had no scheduled time in their daily work schedule for study and personal enrichment. This is an area of chief complaint among DRE's. It is understood that the preaching minister in a congregation must have scheduled time for study, but in many situations there is no scheduled time for other staff members to study or seek personal educational enrichment.

Sixty-two percent of the DRE's state there is no regularly scheduled time for staff worship. There is considerable uncertainty as to whether staff worship is essential, though of those staffs which do have a worship experience, 90 percent feel it is valuable and 10 percent question its value.

Approximately one out of two DRE's say they feel that a difference in theological point of view with the senior minister is a major cause of concern, and one out of five feel it is a major problem in the staff. Associated with this basic difference is a difference in the concept of educational theories and the place of Christian education in the church. This difference is of such magnitude that it deserves much attention by the senior minister and the educator on the staff. It is one of the most serious areas of staff disharmony.

The DRE's were asked to voice their opinion as to what should be emphasized in training for the position. In descending order of importance the DRE's stated: special training in the dynamics and psychology of leadership, administration and methods of teaching, theology, and Bible. Much emphasis was placed upon supervised in-service training and the intern year.

An interesting and revealing phase of the responses of DRE's to the question, What advice would you give to a person considering the position of DRE as a life vocation? is that 46 percent had some reservation. The trend of thought was "do it, provided . . . ." Provided there is a good working relationship with the pastor. Provided one has patience and stamina to get along with people. Provided one is quite secure in himself and sure of his own self-understanding.

In spite of the fact that the number of directors or ministers of Christian education has grown with accelerated speed since World War II and the demand is greater than the supply, there is in some cases uncertainty about the position and a lack of clear understanding as to the role and purpose of the educator on the church staff. There is a large and rapid turnover in the position in the local church. There is also a sizable dropout from the position into secular work. Observation, research, and writings in the field lead to the conclusion that the work of the DRE still needs further defining and much clarification of the position needs to be made. Especially is this true in the relationships with the senior minister.

Standards

A large portion of literature in the field of the professional educator on the church staff reflects the need for sound personnel management policies and good leadership procedures. In a Ph.D. thesis by Wayne M. Lindecker, Jr.,[14] for instance, there are discussed several areas of basic problems in the director of Christian education and staff relationship.

1. Lack of understanding of what the job of a director is.
2. Lack of job analysis.
3. Lack of training for teamwork on the part of both the minister and director.
4. Lack of status for directors on the part of ministers, denominations, and seminaries.
5. Inadequate salaries, housing, pensions, insurance, and relationship to denominational boards.

It can be observed that, with the exception of the first item, all items

---

[14] "A Normative Description of the Certified Director of Christian Education in The Methodist Church." An unpublished Ph. D. dissertation. Boston University, 1961.

are areas related to personnel management, human relations, and leadership. These areas have been discussed at length in previous chapters.

In 1960 under the direction of the National Council of Churches of Christ in America, a consultation on the work of the directors of Christian education was held. The basic objective of the consultation was to define the relationships of the employed DRE in a church staff to other members of the staff and to attempt to formulate normative statements concerning the position. Out of the consultation several specific statements emerged:

1. Titles were defined based upon educational standards and ministerial positions.

(a) *Director of Christian Education.* A person employed for educational responsibilities in a church who holds an A.B. or B.S. degree plus a master's degree in Christian education, or a B.D. degree with a major in Christian education.

(b) *Minister of Christian Education.* The requirements are the same as those for a director, but the person is an ordained minister of the gospel.

(c) *Assistant in Christian Education.* Anyone employed in the educational program of the church who holds a bachelor's degree or who is working toward the degree.

2. Salary compensations should be an amount equal to 65 percent of the amount paid the senior minister, with some variations for years of service and education. (In our study the salary of the DRE was 59.1% of the pastor's salary.)

3. Compensation should be provided for housing, travel, retirement benefits, office expenses, vacations, and time for study and travel.

4. A clear job analysis or job description.

The statements have done much to clarify the position. It can be seen that basically the elements of the findings, like those of Lindecker's, are areas of personnel management and human relations.

An attempt has been made to speak at length to these subjects in chapters 2, 3, 4, and 12, which deal with personnel management, human relations, and the psychology and sociology of leadership. A full job description for the DRE is given in Appendix B.

Observations

Several observations can be made concerning the office of DRE that have come from questionnaires, interviews, and group discussions.

First, the DRE feels his work is gratifying in that it is making a major contribution to the lives of individuals. Many educators stated they derived much satisfaction from seeing persons develop in their understanding of the Christian faith. Others stated they were happy to be a part of a team working together in the local church to help persons develop in Christian growth and maturity. Some stated they enjoyed teaching and working with people.

Unrest and dissatisfaction with the position were voiced most emphatically around four basic areas. (1) A lack of time to get things done, and a lack of time for family and personal enrichment. (2) A feeling that the work of the Christian educator on the church staff is not understood or appreciated by other members of the staff. In relationship with this was voiced the feeling that good leadership procedures in staff relationships were not practiced. Staff meetings need to be held more regularly and meaningfully. Individual rights of staff persons need to be respected. Salary differences are too great, and there are too many "lackey" jobs to do. Some DRE's show considerable cynicism at these points. A case in point is illustrated by one educator, who said, "I can name twelve people who were on church staffs in our city who now are in secular education or some other position." When pressed as to why the persons had left the church vocation the answer was, "A lack of acceptance by members of the staff and congregation as to the work of the Christian educator." Incidentally, the person making the statement soon left his church vocation to return to the university to prepare himself for public school administration.

Salary differences between the educator on the church staff and other professionals, especially associate pastors, is a source of constant irritation and dissatisfaction. If a church employs a professional educator there needs to be adequate salary and other compensations, as well as a complete acceptance of the importance of the office in the church.

(3) A lack of appreciation by the congregation of the work of the DRE. This was expressed in several ways: "Parents feel they are doing me a favor by bringing their children to church." "I become weary in trying to recruit leaders in the church school—after all it is their school and their children." One hostile person stated, "With rare exceptions, the church's treatment of her directors of Christian education is an incredible ritual of hypocrisy. We have no union, no court of appeals, and very few even cry out in the wilderness. Most just leave quietly without a whimper. Four years of college and two or

153

three years of graduate study are lost to the church, and more money is spent to train personnel for secular society."

The fourth problem is related to physical aspects of work: lack of space, lack of secretarial help, lack of equipment, too small a budget, and so forth.

As has been mentioned before most of the problems in relationship to the office of DRE in the church staff hinge around poor personnel management policies and poor leadership practices.

One of the major problems is in regard to the self-image of the DRE. There seem to be two prevailing attitudes among DRE's themselves: the DRE is an administrator of a program of Christian education within the congregation; the DRE is an educator in the congregation. In the first role the DRE conceives of the office as organizing and recruiting. Persons for special educational tasks and emphases are drawn into the church to do the teaching. In the second role the DRE is primarily a teacher with major responsibility in the field of teaching leaders and on occasion teaching a special interest group. There could be, and most likely is, a direct correlation with background and education. When a DRE has been trained in Bible, theology, ethics, church history, and other related fields, there is a natural desire to share such knowledge with others.

It behooves the DRE to work through his own self-image and have this clearly understood by the senior minister, other members of the staff, and the responsible laymen in the church, or conflict is inevitable.

One of the most difficult phases of the work of the educator is that of communicating with other members of the staff. A theory that has emerged from this study may provide a partial clue to the problem. Educators are schooled in the consultative or dialogical method of communicating. The good educator engages his pupil in conversation —not in giving answers, but assisting the pupil to find answers and grow in knowledge. This method is not always understood or practiced by pastors who are accustomed to building their task around preaching. Preaching is a direct method of education. The good preacher will engage the congregation in an imaginary conversation so the listener is brought into dialogue, but there is actually no conversation taking place. There is a tendency to conduct staff relationships in the same fashion, and frustration between the educator and pastor emerges. Some of the principles of leadership as described earlier will help in solving some of these difficulties.

One of the happiest directors of education interviewed in the study of the church staff was in a large church in the Southeastern United States. She had been trained academically in personnel relations and had come into the church office from government work. She had taken extensive work in the field of Christian education in short-term courses and in leaves from church responsibilities.

This DRE conceived of her task primarily as an administrator. Over a period of two years she had been responsible for the entire staff working out carefully stated job analyses. These were printed in one brochure and made available to all members of the staff and leaders of the congregation.

The DRE conceived of her position in regard to the church school as a recruiter of church school teachers and an overseer of church school membership. The church had a basic philosophy in regard to teachers. (1) All classes, with the exception of adults were to be taught by husband-and-wife teams. (2) All teachers were to be carefully selected and invited to prepare to teach. (3) All teachers were required to take three courses in preparation for teaching—Old Testament, New Testament, and methods of teaching—and an examination of literature at the age level in which they would be teaching. Teaching became a coveted position in the church, and there was a waiting list of trained persons for classes!

In attempting to interpret the secret of success of this DRE I should point out that there was a firm commitment to the values and purposes of Chrisian education in the church, a clear self-understanding and self-concept of the position of DRE, a clear job description for her work and that of all members of the staff, and a dynamic sense and ability of leadership.

Day School Workers, Director and Teachers

The day school in the Protestant church dates back to the beginning of Protestantism and was a means of fulfilling the obligation of the church to teach children the catechism and other rudimentary disciplines. In the state church the clergy was (and is) either vitally associated with the education of children in the state-owned school, or giving direction to all education under the direction of the church but supported by the state.

In the United States the parochial school has been promoted and supported quite consistently by the Roman Catholic, Episcopal, and Lutheran churches, with some other denominations conducting schools at various times in history. With the rise of the state-supported schools the role of the church in secular education has decreased until only a minor role is now played by the church.

Increasingly, however, in recent years there has been a return to the assuming of responsibility by the church for some secular education. The day school has become popular, but instead of being a full-blown school, it is confined in the vast majority of Protestant churches to a preschool-age group—that is, children under six years of age. There is still a tradition of the parochial school among some denominations—Roman Catholic, Episcopal, or Lutheran predominantly. There has also been a rise in recent years of parochial schools on the elementary and high school level by some denominations, such as the Church of Christ, with the primary aim of teaching children in their own denomination in an environment protected from the influences of the world.

In the sample of Protestant churches in our study it was discovered that many had a day school. Table 11 lists the percent of day schools by the size of congregations.

Table 11. Percent of congregations by size of congregation supporting a day school

Size of Congregation	Percent with day school
Under 400	7
400 to 699	10
700 to 999	14
1,000 to 1,499	13
1,500 to 1,999	26
2,000 to 2,999	26
3,000 to 3,999	30
4,000 and over	70

The day school as a functioning part of the program of the church increases in number as the size of the congregation increases.

Day schools vary greatly as to their purpose. Some are a kindergarten with the primary purpose of preparing children to enter public school. Some are service organizations with the primary purpose of ministering to underprivileged children in the neighborhood who do not attend the Sunday church school. Some are for the purpose of providing a nursery school where women employed outside the home may leave their children while at work. Some are full-fledged parochial schools providing complete educational opportunity for children through elementary school.

There is a need, especially in low-income residential areas, for day nurseries. Many cities have established rigid requirements for conditions and teachers in such schools. Cities will also provide information by specialists on how to establish and conduct day schools and how to become certified.

Some problems that emerge in regard to the day school are as follows:

1. The day school was established in the church *apart from* the ongoing program of the church, rather than as an integral *part of* the total church program.

2. The senior minister feels no responsibility for the day school, and in some cases is actually irritated that it is in the church.

3. The director of education, or director of children's work in the local church has no relationship with the day school. There is a lack of communication between the members of the educational staff in the church and staff in the day school.

4. Conflicts arise over building use. The same facilities must, in most cases, be used for the day school that are used for the Sunday church school. Teachers in both schools complain that they must spend too much time in putting up and taking out equipment, or there is a lack of respect for space and equipment by the teachers in "the other school."

5. There is no clear understanding of the relationship of the day school staff to the regular church staff.

6. Janitorial considerations are not taken into account in regard to increased work.

7. The business administrator and/or the financial secretary are reluctant to pay the bills of the day school, for there is a lack of clarification as to responsible ordering, authorization, and accountability.

8. In some cases the day school is operated from a separate budget. This leaves much room for misunderstanding and even distrust. Day schools have the potential of self-support by charging a tuition. If there is no clear understanding regarding finance there are many opportunities for misunderstanding.

The most satisfactory arrangement for the day school in a local church that has been discovered in research and interviewing is that school with the following characteristics:

1. The day school is an integral part of the total program of the church. By this is meant that it is authorized and underwritten in ex-

pense by the official board or other governing body. It becomes the responsibility of the education department along with other educational enterprises in the church.

2. The director and teachers in the day school are considered to be a part of the total staff of the church. As such they are subject to all the rights and privileges of the staff, and also held accountable to the ideals and objectives of the staff.

3. The director of the school is included in all regular meetings of the staff and will make reports and requests as do other members of the staff.

4. All teachers in the day school need to be included in total church staff social activities, and two to four times per year they need to be in staff business meetings.

5. Good lines of communication need to be kept open between all persons involved, making sure there are clear definitions of responsibility areas, use of space and equipment, support, lines of authority and accountability.

Local congregations will do well to examine carefully the need for a day school and to observe the above principles as such a school is established. There is much evidence that there will be an increasing need for day schools sponsored by local churches as a part of the regular work of the church.

8

The Church Musician

An ancient tradition within Christendom is that worship is the primary and eternal activity of redeemed mankind. Music in the church is an *aid* to worship and an *act* of worship. Within a one-hour Sunday morning service of worship in a Protestant church approximately thirty minutes, or one-half of the hour, is devoted to music. In addition, church school classes and all organizations within the the church use music in worship, informal meetings, and recreation. It can be readily observed that music has a vital place to fill in the life of a congregation and deserves much attention.

For centuries the organist and choirmaster have held prominent places in the Christian congregation, and in recent years the paid director or minister of music on a part-time or full-time basis has become an accepted position on the church staff.

For purposes of analysis the musicians on the church staff have been divided into three major groups: the *organist-director,* the *director,* and the *organist.* The term *organist-director,* refers to the person who is both the choir director and organist. The term *director* refers to the person who directs the choir or choirs, but does not accompany the choir or congregation on the organ. The term *organist* refers to the person who plays the organ but does not direct the choir. These terms have been widely accepted by church musicians. Some denominations have refined the terms to designate those who hold clergy rights. The term minister of music has been designated, for instance, by The United Methodist Church to refer to a person who has met all the qualifications for full clergy rights in the denomination and is an ordained minister. A director of music in the same denomination refers to a person who is certified by the denomination to direct a program of music in a church, but who does not possess the necessary qualifications for ordination. The three terms—organist-director, director, and organist—serve as descriptive terms. Data from questionnaires received from church musicians were tabulated and processed with the three groups in mind. Church musicians may find it interesting to note some of the differences in the three groups.

One reason for making the above classifications is that there is a difference of opinion among church musicians as to whether there should be one person who is both organist and director, or two persons—a director and an organist. This remains a matter of opinion. To the question, Should there be one or two persons employed to direct the program of music in the church? the following answers were given:

Table 12. Percent of opinions of organist-director, director, and organist about whether one or two persons should be employed to direct the program of music in the local church.

	Two persons	One person	Either way
Organist-director	38.2%	49.4%	11.2%
Director	88.3	5.0	5.0
Organist	67.8	5.3	23.2

Forty percent of the musicians in the study were organist-directors, 29 percent were directors, and 31 percent were organists.

Significant regional differences emerged in tabulated data concerning the type of church musician employed. In the New England, Mountain (Western), West South Central, and Pacific areas there was a larger number of organist-directors than directors and organists, while in the West and East North Central regions there was a predominance of directors and organists. It is quite possible that different regions are influenced by the prevailing attitudes in the different schools of music in these regions.

Size of congregation may be a factor in the type of musician employed. The number of persons who are organist-directors increases noticeably in churches of 1,000 or more members.

The Church Musician, Facts and Opinions

Age comparisons reveal that 58 percent of the organist-directors, 48 percent of the directors, and 61 percent of the organists are between the ages of 40 and 65.

Ten percent of the organist-directors, 23 percent of the directors, and 24 percent of the organists were in their first church position.

Forty-three percent of the organist-directors, 26 percent of the directors, and 24 percent of the organists were serving in their third or fourth church position.

Sixty percent of all musicians had been employed in secular work prior to a church position, and 80 percent of this number had been in professional work.

The educational background of church musicians in the study is listed below.

Table 13. Educational background of church musicians

	Organist-Director	Director	Organist
High school completed	91.0%	97.0%	96.8%
Liberal arts degree	86.8	84.0	61.5
Bachelor of Divinity	4.4	5.6	0.0
Master of Sacred Music	15.0	10.0	3.0
Master of Music Education	18.0	16.0	7.6
Master of Arts	16.0	11.0	9.2
Ph.D. or other earned doctorate	7.6	3.2	0.0

It can be observed that, with the exception of the Bachelor of Divinity degree, the organist-directors have slightly more graduate work than the directors, and both have much more graduate work than the organists.

Approximately one-third of the musicians employed in churches were born in communities of less than 2,500 people, one-third were from cities of 2,500 to 25,000, and one-third were from cities of more than 25,000. Nine percent were born in the open country, as compared with 17 percent of the pastors and 17 percent of the associate pastors. Thirty-five percent of the musicians had parents who were in one of the professions, 7 percent were in agriculture, 15 percent were in managerial positions, 15 percent in sales, 11 percent were craftsmen, and 9 percent were skilled or unskilled laborers.

Seventy-one percent of the musicians had considered making the ministry of music a life vocation by the age of 21 years, and 57 percent had considered music as a vocation by the age of 16. Sixty-three percent of the musicians had made their definite decision to be a church musician by the age of 21. The most important factors in the decision to enter a church music career were in order of importance: parents, teachers, a sense of religious calling, and pastors.

Eleven percent of the organist-directors in the study, 5 percent of the directors, and 1 percent of the organists were ordained in their respective denominations.

A comparison of salaries of employed musicians is given below.

Table 14. Salaries of organist-directors, directors, and organists

Average annual salary	Organist-Directors	Directors	Organists
Under $2,000	33.7%	62.5%	74.1%
Approximately $2,000	11.2	18.7	13.7
Approximately $3,000	14.6	3.1	3.4
Approximately $4,000	7.8	0.0	3.4
Approximately $5,000	11.2	0.0	1.7
Approximately $6,000	17.9	9.3	1.7
Approximately $8,000	3.3	4.1	1.7
Approximately $10,000	0.0	1.5	0.0

It is quite obvious from the above table that there are more full-time organist-directors than directors and organists, and more organist-directors are paid salaries above $2,000.

Nine percent of the organist-directors, 12 percent of the directors, and 2 percent of the organists had either a residence furnished without cost or a cash housing allowance.

Fourteen percent of the organist-directors, 10 percent of the directors, and 2 percent of the organists had a travel allowance, and the same percentages of persons had pension programs provided by the church. Pensions ranged from $1,000 to $3,500 per year.

Ninety-one percent of the musicians in the study participate in the Social Security program of the federal government, with 73 percent under institutional employment and 27 percent self-employed.

Seventy-two percent of the organist-directors, 88 percent of the directors, and 77 percent of the organists were married at the time of the study. Eight percent of the organists were either widowed or divorced, leaving 20 percent of the organist-directors, 9 percent of the directors, and 14 percent of the organists not married. These figures contrast sharply with other members of the church staff in which almost 100 percent were either married or widowed.

Fifty-five percent of all musicians in the study felt their salary was not adequate, and 82 percent supplemented their salary with other income. Thirty percent of the musicians felt their salary was not fair in comparison with other members of the church staff and in the light of their training. Ninety-four percent of the musicians stated there was no system or understood method of salary advancement, and 30 percent felt they had not been treated fairly in their work.

Eighteen percent of the organist-directors, 42 percent of the directors, and 23 percent of the organists indicated there was no stated plan for a vacation. Twenty-three percent of the organist-directors, 18 percent of the directors, and 40 percent of the organists had two weeks vacation annually; and 40 percent of the organist-directors, 18 percent of the directors, and 22 percent of the organists had four weeks vacation.

Approximately 10 percent of all musicians in the study had some funds provided for personal enrichment, such as special schools, workshops, and travel.

Seventy-eight percent of the organist-directors, 66 percent of the directors, and 33 percent of the organists in the study were male.

In attempting to discover areas of concern in regard to the musician's position in the church and relationship with other members of the staff, a series of questions was asked. Answers provide some insights into the problems faced by the musician in the church staff. A brief report of some of the questions and answers follows.

Sixty percent of the musicians reported there is no job description, and 40 percent stated there is some type of job description. Sixty-two percent reported there are regular staff meetings held, and of those having staff meetings, 58 percent are held once a week, 10 percent twice a month, 16 percent on call or irregularly. Eighty-six percent of the musicians felt that staff meetings help create harmony, with 5 percent emphatic that they do not, and 9 percent unsure. Eighty-eight percent felt the staff meetings insured more efficiency in staff work. Of those persons who were in churches where staff meetings are not held, 41 percent felt they should be, 27 percent felt they should not be, and 32 percent were unsure.

Sixteen percent of the musicians felt that theological differences in the staff cause disharmony. Twenty percent felt age differences were a problem, and 22 percent felt that the length of time persons had been on the staff contributed to staff problems. Seventeen percent felt there was one or more persons on the staff who was too domineering.

Seventeen percent of the music staff were dissatisfied with the office space provided, the chief complaints being that the space was too small or there was not enough privacy. Forty percent of the musicians made the following complaints: not satisfied with equipment, improper planning in church architecture, need for new equipment, out-of-date or poor equipment, and lack of funds for maintenance of equipment.

Sixty-four percent felt they had sufficient help, and 30 percent felt they needed help of some kind. Sixteen percent had no secretarial help, with a large number feeling the help they had was poorly trained or overloaded with work. Five percent indicated they had no need for help.

Seventy-five percent of the musicians were members of the church in which they were employed, and 21 percent were working in churches of a different denomination than the one in which they held membership.

Fifty-seven percent of the musicians had no stated time for study and self-enrichment, and 21 percent had a stated time for study and practice which is understood by the pastor and other members of the staff. Nineteen percent of the musicians indicated that the matter of a need for a stated period of self-enrichment was a point of friction in the staff.

Sixty-six percent of the musicians indicated there is no stated time for staff worship. Seven percent stated there was a time for worship but the musician did not attend.

A series of questions was asked regarding staff relationships and various areas of harmony or staff problems. Eleven percent of the musicians indicated the senior minister did not understand the value of music in church worship. Twenty-one percent indicated the senior minister did not understand or appreciate the great music of the church. Ten percent of the musicians stated they disagreed with the senior minister in regard to the place of music in the total life of the church.

In regard to special training for the church musician the respondents felt there is need for training, in addition to the technical skills of conducting and playing the organ, in the areas of: theology of the church, liturgy and worship, music in the church school, and training in group organization and human relations.

The musicians expressed the feeling that students in theological seminaries in training for the pastoral ministry should receive special training in the meaning of music in worship and liturgy, historically and traditionally great music, the place of music in religious education, and how to work with the musician on the church staff.

Twenty-three percent of the musicians in the study have responsibility for the Sunday morning worship service and choir only. Seventy-seven percent of the musicians have a graded choir system in the local church for which they have responsibility. Twenty-three percent of the musicians indicated they work with the church school music as well as with choirs.

When asked to express a philosophy of church music, 86 percent of the musicians stated they felt their task was to assist the congregation in worship. Twenty-five percent stated they were to develop individuals for choir work. Twenty-five percent felt that the program of music should affect all phases of the life of the church. Ten percent stated church music should afford an opportunity for one of the performing arts. It will be seen there is overlapping and duplication in the above.

Male musicians who were married felt, with only minor exceptions, that there was no problem with their wives' feelings toward wives of other staff members.

Thirty-nine percent of the musicians stated they planned the entire Sunday morning service of worship subject to the pastor's approval. Thirteen percent stated they planned the service with the pastor, and 27 percent stated they did not select the hymns but did select instrumental and choral music.

Forty-four percent of the musicians stated they had no relationship with the music in the church school. Three percent stated the choirs are graded in accordance with the grades in the church school. Eighteen percent of the musicians attempt to work with the church school teachers with the music for the church school. Four percent of the musicians assist with the vacation church school or day school music. Forty-seven percent of the musicians stated they give private lessons, and of the persons who do give private lessons 62 percent receive extra pay for the lessons and 38 percent do not.

When asked what they felt were the greatest needs for improvement of staff relations the following were reported in order of number of persons expressing their feelings for each item: a need for a greater respect of staff personnel for each other; a need to understand more fully each person's task on the church staff; a granting of each person on the staff more authority for expressing his specialized ministry; a clearer understanding and definition of the central purpose of the church; more clear-cut job descriptions for all persons on the staff; more sincere support from the senior minister; and more love for one another within the staff.

The most dissatisfying part of the work of the musician was expressed as: unconcern on the part of the congregation and lack of appreciation of the work of the musician (34 percent made such an expression); indifference on the part of the congregation; a lack of communication with the persons who lead the service of worship (senior minister and associates); a lack of guidance on the part of the music committee; and the domineering attitude of the senior minister or other members of the staff.

Musicians, however, in spite of their problem areas stated emphatically that the work in the church afforded an opportunity for self-fulfillment in a church-related vocation (71 percent), and seeing people grow religiously brought great satisfaction. Only 1 percent stated the motive of monetary income was a source of satisfaction.

The Role of the Musician on a Church Staff

It is not the purpose of this writing to attempt to inform the musician what his role is on the church staff. This he should already know. The church musician possesses a self-image which he would like to interpret to his colleagues. This writing will attempt to reflect the thinking of a number of church musicians from different denominations and some of the current trends in the place of music in the church.

The first and basic role of the musician in the local church and as a part of the church staff is as an assistant in worship. As such, the musician expects to have a part in developing a meaningful liturgy; the selecting of appropriate hymns; the perfecting of appropriate voluntaries and offertories; and the directing of a choir or choirs (usually volunteer) to assist with responses, anthems, and leading the congregation in the singing of hymns.

Expressing of the above is done in the traditions of the denomination. There is also a wide variety of interpretation by the musicians and also the ministers within the denomination. In some denominations there is little agreement among ministers and laity in regard to liturgy, rituals, the place of music, and the type of music to be used. Herein lies one of the major areas of conflict between the musician and the minister, other members of the staff, and members of the congregation. In the sample study of musician members of church staffs, 21 percent were members of another denomination than the one in which they were employed. This can lead to a fundamental difference between the musician and other members of the staff in theological positions and basic concepts of worship. Few traditions are more adhered to consciously or unconsciously, than traditions of worship.

Songs or hymns used in childhood, forms of worship, liturgies, and sacramental observances have been so implanted in the worshiper that he feels alienated and out of place with innovations. Worship is like a native language. As long as one is with persons who speak the same language he is at home. When one is placed in a group of people who speak a different language, alienation is felt. Sociologists have proposed a theory that language is basic in communication and "at-homeness."

In my first parish I would call on an elderly parishioner who had been born and reared in Germany. During my pastoral prayer with her she would frequently take the prayer from me and pray for a moment in English. As her prayer became more intense and personal she would revert to her native tongue and finish in German. This was always followed by an apology to me with the closing statement. "But the Lord hears me better in German!" So it is with worship—the worshiper feels the presence of God, is more comfortable in his worship, is more "at home" with a hymnody of his childhood and a liturgy in which he was reared.

As one walks through the corridors of a church school building during the Sunday church school hour one will hear a variety of hymns and songs being used by different classes. In the ordinary Protestant church there will be hymns from the denomination's approved hymnal, probably hymns from a children's or youth hymnal, and songs from a gospel songbook. The adult classes, particularly, will use songs or hymns that they learned in childhood and youth. Here is the opportunity for the group to find a meaningful hymnody. "Meaningful" in this sense means "traditional" and not necessarily the best.

The professional church musician has been trained in what his school of music holds to be the best hymnody and practices in worship. The senior minister has had one or two courses in seminary in the area of music in worship. A quick glance at seminary offerings in the field of worship will reveal the paucity of training that is done in the field. In all likelihood the congregation in the ordinary Protestant church is made up of persons from many church traditions. The one exception to this may be a church with a strong ethnic background and family solidarity. Thus, the church musician is faced with the very difficult, if not impossible, task of assisting persons of many backgrounds and traditions.

In the light of the above discussion, what does the musician do? To compromise with firm convictions in regard to meaningful worship is to destroy one's own vital religious and professional convictions. To hold tenaciously to a concept of worship that is beyond or out of harmony with the staff and congregation is to alienate the musician from the people he is attempting to serve. He has the choice of attempting to meet the needs of the people or changing positions. He needs to recognize that in all likelihood the people are not entirely wrong in their expectations of music within the church. He can be receptive to suggestions with a sympathetic ear and an open mind.

An unbending, arbitrary church musician can quickly alienate himself from the congregation and other members of the staff. The late Hugh Porter, who was director of the School of Sacred Music, Union Theological Seminary, New York, related an experience with a young musician.

> Students and older musicians in their eagerness for fine repertory often fail to remember that they are speaking through music for a congregation of laymen, as well as for themselves. Recently a young organist in his first interview with a minister said, "I must make it clear that I am a professional musician and that I cannot prostitute my art for any minister or congregation." [1]

The musician needs to have the opportunity to be a teacher within the staff and congregation. His task and ministry need to go beyond the Sunday morning service of worship. He needs to have the opportunity to assist a congregation to grow in depth and understanding of worship. This thought is conveyed in an article by John Wesley Lord in *Music Ministry:*

> . . . the church musician must find an enlarged and ennobled place in the thinking and support of the congregation gathered for worship. In the truest sense, he is as much a minister of worship and of education as he is a minister of music. He is more than a chaplain to a music committee; he is a servant of the entire church, youth as well as aged, and bears a unique relation to our church Commission on Education. [2]

The musician needs to discover where the congregation is in their concept of music in the church, and gradually through education lead them to an appreciation and use of better music. Too frequently the musician will make the leap to music in worship that is beyond the grasp of the majority of a congregation, and he wonders why he is not appreciated. This is as foolish as a high school teacher attempting to teach advanced mathematics to students who have not been through

---

[1] "Preparing to be a Church Musician," *Music Ministry,* II, 7 (1961), p. 43.
[2] John Wesley Lord, *Music Ministry,* IV, 2 (1963), p. 11.

elementary mathematics. The teacher must patiently go back and teach, or see that the student is taught, the fundamentals of mathematics before the advanced math is introduced. This principle has caused a number of church musicians to expand their concept of the role or task of the employed church musician. They hold that the church musician should have access to all areas of church life and be given the opportunity to develop a program of church music that will assist all persons to a fuller knowledge and appreciation of music in the life of the church and in worship. Such a program calls not just for graded choirs but for work with church school teachers as they plan their Sunday sessions and extended weekday sessions for all age groups. It calls for work in the day school, where there is one in the local church; for work in vacation church school; for assistance with various special programs throughout the year when music is involved. In such a program there are two major problems. (1) Some musicians do not want to spend the time and energy involved, and conceive of their task to be only that of choir director, or perhaps director of graded choirs. A case in point was a young lady employed in a church of 3,000 members as a full-time director of children's music. She became quite indignant when she was asked to assist with music in the church-sponsored day school. (2) The second problem involved is the opening of the doors for the church musician to the various phases of the life of the church. Church school teachers, for instance, can be quite pointed in their attitude that they do not feel a need for assistance with music. A director of youth on a church staff may be reluctant in using the church musician in youth activities, a special program, or in assisting the youth of the church to a fuller appreciation of church music. The church musician must stand on the outside until he is let in, even though he is fully aware of the inadequacy of the music used in various church departments.

In the process of gathering data for this writing I asked a group of church musicians to meet with me for an informal discussion. Each was given in advance a list of topics related to the work of the professional musician in the church. I moderated the discussion and attempted to keep the discussion close to the subjects. The following positions were represented in the group: (1) an Episcopal director of music who had from time to time served on the faculty of a university school of music, and who at the time of the discussion was serving as director of music in a full-time capacity for an Episcopal church of 2,000 members. He will be known as "Episcopalian." (2) A Disciples of Christ director of music who had served as director of music in a Disciples church of 3,000 members and at the time of the discussion was serving as director of music in a Disciples church of 1,000 members and was a full-time member of the faculty of a school of music in a university. He will be known as "Disciples." (3) The wife of the Disciples director of music who had been for many years a public school teacher of music and had served as a church musician from time to time. She will be known as "Disciples' wife." (4) A Methodist serving as a director of music in a church of 2,500 members. He will be known as "Methodist 1." (5) A Baptist serving as an organist and temporary director of music in a Baptist church of 4,000 members. He will be known as "Baptist." (6) A Methodist serving as director of music in a Methodist church of 9,000 members. He will be known as "Methodist 2." (7) A professor in a school of music and school of theology in a university and the director of the Master of Sacred Music degree. He had served as director of music in several churches and as editor of church music publications for his denomination. He will be known as "Professor." (8) A student doing a Master of Sacred Music degree and serving part-time as a director in a Methodist church of 1,000 members. He will be known as "Student." I will use the denomination or position to indicate the speaker. The first speaker will be Methodist 2. His statement follows:

Methodist 2: We've had a multiple choir program in our church for many years, and just as soon as the situation presents itself we would like to do away with some of the choirs, as such—some of the younger choirs. Some years we have had preschool groups which some people call a choir." I question that greatly. Right now we have the youngest group in the first grade—first and second grade together— and we call that just "music time." Because as far as singing in a church service or having anything to offer, it seems to me that the third grade is low, and fifth grade is better. They can do some things, but as far as really helping a sophisticated (for want of a better word) congregation there just needs to be more age. We are thinking of forgetting about the choir business, as such, and getting into the Christian education business and not having a performing group, as such, for the fourth grade down. We feel we need to supply staff music leadership by going into the church school—to go in and be with 300 children rather than the 40 we have in choirs, and to work with the church school teachers. The choir will come about in this way. What we are talking about does not centralize everything in a choir, but simply broadens the Christian education program with music on a professional level, which we feel is worth trying.

170

Disciples' wife: Maybe a way to get at this matter of children's participation, even at a very early age, is to give strength to their participation in the hymn program. And maybe their best appearance is as members of the congregation, which is what we want always anyhow. If they could learn a hymn adequate to their needs and which serves the congregation, maybe this is a far better way—that they be there as a unifying group prepared to sing one hymn in the course of the service rather than to be sophisticated performers. I don't believe that in any church service where a children's group comes in there is just one thing, the anthem, in which they can really participate. I think this only becomes a demonstration performance. And, of course, here, as in public school and in all performing areas, the performance aspect, unfortunately, has been created to give publicity to an idea and momentum to the business of purchasing robes and instruments and all kinds of things. And the whole picture has become "third-floor" business instead of structural activity which ought to be the "groundwork." And so the multiple choir program has the fault that we have obliged the children to become a display group in some instances. We have put emphasis on numbers and "how we look," "how we act," and so forth, rather than on *how we worship* and *what worship is.* And, of course, they could worship best with a hymn, and they could worship best in the rear of the balcony, except that the folks would have to turn around to look at them.

Episcopalian: This points out the difference in philosophy of what a choir is there for. The music that the choir offers is being offered to God and not to the congregation.

Disciples' wife: That's right.

Episcopalian: And the choir should not be a display group. Now we have a multiple choir system at ———, but every choir that we have sings at a particular service every Sunday. Now we have a Carol Choir, (first, second, and third grades) that sings its own chapel service. The first, second, and third grades go to that chapel service, and the children who are not in the choir are there also. I feel the choir is not on display. They are a functioning group. They are on their own level. They are not being shown off.

Disciples' wife: That's right, but you see this is not the way most multiple choir programs are. This is not the way the multiple choir programs appear. Many times this is a get-together for lots and lots of people. . . .

Episcopalian: But I would just like to pass on something I have learned in working with this group—that the children, the fourth grade boys and girls, are so much better prepared to work with later on after spending several years in pitch training and learning hymns. So I feel the multiple choir system works very well for us.

Disciples' wife: But you define purposes other than assembing multitudes of people. It's an educational program.

Methodist 2: We are not born knowing these things. It has to be educational.

Disciples' wife: Well, an educational program doesn't mean just learning scripture or the names of disciples or something like that. An educational program has many aspects, and music is one of them, and you are just lucky to have set up a program or to have evolved one in which there is a strong flavor of this. This doesn't mean that the ultimate results aren't just as artistic; it probably means that they are more so, because you have trained many, many people. You have prepared them for the fact that when they can sing a difficult number they are singing praise to God.

Disciples: The fact that your young people have participated in these first three years and come out prepared to do better work in the fourth grade—that in itself shows that it is an educational program, it's music education, music training.

Episcopalian: It's more than just music—it's basic sacred music. There is a spiritual training here that is not akin to the public school music program, which is technical. I go to some length to explain the hymn they will sing. And this is educational. I somehow don't think of myself primarily as being in education. I think of it more as musical development.

Methodist 2: Does your church have a director of education?

Episcopalian: Yes.

Methodist 2: Do you work with her, or him, in the selection of hymns that will be taught the children for the season?

Episcopalian: There is coordination and cooperation.

Professor: I would like a word. As I move into the academic vein two words come into focus which weren't used when I was director of music in a church. These two words are *performance* and *excellence*. I find that these words are seldom used because they have a connotation of being snobbish, if you insist upon standards. But I hate to have these two words go out the window and have words like *education* and *integrated quality* substituted. All that I am saying is that it has appalled me to see in students how unimportant a simple piece of music is to them. I think we have somehow taught students they must do difficult and display items whether it is a church recital or whatever. And this has caught on in the church music situation today—that simple music (just because it can be mastered easily—though it seldom is), such as "God So Loved the World," a very sublime piece of music, is just murdered because it isn't done musically. It's just done some other way. A simple thing like this is thought of as being out of the question. There are certain labels attached to it. So I think that if I would say anything, it is that we should keep these two words in the conversation of the church musician—*excellence* and *performance*.

Methodist 1: I think all of us are interested in and striving for excellence in what we do. If we aren't I am afraid we are selling our ministry short. Talking about simple music—in our church I cooperate with the director of children's work and all our choirs learn the church school music that is to be used in the next unit so that these children know it and can help those who are not in the choir. Now maybe this is not the right way to go about it, but it does seem to help, and church school teachers seem to think it helps. We also go over the hymns for the following Sunday because I encourage all our children to attend church. I think they ought to be there. I just don't believe in papa and mama going to the worship service while the children go to Sunday school. They both ought to be in both places in their two hours on Sunday mornings, and they can give time to both purposes.

Professor: Who selects the music that the children are going to use in the church school?

Methodist 1: The music in the church school is suggested in the literature. All our children's literature has suggested hymns to use. Sometimes music is actually printed in the children's workbook they take home. That goes all the way through the grade school now. Then after you get to grades 3, 4, 5, and 6 there are standard hymns from the hymnal most of the time.

Moderator: How universal do you think this practice might be among church musicians?

Methodist 1: I don't know. Does anyone have an opinion on this?

Episcopalian: It would depend on the quality of material used. I have no idea. I'd like to regard the church musician as responsible for seeing that the best quality of hymns is made available for children at an early age and that they be fed a diet of the best hymns in regard to both text and music, so that they form good taste from an early age.

Methodist 1: Of course that has not always happened. We've had some real trite stuff stuck in those little books through the years. And we have had a couple of publications which were definite age-level publications: *Songs for Primary Children* and then a slight improvement in *Singing Worship*, the junior book. That was considerably better than the old books. And now with the inclusion of music in the actual literature it has cut down a great deal. There are very few hymns in these books.

Professor: There has been a transition in education from the use of music as primarily, if not totally, related to the learning experience of the hour. A song would be dropped in at the given moment that could relate to the given text or flow of thought. And now there is a pronounced feeling that hymns can be enjoyed and learned for their own sake. There is an objectivity here in hymn study. This is major—this is way out of the woods.

Methodist 1: We do something at our church which may be somewhat unique. I'll hark back to the total church ministry of music. At the beginning of each unit of study I go to the music room of the church to meet with church school teachers for a planning session. They have these meetings three or four times a year, and we go over the entire unit, including songs, hymns, and music—how they relate, why they relate, and why they were selected. We go over them, and I teach them to the teachers, since in many cases they don't know them.

Moderator: This may be one of the reasons this music has not been used in many of our smaller churches. They just don't know the hymns and don't have anyone to teach them.

Methodist 2: I have been in our church seven years now, and I have yet to attend one church school class—not because I am not avidly interested, but because of the way our services are scheduled. We would like to get into these classes as many times a year as possible to check for ourselves to see that our standard of excellency could be maintained there—not as a singing group, but as a teaching aid in this case, so that it would be getting across to the children. We have had some—I think we are rid of them now—but we have had some of these elderly church school teachers who refused to do the songs in the literature, because they weren't the "good old songs." The good old songs are: "Brighten the Corner Where You Are" and "Blest Be the Tie That Binds," and they did these every Sunday.

Baptist: We have had practically the same problem as Methodist 2. At our church we have people teaching Sunday school who absolutely refuse to work with our music staff—not that we haven't tried to work with them, but they refuse to work with us for this same reason. Perhaps our standard of music is a little higher than theirs.

They asked us for some new hymnals, and we suggested one or two. The Sunday school department leader is a member of the choir, so he went ahead and put the hymnal in the department. The Sunday school teachers came into the department and wanted to know where the books came from. The leader said he had bought them and they would be used, but the teachers refused to let the children sing from the hymnal, and told the children not to sing when the hymnal was used —that they (the teachers) weren't going to be told what hymnal to use. So consequently it made some hard feelings between the music staff and those various people involved. We tried to come to some sort of agreement and asked if we could talk with the Sunday school teachers. They said "Yes." I personally went in to talk with them and found that where I thought people were accepting what we are trying to do in the music department, they really were not. They just hadn't said anything about it. And they did not want the "good music" that we had offered. They went back and told their children that it was not good music that we were offering—that it was highbrow and snobbish, and consequently many of these children are not in our choir program for that reason.

Episcopalian: It seems to me that this would be a case where the director of religious education would have to tell his teachers to accept it or else replace them as teachers, provided your music program had the support of the senior minister. Don't you agree that it is unfortunate to have this conflict?

Baptist: This is under investigation right now.

Disciples' wife: But that's not always the way it's done. It's acceptable in some situations and others it is not. I was hearing this story and I thought, "Well, this sounds like home." I am sure others experience the same thing. This is the educational aspect. You see the material is available not just for entertainment or to satisfy a spot in the service, but as an integral part of the child's development. This is a means of expression. How does a child sing praises if he has no vehicle? This is where the literature of the church comes in. Why do we learn to play the piano? To have a vehicle of expression. Maybe someday it will be a flute or something else, but at least there is a means whereby a sensitive spirit has an outlet instead of remaining caged.

Moderator: Mr. Baptist, I wonder how much the congregation appreciates the kind of music that you and other musicians in the church try to use to bring a genuine act of praise, and where does the role of the musician come in in elevating the total life of a congregation?

Baptist: It's very hard to say what percentage like and what dislike it, because I am usually hit by those who dislike it. Very seldom do I hear from those who appreciate it until we have a problem. If a problem should arise over playing certain kinds of music—for instance, at the organ—I'll have many people criticize that. So we'll make a decision that we just won't play that kind of music any more, then the others rise up and say that they don't want trash, they want better music. It is very difficult to say what percentage appreciate it.

Methodist 1: I think we have to realize how far churches have come in a few short years. Your magazine *The Church Musician* has helped a great deal because the editors have coordinated a lot of work in there to help people along in the education department as well as in the worship area. But too few people see the magazine. Maybe just the musician and the pastor read it—most likely not. We have been doing something in this *Music Ministry* magazine of ours in relationship with children's literature. When we talk about coordinating, the selecting of hymns, we have a page for Elementary I-II. This is, however, for the choir, but it parallels the curriculum of the church school, suggesting other music to use and also suggesting the hymns they are going to be using in the various units. This has helped a lot of church musicians, but here again, our magazine hardly ever hits the pastor's desk. If it does, he puts it in the musician's box, thinking it got there by mistake. The education people don't read it at all!

Professor: We have been talking about attitudes, about appraising attitudes. One of the things that always interests me is to hear people talk (Methodists, at least) about small churches and large churches, when in fact all the attitudes are built in a small church group context. People learn gospel hymns in the small group situation, in nice hard rooms with a nice ring to them, and then these people grow up and go into a large church where there is no reverberation, and they say, "This is not like home, somehow." I think that if you are going to change attitudes you always have to go back and get into small groups—not to break down, but to orient and to relate to the attitude that has been preconditioned through these years of experience. I think that sometimes our approach to "sacred concerts" in the midst of worship are a waste of time, and we could start with smaller groups or in a smaller context somehow. This is where attitudes were built. I doubt that we can change them with large efforts as we sometimes undertake. I'm not talking about seasonal concerts, but just week-by-week attempts to educate at the point of worship. I think that this may be lost effort to some extent, just because of this one fact, most people have been schooled in the small church or small group.

Methodist 1: Our people head for the church school class and small groups where they can sing out of the gospel hymn book.

Baptist: I think this is one reason I am in favor of the multiple choir system, because you can start with the children. The attitude of wanting good music is formed at the very beginning of life itself, and I think the children at ——— Church are most fortunate—where they can have this system of having the good music given them.

Disciples: I think the church musician should set as high a standard as possible. Now granted there will be different standards in different churches and communities. The church musician should lead in the matter of taste, but he shouldn't go too far out ahead or he will lose all contact with his people, and then he simply excommunicates himself; but I think he ought to be definitely leading and at the same time keeping in contact. In this way the congregation progresses in the matter of taste. If he doesn't do this, who does? He must accept the leadership responsibility for this.

The above conversations vividly illustrate some of the fundamental problems the church musician faces:

1. The struggle that goes on within the musician for the development of the best music within the total life of the church. The musician lives in a constant tension, being forced to compromise with his own convictions because of the level of understanding and acceptance of the congregation.

2. The desire of the musician to have entrée to the educational program of the church as a means of teaching the meaning of worship, and the developing of a long-range program in all departments of the church for music appreciation.

3. The desire on the part of the musician to be understood by the senior minister and other members of the staff, as well as the musician's understanding the other members of the staff.

4. The desire on the part of the musician to be understood by the congregation, and to have the chance to be a minister in worship to the congregation.

5. The widespread disagreement among church musicians in regard to basic philosophy of music in the church and the role of the church musician in the church's ministry.

It is at this point that communication needs to be established between the musician, other employed members of the church staff, and leaders in the congregation. Here the roles of the senior minister as enabler and communicator can come into play. He is in the position to make it possible for the musician to be heard and to get together

177

persons involved in leadership for discussion of needs. It is at this juncture that the music committee, the committee or commission on worship, and the committee or commission on education in the local church need to get together. Most congregations are ready for growth when approached from a constructive and educational point of view. The church musician needs to remind himself constantly of the central purpose, goal, and objective of the church staff—namely, *to assist the congregation to be the church*. Being the church involves, among other things, the perfecting of the church in its worship; and the musician, as well as other persons on the church staff, is a *servant* of the congregation, not *master* of the people.

The Church Musician as Minister

It is inevitable that the church musician working with various age groups in the local church will have many opportunities to minister to individuals in their personal needs. Counseling opportunities will be afforded the church musician in regard to vocational choices with young people, marital problems, financial problems, and the usual run-of-the-mill problems of individuals in the church.

It is good to let the church musicians speak for themselves. Following is a quotation of the conversation of the musicians referred to above.

Student: All of us have talked about the music in the ministry of music and the educational aspects of our work. Would you consider a thought about this word *ministry* as related to you? Not necessarily education, or the act of performance in preparation of worship, but *ministry* to persons in their individual needs.

Episcopalian: Many times the music director is closer to the people in his choir than to other members, perhaps, because he is working with them more closely on a more regular schedule, and is with them a considerable amount of time. Therefore, the choir director can be a real minister in a time of help and trouble—sickness or death, and so forth, in the family.

Methodist 1: Sometimes this gets you into trouble with the senior minister.

Disciples: Yes, sometimes it does, but on the other hand, when a member of your choir is ill I think the minister of music needs to take a personal interest. He can't provide the service the regular minister does, but he can take a personal interest and visit in the hospital and can try to be what help he can without trying to be a minister of the gospel.

Methodist 1: There is a very thin line there. Sometimes I have known men who, because of this close contact and because of their almost martyr complex about things "terrestrial and celestial," got into somewhat of a pickle because they started counseling with their choir members in much the same way the senior minister wanted to be doing. In this particular situation it was a large group, 150 or 200 people—adults. These people went to the director or minister of music and soon unloaded all their troubles on his shoulders. The senior minister became quite vexed about this. The music man had to change churches. This is not a singular thing. There are others who have had to come to the conclusion that because of their counseling attitude they have stepped over the little thin line that divides the ordained man from the director of music. Now if the minister of music happens to be an ordained man, then this is a little different thing. But yet you have to cope with the fact that there is a head of the local church, and you have to be careful about that.

Episcopalian: I don't really think it makes any difference whether he is ordained or not—I think that what makes the difference is whether that is his function in being there. I mean the director of music may be better qualified to counsel, but if the senior minister is there, and it's his function, then the minister of music should not usurp it.

Disciples: I think that this matter of ministering to choir members is a part of the area of his responsibility when he takes that kind of position.

Professor: I think one of the worst shocks I ever had my first year out of school was when I was on a multiple staff and found out, quite by accident (because I went to the church in summer when the minister was away) that there were certain families in the parish that no one called on but the senior minister. Some senior ministers who have come up the road, say for 20 years, in which they have done all of the ministry of the church, are really unable to delegate responsibility. For twenty years they have done all the work. Now there is a staff thrust upon them, and they do not know what to do with the staff.

Methodist 1: This is a desperate problem—the interpersonal relationships of the church staff. It happens in more cases than any of us would like to believe. I believe everyone in this room has drawn a different line—where we know we have to decide in relationship with our senior minister what we can or cannot do in regard to his work. In my own case, I don't bother with counseling—serious counseling. If someone comes to me with a problem, and they quite often do (our church is a young church of rising executives—they are changing positions rapidly), I refer him to the senior minister.

Summary

Interpersonal relations, communications, and understanding of the work of the musician on the part of church staff and members of the congregation are the main factors for consideration by the church staff in regard to the professional musician.

The musician is frequently caught in tension between his concept of the place of music in the church, both in worship and education, and concepts of other members of the staff. Much time needs to be devoted to discussion within the staff of the place of music in the church. The musician needs to be heard by other members of the staff, and he needs to hear them.

It may be advisable at this point to go back and review Chapter 3, "Personnel Management: Policies and Methods and the Lay Committee on Personnel," and seek to put every aspect of the chapter into practice. The job description is of special importance. This, like all job descriptions, needs to be worked out with other members of the staff, the music committee, and a committee on worship. Clear lines of responsibility need to be drawn in regard to the musician and his responsibilities in Christian education, as well as worship, choir program, and any pastoral responsibilities.

The musician is an educator. As such, he needs to have the opportunity to lead children, youth, and adults in the meaning of worship and the place of music in the total life of the church.

If we are faithful to the basic premise of this work—namely, that the employed staff of a church is to assist the congregation to be the church in worship, nurture, and at work in the world—the musician carries a major responsibility within the church, especially for worship and nurture. Good teamwork, cooperation, and communication will go far in maximizing the work of the musician as a member of the professional staff of the local church.

9

The Church Business Administrator

While interviewing members of church staffs I talked with a church business administrator in a large Episcopal parish in the South. Here was a middle-aged man who had been in private business for some twenty years before going into full-time church work seven years ago. To the question, How do you look upon your position in this church? I received crisp, concise, rapid-fire responses. "I never look down upon an employee. I attempt to sell everyone on his job. I'm never too busy to help anyone with anything. I don't have a position, I have a job. I try to take as much work off the pastors as possible so they can do their 'pastoring.' I am at the church for weddings, funerals, and any special events to see that everything goes smoothly."

Interviews with other members of the staff indicated the church business administrator fulfilled his self-expectation roles well. There was a keen sense of appreciation and high admiration of his work by every member of the staff. I felt he did more than was necessary and carried some responsibilities that should have been shared by others; however, he seemed to be "joyous in the service of his Lord." In actuality the entire administration of the church was centered in the CBA (church business administrator). This was reflected by the arrangement of the offices. His office was at the hub of a large wheel, with other offices—including the senior minister's—around him. At the same time he had the ability to do the job needed, but also to recognize the abilities and positions of others. He seemed to carry the servant role fully.

The position of church business administrator is growing in the Protestant church. There have been similar positions for some forty years, but only a few instances could be cited up until the last two decades. It is estimated that at this time there are one thousand to twelve hundred positions in local churches that can be classified as church business administrator, though there are some forty different titles for the office.

The term church business administrator (hereafter referred to as CBA) has been recognized by the National Association of Church Business Administrators, which was established in 1957. The position is now recognized by the national organization with formal membership and certification standards. More will be said about this organization later.

The Office, Its Function and Work

A church with a thousand members and a budget of $100,000 has reached a size or achieved a degree of complexity that should give reason for reviewing its internal administration and its business practices and procedures. This review often results in a conclusion that an administrative assistant, a business manager, or an administrator would be able to solve a great many problems and add substantial strength to the work and ministry of the church.[1]

Fitch continues, stating that with a thousand people involved in a church:

There are committees and departments and all of these things go with them: personnel, budgets, supplies, services, building use, meetings, programs, schedules, and many interrelationships.

A budget of $100,000 means an extensive amount of work to raise the funds required, it demands control of how the money is spent, that it is done wisely and carefully, and it requires books and records to account for the expenditures. A church office that should be supervised has come into being. There are a number of staff people that require direction. Payrolls must be met, and the increasing number of employee benefits must be administered. Wages, hours, and all of the elements of personnel administration come into being. The church is an employer, and because it is a church, it should be the most responsible kind of employer.[2]

In addition to personnel and budget a church of a thousand members must maintain a building of some dimension representing large investments and requiring maintenance, upkeep, and insurance. A church soon gets into a number of large-scale operations, such as communications by mail, publications, news, radio, television, parking lots, additional property, church camps, a dining room, and recreational facilities.

All the business activities of the church require specific supervision and guidance. In the small church much of this work can be done by volunteer laymen under the supervision of the pastor, but as the

---

[1] Carroll B. Fitch, *Church Management,* Vol. 39 (May, 1963), p. 7.
[2] *Ibid.*

church grows needs increase until it is necessary to add personnel to give direction. Too much of the responsibility for the necessary administration of a church has been placed upon the pastor. He does not feel capable of giving guidance to the needs, nor does he feel it is a wise investment of his time.

When Should a Congregation Employ a CBA?

With increasing demands for a larger church staff and a fuller program of the church, there are many operational tasks to be done. Herein lies the major work of the CBA. Congregations will ask the question, "Should we employ a CBA?" or "What are the criteria for a CBA in the church?" These are justified questions and deserve consideration.

It is difficult to give a universal answer to the above questions. A rule of thumb is: a CBA should be added when the congregation has grown to the dimension that the operational tasks of the church are too large to be handled by volunteer help and the paid staff. Here, however, there are problems, for the paid staff may be performing well in the operational tasks of the church but failing to perform in the professional roles for which they have been employed, thus causing the major works of the church to be neglected.

Size of congregation and amount of church budget may be a partial key. In a study done in 1964 by Kenneth Zinn (CBA in a Presbyterian church) of 175 churches employing a church business administrator, 7 percent had under 1,000 members with annual budgets of $50,000 to $137,000. Eleven percent of the churches had from 1,000 to 1,500 members with budgets of $54,000 to $175,000, with two churches of $200,000 budgets. Nineteen percent of the churches had a membership of 1,500 to 2,000 with budgets of $66,000 to $300,000. One-fourth, or 25 percent, of the churches had memberships between 2,000 and 3,000 with budgets ranging from $134,000 to $400,000. Twenty-one percent of the churches were in the 3,000- to 4,000-member size, with budgets of $150,000 to $667,000. This leaves 17 percent of the churches with more than 4,000 members. It can be seen by these figures that some churches employ a CBA at one thousand members, and a large number of churches will employ a CBA when the membership reaches 1,500 to 2,000. There is a clear indication from the study that in the smaller churches a number of the CBA's were part-time employees.

Salary ranges were from $2,000 for part-time work to $12,600. The smaller the church, the larger the percent of funds spent for total salaries put into the salary of the CBA. An overall average for churches of 1,500 members or less would require an expenditure of some 15 percent of all budgeted salary funds for the CBA. For churches of 1,500 to 2,000 members, approximately 12 percent of budgeted salaries is spent on the CBA. For churches of between 2,000 and 3,000 members approximately 9 percent of budgeted salaries is spent for the CBA. Churches of 3,000 to 4,000 members spent approximately 8 percent of the salary budget for the CBA. Churches above 4,000 varied considerably, but spent, on an average, 7 percent of all budgeted salaries for the CBA.[3]

From the sample of church business administrators in our staff study, the following information has been compiled. This information is not to be considered normative, but may be of value in assisting to understand more fully the persons in the office.

Seventy-seven percent of the CBA's are in churches located in cities of more than 100,000 persons, and 55 percent of the churches have 2,000 or more members. Fifty-one percent of the churches have operating budgets of $100,000 to $200,000; 28 percent have budgets of $200,000 to $400,000; and 5 percent have operating budgets of more than $400,000.

Thirty-five percent of the CBA's are sixty-five years old or older, with 20 percent between 55 and 64 years old, and 25 percent 45 to 54 years old. Twenty-seven percent have served in the church in which they are employed at the time of the study less than two years. Twenty-two percent have served in the local church for two to three years, and 15 percent for 4 to 5 years. Ten percent have served in the same church for thirteen to fifteen years.

Sixty-four percent of the CBA's have completed high school, and 21 percent hold a liberal arts degree. Forty-two percent of the CBA's have had special training in a business school.

Twenty percent of the CBA's were born in the open country, 40 percent in communities of 500 to 2,500 people. Twelve percent of the CBA's were born in a city of 500,000 or more.

Eighteen percent of the CBA's were born in homes where the father was in one of the professions, 13 percent were in agriculture, 23 percent were in managerial positions, 20 percent were engaged in sales work, and 10 percent were craftsmen.

---

[3] Edward B. Wycoff, "The Church Business Administrator, A Christian Vocation," a publication of the National Association of Church Business Administrators, 1964, p. 104. Kenneth Zinn, "National Salary Study of Church Business Administrators."

Seventy percent of the CBA's in the study did not consider a church vocation until they were beyond their thirtieth birthday, and 34 percent did not go into a church vocation until they were 40 years old or older. An additional 42 percent were between 30 and 49 years old before entering a church vocation. There is a clear indication that church work as a vocation came rather late in life and was chosen after working at some other type of vocation for a number of years.

Influences that assisted in the decision to enter a church-related vocation were strongest from the pastor, home, and church people. One-fourth of the CBA's have had some adverse type of experience in the business world, military, or personal life that caused them to consider a church position for a vocation.

From the above statistics it could be stated that a local congregation will need to decide if it feels the expenditure of from 7 to 15 percent of its budgeted salary funds for operational administration is a wise investment. In the light of the highly skilled ministerial staff who must carry heavy operational responsibilities if there is no employed CBA, the answer may be the employment of a CBA. I feel the office of CBA will gain increasing importance in the church as congregations and ministers become aware of the value of such an office in the church staff.

The Work of the CBA

No universal job description can be given for the work of the church business administrator. The size of the congregation, the number and types of persons on the church staff, and the dimensions of the program of the local congregation are determining factors for a job analysis or description of the CBA. A number of areas of concern have been described and quite adequately covered in a paper prepared by Carroll B. Fitch for a special Consultation on the Church Staff conducted by the author. Fitch is the CBA for Riverside Church, New York City, and served as president of the National Association of Church Business Administrators in 1962–63.

The CBA as Coordinator

"The job descriptions of some CBAs provide for responsibility in three broad areas: physical plant, finances, and personnel. An examination of these areas indicates that they have church-wide implications touching both the staff and the membership.

185

"It is obvious that in operating and maintaining the church properties, buildings, and equipment the CBA becomes involved with virtually every phase of church activity. In making arrangements for the use of the physical plant he comes to know the requirements of various functions and a great deal about them. If, within one of his areas of work, he serves as purchasing agent, he accumulates further detailed knowledge. These activities on his part also keep him in a working relationship with other staff people and frequently with the chairmen of boards and committees.

"As financial officer the CBA may function in several capacities: budget director, accounting supervisor and/or controller, and fund raiser. In his financial role, particularly in the preparation of the budget and in controlling expenditures, the CBA again works with various staff colleagues and normally with every church department and group that has a budget allocation. The budget is often described as a program plan expressed in terms of dollars. A church budget director or controller can hardly do a conscientious and intelligent job if he is not familiar with the facts behind the figures. More than plain facts are important; the spirit and purpose involved are essential factors. The CBA becomes the channel, the means through which the plans and requests for budget appropriations from the various areas of the church are brought together, transformed into a unity and put into form for consideration by the official board and action by the congregation. The CBA has the opportunity and the responsibility to assure an adequate presentation and a full hearing for each budget request. He readily becomes in this process both a source of information and a counsellor and advisor. A particular obligation that he should feel is to maintain an objective and impartial position with respect to all departments and church groups, helping to make possible budget decisions that will contribute to the best interest of the total church ministry, program and operation.

"The CBA's personnel role may be a limited one initially, related to office and building employees within his own department. This role has built-in tendencies to grow and expand. The Church Salary Committee (or other group responsible for this function) requires various kinds of data which the financial office must provide. Sometimes a salary study or survey is requested. Various kinds of fringe benefits are being granted increasingly by churches to their employees. Materials must be obtained and information gathered. In all of these processes, the CBA is likely to be the individual assigned the task. In the area of evaluation of the work of employees, the CBA will be consulted with respect to people who work for him. Because he works with other staff members, his judgment often is sought with respect to them. The result is that the CBA frequently comes to have a distinct role as Personnel Director that eventually covers nearly every aspect of the personnel process.

"All of the three areas described above (physical plant, finance and personnel) indicate the service character of the CBA's basic job. His responsibility is to provide the various facilities, mechanics and processes, and personnel that undergird and support the ministry of the church and the various specialized activities that relate to it.

"The nature of the work of the administrator and the associations throughout the church that evolve from it can very well make him the best informed person on the staff, not about the details of specific programs, but about the overall content of the ministry in the broad sense of the term. The CBA is a cooperator. He must be, or he is not effective.

"From this develops the role of coordinator. This is often an informal function, but in an increasing number of churches it is a designated or delegated responsibility added to the CBA's portfolio. It is a logical one for no other staff person has a less specialized job, and there is probably no one else who has as frequent contacts throughout the church organization.

Organizational Relationships of the CBA: To the Senior Minister

"The senior minister in a large number of churches with a multiple staff is without question recognized or designated as the head of the staff, responsible for its work. In some cases he has virtually absolute authority to hire and fire any staff member. More frequently, he must work in consultation with a committee or board, particularly in matters relating to his professional staff. In some churches ministers, and even the church business administrator, are called by the congregation and can only be discharged by the action of that body. In those cases where the senior minister is the chief administrator, the CBA usually reports directly to him. Organizationally, the CBA is on the same level as ministers in the associate clergy.

"There are exceptions to this, however. Some CBAs have a lower rank. Others are only nominally responsible to the senior minister and, instead, work directly under an official board. One reason for this is a variation in state laws. A church can be two separate entities— a religious fellowship and a religious corporation with mutually

187

autonomous boards. A CBA employed as an agent of the corporate board which has no jurisdiction over the senior minister cannot logically be responsible to that senior minister.

"An additional factor is that the CBA tends to have a close and often direct working relationship with the church body that has responsibility for temporal affairs. His position may have been created because of their initiative. They were undoubtedly active in his recruitment and selection. He works with them on matters that are within their own field of competence and he speaks their language from what is often a similar background of experience. Whereas church bodies often extend a degree of deference to the minister because of his role as 'the man of God' and defer to his judgment in religious and program matters, they face the CBA on their own terms, demanding facts, figures, and proof. From this relationship a rapport can develop that, to some extent, will by-pass the senior minister even when he is unquestionably the chief administrator of the staff. The senior minister may acquiesce in this and be glad to be relieved of non-ministerial responsibilities. Yet, this can still become a matter of friction, offering the CBA the opportunity to build his own special sphere of influence, independent of his chief.

"This, and any other barriers between the senior minister and the CBA, should not be permitted to develop. Despite the dedication and devotion that both may have, they have human qualities such as fear, pride, jealousy that all people possess. Every possible step should be taken to avoid conflicts and misunderstandings.

"Some ministers are blessed with skills as administrators; others are not. Few have had administrative or advisory experience outside their own churches. Many ministers are poorly prepared to discharge a major executive function when it is thrust upon them as a result of church growth and a multiple staff.

"The CBA, on the other hand, has probably had specific training or experience that gives him strong qualifications in this area. If his senior minister is impatient with his executive role, dislikes it, feels insecure, and permits his CBA to assume his function, the CBA may achieve a position that threatens the relationship.

"The relationship of senior minister and Church Business Administrator can be one of the most important in the church. The minister is the leader of the congregation with special and overriding concern and responsibility for its spiritual life. The CBA often has a major responsibility for the structure and organization—the machinery, procedures, and personnel that support the ministry. Unless there is the best kind of coordination between these two areas and functions, the life of the church suffers and its resources are not used with maximum effectiveness.

"The CBA can perform a significant service if he accepts the responsibility for assuring the best kind of relationship with his senior minister. He will have to use wisdom and tact in many instances to achieve this. Basic to his efforts will be a conscious and planned process of keeping the senior minister informed, of seeking his advice and counsel, and of having the judgment to secure the senior minister's decision on matters that he should decide. And the CBA should accomplish this without consuming time that should be devoted to other purposes.

"When there is complete trust and mutual confidence between minister and administrator, an effective working relationship will result. Moreover, this will be evident to others and will have significant benefits throughout the rest of the staff and will reach to the church membership.

Organizational Relationships of the CBA: To Other Professional Staff

"It would seem that the nature of the relationships of the CBA to the ministers (excepting the senior minister) and other professional personnel would depend upon the job description of the CBA, the extent of his responsibilities, and the authority vested in him. This implies that these relationships are based primarily on position and status. Unless the CBA can develop a stronger foundation than these, he will find himself frequently in difficulty. To be effective, the CBA must operate from a position that is founded on the confidence and trust of his associates, their respect for him and his competence as a staff member, their appreciation of his qualities as an individual, and their awareness that he shares the same concern for their work that they have. This may not be easy to achieve for the CBA's presence on the church staff is often resented.

"There is never sufficient money in the budget to meet all of the needs or support all of the plans of a vigorous and imaginative congregation. Having to allocate funds to the business office and to pay the salary and expenses of an administrator seems on the surface to be diverting money to non-program purposes. Even when the position has been well established and its value demonstrated, the CBA is sometimes seen as a competitor rather than a colleague. Because of his role in controlling expenditures, which often means saying 'no' to requests, he is interpreted as being opposed to the program ideas of the staff or of church departments.

"The administrator can become a middle man between an official board and the staff or other groups, subject to pressures from both directions. For example, in a healthy church, the budget is constantly increasing, new projects are initiated, additional staff jobs are created, and expense totals rise regularly. Conservative factions want to hold the line. Enthusiasts press for new and larger appropriations. The result is a compromise with neither side fully satisfied, the administrator being held responsible by both sides. This is indicative of what may happen in other church situations.

"The CBA's job is unique in another way. He may well be the only layman among the professional staff group. The ordained people have many elements in common in their background of experience and training. To some extent, they speak a different language than the man who came from the commercial world. Perhaps, unthinkingly, the administrator is excluded from the fellowship of the 'fraternity.'

"Yet, contradictory as it may appear, a church business administrator not infrequently becomes the 'pastor's pastor.' There is a sense of pride among some ministers that makes them feel that they should be able to work out their own problems, face their difficulties without counsel, and find solutions unaided. When they can reach the point where they must talk with someone, preferring not to go to a ministerial colleague, they turn to their CBAs.

"To earn the confidence and respect of the staff, the church business administrator must have wisdom, patience, a working level of knowledge of human psychology and the ability to work well with people. Perhaps of all the qualifications a CBA should possess, it is in this area that he should have his greatest strength. It is also in helping to mobilize and use the *human resources* of the church—both within the staff and among the membership—that he has an opportunity to make a major contribution to the total ministry.

"An unlimited number of elements are basic to good staff relationships. There are some important ones that the administrator should keep in his thinking. Heading the list would be the requirement of full loyalty to his senior minister. Any legitimate differences of opinion or appropriate questions should be discussed personally, not publicly, nor in the minister's absence. Related to this is the importance of the CBA avoiding being a part of any faction or clique that might develop within the staff—or the church. Also, the administrator should avoid

190

being a tool or means through which special favors are distributed or obtained.

"Laymen tend to invest the clergy with special traits of goodness, charity, wisdom, patience, faith, and the like to a degree that is inconsistent with basic human frailties. The CBA must know his clergy, respect them for their dedication, leadership, and service and love them greatly despite human weaknesses they may display.

"Such weaknesses occur within the staff in various ways. Competition goes past a healthy point. 'Politics' develop. Status and position, rights and privileges become issues. As another example, pressure groups are encouraged to secure favorable budget consideration. Similarly, individual staff members draw groups about themselves that can come to be 'little churches' within the church. No one is more likely to become aware of developments of this kind than the administrator, and with tact and wisdom, and in consultation with his senior minister, he can help maintain a balance so that the overall ministry and interests of the church are not subordinated to the narrower interests or enthusiasms of a part or of a group. Above all, the CBA should avoid becoming a part of a competition or he loses his value in his broader role of coordinator and stabilizer.

"The administrator needs to be clear about his place, his role, and intended function and accommodate to it. He is on the staff to serve the whole church and his actions should demonstrate both understanding and ability concerning this. He is essentially a person who works 'backstage' and seldom occupies the spotlight. Whenever possible, he shifts credit to other participants, finding his reward in the progress, growth, and the effective ministry of his church.

"A professional ailment that occurs among church business administrators is the development of a proprietary attitude toward church monies that goes beyond his function as controller. The CBA, so afflicted, evidences an attitude that the expenditure of church funds is improper unless for a purpose that he personally thinks is proper and which he endorses, whether or not the item was planned when the budget was prepared. He ignores the reality that budget appropriations are meant to be spent and that it is his job to see that they are disbursed properly, used wisely, and that value is received. By being cooperative and constructive, he can render a real service. By being an obstructionist, he can damage morale and make money of disproportionate importance.

"People are more important than budgets, buildings, or bonds. It is this approach that should be basic to the CBA's relationship with the staff. Just as his job tends to be openminded, depending on what he brings to it, so his relationships with the staff are likely to be what he creates.

Organizational Relationships of the CBA: To the Non-Professional Staff

"To the office and building employees in a large number of churches the administrator is the 'boss.' While he may have a limited personnel function to perform with other church staff members, these are people who look to him for supervision and direction. They depend on him for recognition and reward. They expect help and understanding with job problems and often with personal ones.

"Using human resources creatively (so that the individual finds satisfaction in his job—and maximum ability is brought to the task at hand) is the obligation of the CBA and requires of him more than a superficial acquaintance with the people he supervises. Because the nonprofessional staff of even the large church is relatively small, it is possible for the CBA to know each person in a way that is impossible in organizations where employees number in the hundreds and thousands. It should be practical to develop far better employer-employee relations in the church than in most places. This should be seen as an opportunity and accepted as a goal.

"The reality, in at least some churches, is far from this goal. Few of the good personnel policies and practices now common in business and industry have been applied widely in churches, particularly with respect to the nonprofessional group.

"In addition to his role as supervisor and his obligation to obtain an appropriate quality and quantity of work from his staff people the CBA has the responsibility for seeking reasonable rewards, needed fringe benefits and good working conditions for them.

"The church has much to say about justice, mercy, love, and understanding. It should demonstrate a working knowledge and the practical application of these concepts in its relationships with those who earn their daily bread as church employees. When outsiders scrutinize the church, they should find that the church is a good employer. The CBA should consider it his obligation to see that this condition exists.

Organizational Relationships of the CBA: To the Official Boards and Officers

"Except in an extremely formal and rigid church organization, the church business administrator will have many contacts with the official

192

board (s) and its officers. (The senior minister will not be concerned and should not needlessly be burdened with a variety of business matters involved in the board-administrator relationship. Yet both the board and the administrator should be conscientious in keeping the minister informed, and involved personally, when appropriate.) The organizational line from the official board to the administrator will frequently be through the minister. In practice, there will be many lines as the board gives authority and responsibility to its officers, members, and committees who will then work with the CBA. While these lines will usually be gathered together in board meetings through reports and discussions of items of business, the CBA still needs to be continually aware of keeping the proper board personnel informed. He can and should serve to coordinate various efforts and to help avoid overlapping and even competition. Diplomacy of a high order is often required.

"The CBA will provide an important service if he will help to see that the time of the lay officers of the church is used wisely. When their time and abilities are used effectively and efficiently, they find satisfaction in their work. When they are burdened with trivia, or inordinate demands are placed on them, they tend to seek escape from office.

"The official board may invite the CBA to meet with it occasionally or regularly. If he does, he should be particularly aware that his is not a policy-making function. He is a resource, providing facts and information. He may also be the agent of the board. When serving in this capacity, his obligation is to avoid seeming to be the source of authority. The ready access that he may have to church policy-makers should never be used to promote or advance his own special interests.

"Church boards and officers tend to become more involved in actual administration than their counterparts in business. This can have values and it may create problems. When a board chairman of a large church becomes the church executive, a cumbersome and ineffective system may eventuate. This should not occur, except by plan—and that might be challenged with strong leadership from the senior minister. It should be unnecessary with a skilled and competent CBA on the staff. One value that a CBA can provide is to assist the board to distinguish between its functions and those of the staff. Situations develop in which senior board officers fail to perform. This creates a vacuum. The responsibility of the CBA is not to fill this vacuum, but to help in having the problem solved.

"The wise CBA will be sensitive and alert concerning his relationships with the board (s) of the church. From it he gets his authority (although it may be exercised under the senior minister). His rewards must follow its action and his tenure is largely dependent upon its pleasure. But more important is the fact that much of the strength of the church is found in the board and its members. To conserve, develop, and use this resource is not necessarily a primary responsibility of the CBA, but it is one to which he will be able to contribute significantly in many ways.

"For its 10th Biennial Convention held in Washington, D. C. in 1961, the National Association of Temple Administrators chose as its theme, 'Coordinating our Human Resources.' The National Association of Business Administrators had a representative present. His notes reporting the meeting contained the following on the subject, 'The Administrator, the Board of Trustees and Committees.'

" 'A partnership concept should exist between the people involved, some of whom are working as part-time volunteers, while at least one is a full-time paid person. Too often the administrator tends to act like the owner (the congregation). A major function of the administrator in the partnership plan would be to help locate, identify and develop leadership for the Board and committees.

" 'The administrator's job on behalf of the Board has a number of facets. He should prepare information that will be required. He often must prepare people; sounding them out, obtaining spokesmen for various matters, preparing the ground so that obstacles to action can be discovered and removed. If there are hostilities of an irrelevant nature, he should help remove them. Key people related to a proposal should be briefed in advance. The administrator should help prepare alternative plans should a given proposition not be approved.

" 'The administrator is in some respects a traffic manager, seeing that approprate committees or others groups are assigned projects or other work. The administrator is necessarily a political leader but never a candidate for office. He is constantly dealing in public relations and in all that he does, he is seeking to get committees to do their jobs to advance the work of his temple. He should work to keep committees that have specific jobs to do small in size. While large groups decide policy satisfactorily, work is done most effectively by just a few. (If Moses had had a committee we'd still be in Egypt.)

" 'The administrator is often tempted to manipulate, to form policy by indirection, to let a committee provide the form while he provides the substance.'

"There are differences between the role and function of the Temple

Administrator and the Church Business Administrator. For one thing, the operational and administrative patterns in temples have more uniformity than in churches. However, the content of the quotation from the report of the N.A.T.A. meeting has much that is immediately applicable to the relationship of the CBA and his official board.

Good Organizational Relationships: A Basic Need

"Throughout the church organization there is need for clarity and understanding concerning function and responsibility. Every member of the church staff should know *to whom he or she is responsible.* Those who have supervisory roles should know *for whom they are responsible* and the extent and nature of their authority. Related materials such as job descriptions and organizational charts are useful and important. Written procedures are often desirable. Staff relationships should be clear and overlapping, if it exists, should be understood and a means provided to deal with it.

"The principles involved apply with equal force to the volunteer sector of the church—the board (s), committees, departments, and various groups. In those churches possessed of more than one established official body, there is urgent need for written material covering their functions, areas of responsibility, various procedures and policies, and a means established for coordination.

"The Church Business Administrator may never be given responsibility for the preparation or development of such material, but he will have many opportunities to give leadership that will result in its being written. The result need not be rigidity and inflexibility, but, instead, a breaking down of barriers that have been built because of a lack of understanding. When individuals or groups know their jobs, what is expected of them, the limits of responsibility and authority, accepted procedures and resources available, they will produce results and find rewards in their work.

Problems, Concerns, and Comments

"One problem that may be faced by the CBA is to know what his job is, what people expect of him. The essence of the difficulty is that there are differing viewpoints within the church. An official board may see him as the person to relieve its officers of a burden of work. The senior minister, on the other hand, may think of the CBA as his assistant. The more competence displayed by the CBA, the more things

195

he may be asked to do with the consequence that he spreads himself so thinly that he fails to be thorough in his work.

"The staff of a large church tends in the direction of a series of specializations. The administrator is a generalist. The result for him can be the frustration of never feeling fully qualified for many things given him as a responsibility.

"When the CBA is a really good administrator and good administration develops, he is not unlikely to find church people who think it somewhat unchristian for a church to be business-like. Sound management curtails certain kinds of freedoms. Efficiency puts the spotlight on vested interests and nonproductive efforts. Resistance develops and the plea is made, 'This is a church, not a business. Let's operate on the basis of goodwill.' What is actually meant is, 'Don't interfere with us.'

"The qualified layman coming to the church staff may bring ideas and viewpoints that call for revisions and changes. A defensive attitude can develop on the part of the ministers and staff for they may feel there is an implied reflection on their past conduct. The senior minister may become enamored of the idea of 'administration' and devote a disproportionate amount of time to it. There should be no competition between ministerial functions (such as preaching) and administration. Yet the skilled executive or administrator seems to gain more recognition than the minister. Hence, a minister can come to believe that it is more important that he do a good job of 'running the church' than giving religious leadership.

"The reverse side of this is the administrator who believes that to have status or recognition in the church, he must be accepted as a minister. He seeks opportunities to fill the role of a minister. He becomes more interested in the broad purposes of the church in the world than in doing a superior job of the task for which he is employed. And yet administration is a part of the total ministry of the church, not a thing apart. It is because this has not yet been fully understood that congregational resistance to the concept of church business administration occurs with people feeling that the funds used for the CBA's office might better be spent for missions.

"The place of the CBA in the future of the church, however, seems to be assured. The urbanization of the country, the increasing number of churches with institutional characteristics, the complexity demanded of the church to meet the rapidly changing conditions and, in some areas, a shortage of qualified ministers, are all factors for a good church business administrator.

"The denominations are taking steps to give the CBA their blessings. When these national bodies give formal sanction to the administrator's job as a recognized position, they will have advanced the cause considerably, benefiting both the CBA and the local church. The basic concept that must be achieved is to see the CBA not as a man provided to insulate the minister, nor to run his errands, but as a professional church worker with responsibilities for a part of the total church job.

"To sum up the Church Business Administrator's job a further quotation from the National Association of Temple Administrators' 1961 meeting is appropriate:

" 'The administrator must learn to live and to work with integrity, serving multiple functions. He is servant, executive, leader, follower, and catalyst. He must avoid the limelight and be content to sow seeds and watch them grow.' " [4]

The National Association of Church Business Administrators (NACB)

In 1955 a group of persons interested in the work of the CBA met at Lake Junaluska, North Carolina, to discuss the work of the CBA. In 1956 Mr. Webb Garrison of the General Board of Education of The Methodist Church called a meeting to be held in Oklahoma City for church administrators, financial secretaries, and treasurers of local churches. Seven denominations were represented among the forty persons present. It was felt by the group that they would like to see such a meeting made available nationwide. Tillman Carter, CBA of First Methodist Church, Lubbock, Texas, was selected by the group as organization chairman with authority to move forward with plans for a meeting.

The meeting was held in Dallas, Texas, July 10-12, 1957, in First Methodist Church with one hundred delegates present representing seven Protestant denominations from seventeen states. At this meeting the name National Association of Church Business Administrators was adopted. Mr. Bryan Brawner, then Executive Director of Highland Park Methodist Church, Dallas, was elected president. Since that date meetings have been held annually, and there are at this writing more than four hundred members of the Association.

Annual meetings have served as a solidifying and coordinating agent for the CBA's. Discussions in the meetings have been centered,

---

[4] Carroll B. Fitch, "The Church Business Administrator," *The Appropriate Functions and Relationships of the Church Staff in the Protestant Church,* Marvin T. Judy, ed. Copyrighted by the editor, 1964.

by and large, in basic "how to" areas, such as church insurance, wills and legacies, personnel management, bookkeeping, operational budgets, building management problems, role definitions, and the like. The 1966 conference in Dallas concerned itself primarily with the basic theological role of the CBA as a member of the church staff.

The organization has had no official publication, but there have been periodic newsletters from the presidents. *Church Management Magazine* did a series of articles on the CBA January through June, 1964. The magazine provides space each month for news and work of the CBA. The late William H. Leach, former editor of *Church Management* was quite influential in the development of the organization.

Through the years of its organization a code of ethics has been established, job descriptions designed, and a standardization of membership established. There is now a prescribed set of examinations to determine the ability and qualifications of those seeking membership in the National Association of Church Business Administrators. Examinations are in: Protestant Perspectives and Polity, Church Finance and Business Law, Property Maintenance and Insurance, Office Management and Personnel Administration, Public Relations and Communications.

The Future of the Church Business Administrator

The office of the CBA has within it the potential for answering many of the problems of the multiple staff in the local church. The office has been in existence long enough to have proved its worth in helping create more efficient staff and church operations, and for paying for itself financially. It has also been in existence long enough to reveal potential trouble spots that may occur. An alert CBA will be aware of such potential troubles and avoid falling into a trap. I mention some of the problems that seem to be the most acute.

First, as has been pointed out earlier, the CBA can become quite possessive in his work. It is a long known law of human relations that the person who controls money and personnel *controls*. Church budgets of $100,000 to $500,000 or more become a sizable responsibility. Also the nonprofessional staff may be quite large.

Second, it has been observed that if a senior minister wants to rid himself of administrative responsibilties and the CBA is willing or even anxious to take on more responsibilities, the CBA in practice, though not in theory, becomes the administrator of the local church.

Church staffs are not ready to accept the CBA as administrator and continue to look to the senior minister as the director of the staff.

Third, most CBA's have been schooled in the business world. Business practices are brought into the church, which in most cases is good and necessary; but the church is basically an institution that has grown out of a theological foundation. The business world has a philosophy of making as much profit for the stockholders as possible. The church is not a money-making, but a money-spending institution. It is mission. It is quite possible for the CBA, who has, as a rule, not been schooled in theology or church tradition, to become quite calloused in the central mission of the church.

I must hasten to say, however, that by virtue of being the comptroller of funds the CBA has a stewardship to perform to see that there is wise spending. Much friction will originate between the CBA and the other members of the staff if the CBA feels a request for some item is not wise. Clarification of such conflicts can be obtained through proper discussion and policy.

I feel emphatically that the work of the CBA in the local church is important and can provide a means of staff efficiency. In spite of the problems that may arise in the office, it is an asset to the congregation and church staff well worth the risks of personality problems and worth the financial investment.[5]

---

[5] For a further discussion see Robert N. Gray, *Church Business Administration: An Emerging Profession* (Enid, Oklahoma: Phillips University Press, 1968).

10

The Church Secretary

"If you can work independently, love people, are a good organizer, have a degree of patience, like mental and spiritual stimulation, and don't mind being alone from time to time, there is no job more rewarding," writes a church secretary in a Congregational church in the Midwest.

The above statement summarizes the feelings of a vast majority of church secretaries in spite of major and minor irritations and dissatisfactions with the position in the local church. The position of full-time secretary on the church staff has increased in importance in recent years. Churches of 400 to 1,000 members have, on the average, one full-time secretary, churches of 1,000 to 2,000 members have 2 secretaries, churches of 2,000 to 3,000 have 3, churches of 3,000 to 4,000 have 4 and churches over 4,000 have 5 or more. A rule of thumb may be: one full-time secretary for each 400 to 1,000 church members and one additional secretary for each additional 1,000 members. In addition, many churches have part-time help or specialized secretarial positions, such as financial secretary or membership secretary.

Secretaries, like church business administrators, have entered into full-time church employment from a variety of secular positions, motivated by a desire to do work in the church rather than by a compelling call to a church-related vocation. Many secretaries, however, possess a compassion for their work and a dedication to the church which may be as strong as that of a pastor or educator. In numerous cases the church secretary is the permanent member of a church staff and will survive the coming and going of pastors and other members of the staff. With the proper spirit, the church secretary can be one of the most valuable persons on the church staff. She is called upon to be the liaison between congregation and staff. She must possess the graces necessary to meet the public in person and by telephone. She must have at her fingertip the church files, records, and correspondence. She must be able to remember names and identify persons both in and out of the church membership.

The secretary is in the position of understanding the condition of the local congregation as does no one else. Laymen will share with her their real feelings regarding the work of the church and also how they feel about persons on the church staff. A competent church secretary can assist the church staff in understanding the attitudes of the congregation and status of the staff with the congregation and community.

In our study of the church staff data were compiled for 355 secretaries from eight leading American denominations representing every section of the United States; towns and cities of 500 to more than 1,000,000 population; and congregations of less than 400 members to more than 4,000. In addition to formal questionnaires, interviews were conducted with more than 100 secretaries in churches of different denominations across the nation and in Canada.

Thirty percent of the church secretaries in our study were 55 years old or older, 34 percent were 45 to 55 years old, and 23 percent less than 35 years old.

Thirty-one percent of the secretaries had been in their present position less than 2 years, but 33 percent had been there 6 years or more. Seventy-six percent of the secretaries had worked in no other church, and 19 percent had worked in one other church. Sixty-five percent of the secretaries had worked in secular positions prior to becoming church secretaries, and of that number 85 percent had done secretarial work in the business or professional world.

Eighty-eight percent of the secretaries had completed high school, 14 percent had a 4-year college degree, 1 percent had a master's degree, and 67 percent had specialized training in a school of business or commerce. Twenty-four percent had been to college but did not complete the degree program.

Sixty-five percent of the secretaries were born in communities of less than 10,000 persons. One out of 4, or 25 percent, of the secretaries came from homes where agriculture was the way of making a living, 22 percent of the secretaries' parents were in one of the crafts, and 18 percent were in one of the professions.

Unlike ministers and church educators, the majority of church secretaries considered a church position comparatively late in life. Fifty-six percent of the secretaries considered a church position after they were 30 years old, and 46 percent entered a church vocation after they were 40 years old. The most decisive factor in becoming a church secretary was the necessity of making additional family income, with 54 percent of the secretaries having this reason. There are, however, a number of church secretaries who feel their position is the fulfillment of a vocational calling to invest their lives in a meaningful church-related position. Ten percent indicated they had experienced a secret call to the ministry. Eleven percent indicated their parents had been influential in the selecting of the position, and 12 percent had been influenced by their pastors to become church secretaries.

The average salary of all secretaries in the study was $3,000 per year, with 45 percent receiving this amount, and 21 percent receiving an average of $4,000 per year. Only one secretary in the study had housing furnished, and none had a housing allowance. Four percent had some travel allowance. Ninety-three percent of the secretaries participated in Social Security, with 89 percent of the number listed as institutionally employed and 11 percent as self-employed.

Fifty-one percent of the secretaries felt their salary was not adequate, although 79 percent felt it was "about right" considering the position and other factors involved. Only 12 percent of the secretaries felt the inequities of salary arrangements in the church caused friction in the church staff. Only 8 percent of the secretaries reported there was any type of systematic salary advancement scale.

Twenty-one percent of the secretaries were provided with medical insurance by the church.

Fifty-eight percent of the secretaries were granted a 2-week vacation annually, 5 percent had 3 weeks, 4 percent had 4 weeks, and 15 percent reported there was no plan for a vacation period.

Seventy-two percent of the secretaries were married at the time of the study, 17 percent were widowed or divorced, and 11 percent were single. Twenty-three percent of the secretaries had no children, and 67 percent had one to three children.

Since there is good literature available on the church secretary and an abundance of literature on secretaries in general, only a little will be said in this writing concerning the actual work of the secretary. We are concerned in this book more with human relations in the church staff than with actual details of work of each person on the staff.[1]

---

[1] See Virginia S. Ely, *The Church Secretary* (Chicago: Moody Press, 1956), and Lowell Russell Ditzen, *Handbook for the Church Secretary* (Englewood Cliffs, N. J.: Prentice-Hall, 1963).

Some Problem Areas

To approach more adequately the ways of developing good staff relations some of the major problems faced by the church secretary are recorded. The problems have been listed by the secretaries themselves through correspondence and interviews. To see the problems may assist church staffs to face more realistically the position of the secretary, to make her work more valuable, and to help her as a person.

Many church secretaries feel their work is not clearly defined. Responsibilities are hard to define for a church office, but too often there are loose ends that need to be attached to someone's responsibility. There is overlapping of work and also areas that are not clearly designated. A job description is essential, especially as secretaries begin their work, and a review of the job description needs to be made within three months, six months, and annually after the first year.

Along with the vagueness of the job description is the failure on the part of pastors and other members of the staff to be specific in their assignments of work to secretaries. This problem is no more characteristic of the church than of the business world. Frequently an executive will leave too many decisions to the secretary, either because he does not want to be bothered or because he has complete confidence in the ability of the secretary to handle the situation. Many secretaries, however, feel incapable of assuming this much responsibility and desire more specific directions. Usually after the various aspects of the work of the office have been worked through, the secretary learns how to proceed in each situation and is capable of using initiative without frequent direction from the executive.

The most often mentioned problem of the secretaries is in regard to planning work. Many feel they are overloaded with jobs that call for immediate attention, or, "I have long periods of time with nothing to do," as one secretary stated. Most secretaries enjoy being busy, but they like consideration in having time to get jobs done. A frequent complaint is that the staff will meet, decide on some action, and dump a load of work on the secretary to get out as soon as possible, or expect an impossible production of the job in the time allotted. This leads to frustration because of the pressure of time, demand for overtime work, and inability to do the best work. All offices have their peaks and dips in work load, and it is difficult to keep a steady flow. Wise planning, however, can make the problem minimal.

A second major problem is lack of information about the ongoing activities of the church. The secretary is frequently asked questions about church meetings, programs, staff decisions, and board or committee decisions about which she has insufficient knowledge to answer intelligently. It is a bad reflection on the secretary and on the church staff if she is constantly found to say, "I don't know," or "I haven't been informed about that." A secretary is supposed to know, and if she does not have all the information she should be able to turn to the file where it will be, refer to correspondence about the subject, or put the person who does know in touch with the inquiring party. Secretaries, for this reason should be included in staff meetings, and, as far as possible, various business meetings of the boards and committees. There is a limit to what can be expected, but at least the staff meetings that are held during the normal workday should include the secretary.

I interviewed a church staff in what appeared to be the most ideal of staff relations. Pastor, associate, minister of education, minister of music, director of youth and children's work, and church business administrator seemed to work as a team in complete harmony. All was well in my interviews until I talked to secretaries. I discovered there was an invisible wall between ministerial staff and secretarial staff. Communication was poor, and secretaries felt left out and that they were doing the chores for the staff without being a genuine part of it. Knowing the ministerial staff quite well, I mentioned this. After some deliberation one member said, "You are right, we have been enjoying our fellowship so much that we have completely ignored the church secretaries."

A good church secretary can be trusted with confidential information. If she cannot, she has no place on the staff and must be replaced. She needs to know the problems faced by the ministerial staff and be apprised as to how best to meet the problems as they arise. She needs to know of church programs and plans that are being made by ministers and lay groups in the church. The church calendar and schedules of the staff need to be at her fingertips. The church secretary can serve as a "clearinghouse" to avoid conflicting programs and dates, and she needs to have the freedom and authority to keep all members of the staff clear on dates and schedules.

Another chief complaint of secretaries is in regard to the schedule of the ministerial staff. When the ministers are not in their offices, the secretary has to answer their calls. She is at a loss if she is unable to say to the calling party when the minister will return or how he can be reached. It is a simple thing for the minister to say as he leaves the office, "I will be back at 3:30. Should an emergency arise, I can be reached at St. John's Hospital." There could be an agreement as to when the minister will call back to the office to inquire if there are messages for him. It is poor business for the secretary to have to constantly say to callers, "The pastor is out. No, I don't know when he will be back. No, he didn't say where he was going." How much better it is to be able to say, "The pastor is making hospital calls. Can you leave your number, and he will call when he returns about 3:30." Or, "The pastor is not in his office now. We can reach him shortly if this is an emergency, or he can return your call in the morning." Some ministers may object to this close a tab on their activities, but after all they are the servants of the church. Recently while I was in conference with a layman from a large city church he noted, "I call the office every thirty minutes while I'm out like this—even while playing golf." He sells television commercials!

One large church has installed a two-way radio communication between the church and cars used by the ministerial staff. Instant contact can be made in this manner for not only emergency calls, but routine church business. Such equipment is expensive, but is a valuable time-saver and makes for greater efficiency. This is common practice with large plumbing firms, public utilities, police, and business organizations. Medical doctors now carry small transistor radios so they can be contacted on a moment's notice.

Another complaint of secretaries is the mutilation of their time by loiterers in the office and compulsive talkers on the phone. These are usually laymen in the church membership. Every church has at least one! Sometimes it is a retired person who in all good faith is trying to do church work, but is really finding some way to meet his own loneliness. It is a part of ministry to meet human needs, but laymen should be more sensitive to the time of all members of a church staff. A secretary needs to develop the skill of being able diplomatically to help the person to move on into something else, or let the person know there is a pressing assignment. I once heard a Methodist bishop call on a retired minister to pray at Annual Conference. After twenty minutes of praying the bishop said, "Let us sing hymn number 20 while Brother——finishes his prayer!" Unfortunately secretaries do not have the authority of bishops, but they can be diplomatic.

Another problem that arises with secretaries is to whom is she directly responsible, and from whom should she receive her directives. A good job description would clarify the issue. Most churches are short on secretarial help, which means two or more members of the church staff will be using the same secretary. A conflict of time, work that must be done, and responsibilities, as well as loyalties, is inevitable. It is quite easy for ministerial, educational, or music staff members to make the work of the secretary quite confusing unless clear lines of communication between all parties are maintained.

In the church office where there are two or more secretaries it is necessary to work through lines of authority and responsibilities. Probably no persons on the church staff are more prone to assume authority over other persons on the staff than secretaries. A secretary who has been in a church a number of years may have a tendency to become authoritative over other secretaries. Small things—overtime schedules, mistakes, how the secretary spends her time—may become the object of criticism and needling. Communications can go to pieces quickly when this becomes the case. The senior minister needs to keep his finger on the pulse of the situation and attempt to minimize the problems as they arise.

A chief complaint of secretaries is overtime work. A number of secretaries reported they were expected to spend every workday at the church—usually eight or eight-thirty until five o'clock—half a day on Sunday, sometimes half a day on Saturday, and one or more nights per week. One secretary responded to the question "State the most dissatisfying part of your position," by reporting, "Being tied to my job every weekend. Sunday is the only day my husband has off from work. I would like to have at least one day a month that I could stay home and rest or do as I please. I would find my job almost perfect if three weeks out of the month I could have Friday afternoon off and the fourth week Friday afternoon and Sunday." A number of expressions from other secretaries were of similar nature. One of the difficulties in church work is that ministers do not work by the clock. Usually there is some adjustment in schedule if there is a heavy demand for night work. Secretaries can hardly make the adjustment. One secretary did report that if she were expected to be at a night meeting or to work on Sunday, she would be compensated with equal time off during the day rather than being paid overtime.

The question has been asked many times, Should the church secretary be a member of the church in which she is employed? No firm answer can be given to the question. Some secretaries feel they should be a member of the employing church while others are emphatic they should not. Some denominations, especially some branches of the Lutheran Church and the Southern Baptist Church, have standing policies that the secretary, as well as all other employees, must be members of the denomination, and many require the person to be a member of the local congregation.

Arguments for the secretary *not* being a member of the local church are: (1) It is much easier to dismiss a person if work is not satisfactory without causing a disturbance in the congregation. (2) A secretary does not become emotionally involved in the life of the church and can more objectively do her work. Arguments *for* a secretary being a part of the congregation are: (1) the secretary will take a more vital interest in her work since it is "her" church. (2) The secretary understands the program of the denomination and is aware of the doctrinal standards and church polity. This assists greatly in the promotion of the work of the local church.

Many secretaries have stated they feel it is essential that the secretary have a firm knowledge of the doctrines and polity of the denomination. Efficiency of the work of the secretary is increased as she is knowledgeable of the inner workings of the denomination. A secretary who does not understand the doctrine and polity of the denomination in which she is working will do well to read extensively in the field.

Interviews and questionnaires show a bias toward the secretary being a member of the church in which she works. The feeling is that the work of the secretary becomes a part of her life and religious practice. A number of secretaries stated they did not mind night meetings because, "I would be there anyway as a member of the church, even if I were not a secretary."

In our study 266 secretaries out of 355, or 76 percent, were members of the church in which they were employed. Thirty-three of the secretaries who were not members of the church in which they were employed were members of the same denomination, and 55 were members of some other denomination. One did not give the information.

Following is a summary of basic considerations in regard to the church secretary.

Basic Considerations

1. Define clearly the position and work of the secretaries. A clear-cut job description is essential.
2. Define clearly lines of authority—to whom is the secretary responsible for instruction, work, complaints.

3. Level the work load; avoid, as far as possible, overwork and under-work periods. Plan far ahead.
4. Take the secretary into confidence. She needs to be thoroughly informed concerning the work of the local church—policies, programs, and planning.
5. Keep the secretary informed of the minister's schedule so she can inform callers intelligently concerning calls or appointments.
6. Secretaries need to possess a knowledge of the doctrines and polity of the denomination in which they work.
7. Secretaries' salaries need to compare favorably with secretaries doing comparable work in secular business with considerations such as Social Security, retirement plans, hospital insurance, stated vacation time, and salary advancements.

11

The Multiple Staff
in the Cooperative Parish

In its most simple definition a cooperative parish consists of two or more congregations and two or more employed staff cooperating for an effective ministry within a given geographical area. The area may be rural, town and country, small city and its surrounding countryside, or any part of a city or metropolitan area.

Cooperative parishes have been a form of church administration in town and country areas for more than a half-century in the United States and England. They have emerged primarily as a means of effecting the work of the church where there has been an "overchurching" through denominational competition, or a severe change in population structures. In the United States, Harlow S. Mills, a Congregational minister in Benzonia, Michigan, is usually credited with the origin of the larger parish idea in 1910.[1] Mills conceived of a staff of specialists in ministry—namely, a senior minister or director, a minister of evangelism, and a minister of education, working together to lead a group of congregations in town and country. Mills's basic philosophy was built around five convictions: "1. The real object of the Church is to *serve* people, and . . . its claim for support should rest upon the same ground upon which every other institution bases its claim for support—that it gives value received. . . . 2. The Church . . . must serve *all* the people. . . . 3. It [the church] must serve *all* the interests of the people. . . . 4. The village church, if it would fulfil its mission, must be responsible for *country evangelization.* . . . 5. If the village church would fulfil its mission, it must be a community church." [2]

By 1925 there were a sufficient member of larger parishes in ex-

---

[1] Mills's own account can be found in his *Making of a Country Parish* (New York: Missionary Education Movement of the United States and Canada, 1914).

[2] *Ibid.*, pp. 13, 15, 18, 20.

istence to warrant a systematic study. This was done by Edmund deS. Brunner, director of the Institute of Social and Religious Research. His findings were published in 1933 in a book bearing the skeptical title, *The Larger Parish, a Movement or an Enthusiasm?* [3] In this work Brunner established nine criteria for successful parishes that became basic for further development.

1. The territory included is an economic and/or social unit.
2. The territory has adequate resources, under normal economic conditions, sooner or later to support the larger parish.
3. The churches of the parish combine their finances, at least as regards the salary of the staff and preferably for all items.
4. The staff consists of two or more persons with special training or interest in the field of responsibility to which each is assigned.
5. There is a functioning parish council.
6. The parish gives, or at least sincerely aims to give, many-sided service to the whole territory it serves and to every person within it.
7. The parish has exclusive possession of its field so far as Protestant work is concerned, or at least has cooperative relations with other religious groups and with community organizations.
8. The parish recognizes its interdenominational obligations.
9. The parish is assured of the continued support of the denomination or denominations concerned regardless of changes in administrative personnel. [4]

From these ideas there have developed numerous variations of larger parish or cooperative parish structures.

The group ministry concept was developed first within the structure of The Methodist Church by Aaron H. Rapking, in 1938 during his tenure as Secretary of Town and Country Church in the Division of National Missions of the Board of Missions in The Methodist Church. [5] The basic idea was to effect a ministry between a number of congregations and their ministers within a natural sociological area such as a county or trade area community. The work would be coordinated through a council composed of lay representatives from each congregation. The group ministry has been a fruitful means of effective witness within Methodist congregations as well as other denominations.

In more recent years both terms, larger parish and group ministry, have been adopted by ministers within the inner city or large metropolitan areas. A 1966 publication by Douglas W. Johnson is entitled *A Study of Methodist Group Ministries and Larger Parishes in the*

---

[3] (New York: George H. Doran Co., 1933.)
[4] *Ibid.*, pp. 67-68.
[5] Rapking's plan is described in his *Stick to It, Farmer Boy,* ed. by Roy A. Sturm (Nashville: Parthenon Press, 1967).

Inner City.[6] The study describes the organization, structure, and working program of twelve inner city parishes. It is interesting that the first footnote in the report is to Rockwell C. Smith's *Church in Our Town,* and the second to my *Larger Parish and Group Ministry.* Both books are directed toward the work of the church in town and country areas!

In the light of the above résumé of the beginnings of cooperative parishes, several generalizations can be made: (1) A cooperative parish generally comes into existence after there has been a radical social, economic, or population change within a given area. In many rural areas the major changes have been depletion of population due to the agricultural revolution and technology, and modern means of travel by automobile and good roads. In the inner city, the transition has generally been from a stable, socially and economically advantaged population to a mobile, economically deprived and often ethnic or racial minority. (2) In most cases there have been long-standing established congregations of several denominations. (3) Ministry has been difficult due to old self-images of the church held by the people who have remained loyal, but there has been an inability of congregation and ministry to adapt to the community changes that have taken place. (4) Cooperative parishes are developed to meet immediate needs of the residents of the area. Such needs are in the areas of economics, education, recreation, health, and religion. (5) Cooperative parishes, especially in the inner city, tend to focus their ministry on the physical needs of people first, and eventually develop a program of ministering to the religious needs.[7]

Due to the above factors many cooperative parishes are designed to save a situation—a sort of last-ditch stand. There is no area of ministry that demands more creative imagination and personal dedication than the cooperative ministries. Social pressures are upon persons who enter into such ministries. In town and country areas, the mind of the ministry in general, and particularly the administrative executives, frequently has been conditioned to feel that serving in a rural area is a less valuable ministry than in the urban areas. Feelings are not the same concerning serving in the inner city. At this writing it is a

---

[6] (Chicago: Chicago Home Missionary and Church Extension Society, Rock River Conference of The Methodist Church, 1966).

[7] For literature on cooperative parishes see: George W. Webber, *God's Colony in Man's World* (Nashville: Abingdon Press, 1960) ; Bruce Kenrick, *Come Out the Wilderness* (New York: Harper, 1962) ; Marvin T. Judy, *The Larger Parish and Group Ministry* (Abingdon Press, 1959) ; Judy, *The Cooperative Parish in Nonmetropolitan Areas* (Abingdon Press, 1967).

rather popular thing for the young seminarian to be challenged by the inner city ministry. However, it takes only a few months of working in the inner city for a person to become aware of the problems involved in identifying oneself with the social class with which one works. If a minister or member of a staff of an inner city ministry does not live in his geographical parish, he curtails his effectiveness as a minister to the constituency of the parish. (There is some disagreement at this point among leaders.) Identity means a "living with" the people of the parish. This may involve tenement residence, or occupying a low-grade rooming house, or living in an old house in an undesirable neighborhood. Such pressures in either rural or urban areas force church staffs to face the decision for such ministries with their families. Families must be involved in cooperative ministries in a way not necessary in the routine type of pastoral ministry in a social situation that is not too different from the culture of one's rearing. The pastor of a downtown first church can live in suburbia and get by with it—this is where many of the members of the church live—but this will not prove true with a pastor in an inner city parish.

Motivation for one entering into a cooperative parish, either in town and country areas or in the inner city, must be quite well defined, or frustration will soon mar one's effectiveness. The motivation needs to be more than service to humanity—this is essential—but it needs to be evangelical in the finest sense of the word. Motivations must be maintained, as days of discouragement are numerous. This means staff associations and family relations must be maintained at an intensive level for mutual support. The nature of cooperative ministries will automatically call for a structuring of staff relationships that emphasizes fellowship and spiritual enrichment. A monthly family get-together for staff fellowship is essential. This helps to maintain morale and motivation. Many staffs make the monthly fellowship around a covered dish meal, meeting in the home of one of the members or in one of the churches. Emphasis is again placed upon this being a *family* gathering of members of the employed staff. Some staffs unite the fellowship with a retreat for spiritual renewal and planning.

Weekly staff meetings are essential in a closely integrated type of cooperative parish. There is no type of multiple ministry that demands so much planning for creative leadership as does the cooperative parish ministry.

One of the areas in which confusion arises in cooperative parishes is in regard to the various church bodies that are directly related to the parish. These are of two natures: (1) the local congregations involved, and (2) the boards and agencies of the denominations involved. In the normal church with a multiple staff there is one congregation, which retains a great deal of autonomy because it is completely self-supporting. As long as it remains loyal to the denominational policies and supports the various denominational administrative and benevolent programs there is little interference from denominational executives. Nor is there a need for dependence upon the executives by the local church staff for direction and guidance. In a cooperative parish there are usually several local congregations involved. The churches may be in a rather close proximity in an inner city, covering a distance of only a few blocks, or they may be scattered over many miles in a rural area. In an inner city they will most likely be of different racial and ethnic backgrounds: Negroes, Whites, Latin Americans, Puerto Ricans, Japanese, Chinese, Indians, and so forth. They may also be of diffent denominations.

In all likelihood the cooperative parish will be receiving financial support from various church boards of missions and other agencies. One of the basic laws of economics is: Wherever there is support, there is supervision. In the light of the cooperative parish this means that when a church board or agency puts financial support into the project, that board or agency expects to have some voice in the administration of the funds. This supervision is generally made through a coordinating committee, a denominational field representative or executive, or both. It does not take much imagination to conceive of the complications that arise when there are several agencies of one or more denominations involved. Only through many hours of committee meetings and personal conversations between the director of the parish, the employed staff, and the denominational bodies can any sense of balance be maintained. A director of a cooperative parish *must* be an executive of the finest sort, or chaos will result.

Some denominations have trained workers, usually women, who are specialists in church and community work. In some cases the persons are deaconesses filling positions in the traditions of New Testament and church history. The women may work in rural areas or inner city. They are usually specialists in that they are trained in some aspect of Christian education, recreation, nutrition, social work, or case work. In the inner city parish workers are assigned by the denominational office to be directors or workers in community houses, directors of education, social service workers, and so forth. In town and country areas workers are generally assigned to a larger parish or group ministry staff to do both church and community work. By community work is meant cooperation with various governmental and social agencies for the betterment of mankind. It is quite obvious that if a denomination recruits and trains church and community workers, and dispatches the worker to the field of service, there is a line of administrative autonomy which will be maintained by the national office. Confusion can arise if the national office and the co-operative parish staff have different conceptions about the area of church and community work. The staff, and especially the director of the parish, has to be alert and aware of the objectives and goals of the national office and be in a position to hear the national director, or trouble is in store.

Another area of involvement in the cooperative parish which is not in the regular church program is the intense relationship between the parish and the government and private social agencies. Social agencies are at work in the geographic region of the cooperative parish for the same reasons the cooperative parish is there—namely, because of a radical social, economic, ethnic, or population shift which has led to a disorganized society. Some of the oldest and most effective government agencies are found in rural areas. By the middle of the nineteenth century the agricultural revolution had grown to such proportions that the federal government established the Department of Agriculture and the Federal Land Grant College. The latter was to experiment in agricultural methods and to train persons in the field of agriculture. By the beginning of the twentieth century great strides were taken to carry training outside the college to the land where the farmer was working. This brought into being the county agricultural program with the county agricultural agent—a member of the extension staff of the land grant college and teacher in residence in a local county. This soon led to the development of the position of home demonstration agent to assist the farmer's wife to be a better home-maker, nutritionist, and community-minded person. Then developed the program of the 4-H Clubs for the farmer's children so they could learn through the project method a better agriculture and home management. Soon to follow were vast conservation programs and the many so-called alphabet programs in agriculture. At this time the largest single agency of the federal budget, outside the military and space programs, is agriculture. Much has been accomplished through the programs, and cooperative parish workers in rural areas have a vast resource available for community betterment through such agencies. In addition to agriculture there is rural development, the

War on Poverty, programs of education, and other government programs for the elevation of life outside the metropolitan areas.

In the inner city the same is true. Health and welfare agencies, housing, education, law enforcement, recreation, family life, job training, vocational guidance, counseling services, legal services, and many more agencies are at work. All are attempting to elevate the life of persons living in the region. One of the great needs of the staff in a cooperative parish is to understand the agencies and their work, and to know how the agencies can be of assistance in their work and how they can be of assistance to the agencies. In other words, how can the two cooperate to do the most effective job without duplication of effort and without missing areas of genuine need?

An effective tested method of establishing a working realtionship between church and agencies is to bring together for a full day's discussion the leaders of various agencies and church leaders. In a town and country area the county may be the working unit. A well planned meeting can bring together ministers and laymen in the cooperative parish along with the county agricultural agent, the home demonstration agent, the county or regional director of conservation services, the county school superintendent, the county law enforcement agents, the county health and welfare director, county or regional planners, and representatives of various farm organizations. In a rapid order each agency representative is asked to (1) state the purposes and goals of his agency in the region, (2) state what he feels is the most effective way the church can be of assistance in doing his work, and (3) how he feels he may be of assistance in the work of the church. Each agency is asked to bring charts, maps, and other visual aids to illustrate its work. Representatives of the cooperative parish are asked to prepare similar visual materials concerning the churches of the region.

The same type of day's activity can be planned in an urban area. It may be necessary to schedule the meeting from four in the afternoon until ten at night with dinner at the church. As in rural areas, the representatives of various urban agencies are asked to participate. A geographic boundary is arbitrarily established that will include the area served by the cooperative parish. Agency representatives are apprised of the area and asked to speak to the needs in the specific area and what their agency is doing there. It is good to begin the discussion with the city planner or a representative from his office. He will be asked to bring to the meeting a map of the area showing land use, major traffic flow, proposed changes in zoning, age-sex distribution of population, ethnic and racial distribution of population, educational levels, economic levels, housing, and other relevant data.

The principal of the public school in the region is asked to describe the situation in regard to elementary and high schools. Health and welfare personnel, nursing services, law enforcement officers, housing authority directors, day nursery directors, alcohol and narcotics officers, and persons in related fields are all asked to be present and describe their work. Each is asked to focus his attention upon the immediate needs of the area under study and to state how the church may be of assistance to him and how he may assist the church.

As the result of participating in a number of such meetings in both rural and urban areas I have seen several valuable results. (1) Personnel in both church and community agencies get to know each other. (2) A new appreciation of the work of the other is born. (3) Areas of common concern are established. (4) A working relationship for continued conversation and working together on common problems is established. (5) Areas of common need and resources for meeting needs are discovered.

From the above description of the work of a staff in a multiple ministry it can be readily seen that there are many occasions for serious staff problems. While talking to a director of a very effective inner city parish in a Midwestern city, I was told, "When in seminary I shunned any courses which dealt with administration or human relations. I wanted the courses in Bible, theology, and philosophy. I did the same thing in my Ph.D. work, taking it in philosophy. Now that I am a director of an inner city parish I find that 90 percent of my time is devoted to administration—this is the area of my greatest need for training." As we talked we were surrounded by a group of Negro women practicing typing. They were learning a skill to assist in making a living. During our conversation a Negro secretary brought some papers to the director for his signature. He said to me, "This woman was a prostitute. She was trained for secretarial work right here and is now serving as secretary in the parish."

It is impossible in one chapter of a book on the church staff to give complete direction to the staff in a multiple ministry. There has been, however, in this chapter an attempt to lift out the additional problems and interrelationships found in a cooperative parish staff that are not in, at least to some degree, the staff of a single well-established church.

It has been observed that in cooperative parish staffs there is a wide diversity of persons. In rural areas, as a general rule, some of the ministers may not have seminary training. A recent study, for instance, in a sample of Methodist larger parishes and group ministries indicated that 46 percent of the ministers had not attended seminary. An increasing number of cooperative ministries in cities involve churches of different denominations. In most inner city parishes there are staff members of different racial and ethnic backgrounds. In practically all cooperative parishes there will be persons of wide differences in age. All this leads to many distances between the members of staffs of multiple ministries—age, denomination, race, ethnic background, sex, theological differences, and education. Such distances can be lessened only as persons work in close harmony with well-defined goals and objectives, an evangelical fervor, and dedication to their task. It can be seen why frequent staff meetings and occasional prolonged periods of fellowship with spiritual renewal retreats are essential. Many cooperative parish staffs have come to a bitter end because of a failure to establish proper communication through the natural barriers which held the individuals apart.

Figure 6 diagrams some of the relationships in cooperative parishes. Four churches are involved in the diagram. The churches may be (1) of the same denomination and all of the same race, (2) different denominations and of the same race, (3) same denomination representing two or more races or ethnic groups, and (4) different denominations and representing two or more racial or ethnic groups. In addition to the churches there may be a storefront center, a recreation center, a community house, or other centers representing the work of the parish. The diversity of operation in various physical buildings necessitates a division of the work of the staff.

Within the parish will be found the employed staff with a number of specialties and, in many cases, numerous volunteer staff persons. This is particularly true of the inner city parish where volunteers from churches outside the parish devote time to the work of the parish.

Each local congregation will have some organization which will vary from a skeletal set of offices to a full-scale organization according to the plan of the denomination. In addition to local church organization it is essential that there be, to coordinate the work of the parish, some type of organization composed of the employed staff and lay representatives from each church and center within the parish.

Outside the physical parish there will usually be, especially in the inner city, some type of council composed of representatives of various denominational interests who have the responsibility of coordinating the resources, consisting of finances, personnel, buildings, and equipment, and to give some direction to the work of the parish. In addition to the council there will generally be one or more denominational executives, such as a district superintendent, who will be directly related to the parish, with his denomination expecting him to keep a close watch over the project, giving counsel and guidance where needed. Boards of missions may also feel some responsibility to the parish since they are supplying some financial assistance and, in some cases, assigning personnel to the parish.

In addition to the church-related resources there will be many private and government agencies working in the geographic area of the cooperative parish which can become valuable resources for the parish.

The complicated structure of a cooperative parish creates many staff problems. In addition to the suggestions which have been made throughout this book in regard to the multiple staff ministry, it must be emphasized that the director of a cooperative parish needs all the basic qualifications of a good administrator, public relations specialist, and personnel manager, and should be deeply motivated with humanitarian and evangelical interests.

Boards of Missions—National and Local
Coordinating Council outside of Parish
Denominational executive(s)
Private and Governmental Agencies

Church Board	Staff	Church Board
	Ministers	
	Associates	
	Church and Community Worker	
	Interns	
	Specialized Ministries	
	Education	
	Music	
	Social Service Worker	
	Others	
Church Board	Few or many volunteer workers	Church Board
	Council of laymen and staff in the Parish	

Fig. 6. Church boards, denominational boards, councils, agencies, staff and personnel relations within the cooperative parish

It needs to be clearly understood by all persons in representative groups related to the parish, but outside the parish, that there must be maintained within the parish structure a high degree of local autonomy. A case in point would be the working through of job descriptions by members of the employed staff. Each person on the staff needs to have a clear understanding of his work in the staff. If there are, for instance, persons assigned to the staff by boards of missions, their work within the staff must be in the general framework of the assigning agency, but in the light of the specific needs of the local parish.

12

The Creative Staff

Creativity as an academic discipline has been recognized since the mid-thirties. Like most disciplines, however, it has had slow acceptance and has emerged in strong favor only since about 1950. In some circles the word has now been used to the point of weariness and a new term is being sought. Persons in the Judaeo-Christian tradition should be at home with the term, since it is the beginning and ending of the Scriptures. "In the beginning God created . . ." are the first words of Genesis. "And I saw a new heaven and a new earth" are the opening words of Chapter 21 of the Book of Revelation. Between those pages are the recordings of the mighty acts of God in the life and work of his highest form of creation—man.

Prior to the time of the acceptance of creativity as a valid academic discipline, it was thought that only persons in the field of the arts or persons possessing special abilities and talents making them geniuses in their respective fields possessed creative abilities. These were musicians, artists, inventors, poets—the Beethovens, Edisons, Longfellows, or Rembrandts. No longer is this attitude held. Contemporary teaching holds the concept that within all persons there are creative potentials, varying to be sure, with individual native ability. Creative ideas lie dormant until motivation and the situation call forth the best that there is within a person. Roger Bellows states, "Creative leadership is needed if our present civilization is to survive. The thought has been voiced that the physical science has made it possible for all men to die together; our growing knowledge of creative leadership must make it possible for men to live together." [1]

The church staff is composed of individuals with creative potentials. The staff as a whole can become a creative corporate body within a local congregation of Christian believers to assist in fulfilling the

---

[1] *Creative Leadership* (Englewood Cliffs, N. J.: Prentice-Hall, 1959), preface, p. ix.

needs of the congregation in worship, nurture, and work. The process of bringing new ideas into existence is, like physical birth, often slow, painful, and costly. Church staffs must pay the price in self-discipline, study, and worship if they are to fulfill their mission. Eliot Dale Hutchinson summarizes the process by which creative ideas are born by stating four stages through which the individual or group will go. The stages are:

1. Preparation centering upon a problem. This may be a long-term or a short-term problem. Within the church staff problem-solving is an everyday concern. Defining the problem is of major importance.

2. A period of frustration. This is a period when the problem seems to be impossible. There is no forseeable solution. There is a temptation to give up in despair. Many persons stop at this point.

3. The period of insight. Ideas will begin to flow as new thoughts and insights come to mind. There must be choices made. Each idea deserves to be refined resulting in:

4. The period of testing. Ideas need to be tested for verification, validity and usefulness.[2]

Motivation and creativity are closely related. A church staff becomes a creative body as it is motivated to work within the framework of the church. A great deal has been said in previous chapters concerning the defining of central goals and objectives. Creativity and motivation are dependent upon a climate in which personal goals and group goals can be fulfilled. J. D. Batten states, "When the majority of employees realize clearly that the action needed to accomplish their performance requirements also is the action best calculated to achieve their own goals, you have the principal elements of a highly charged motivational climate." [3]

Creativity in the church staff is dependent upon establishing: goals and objectives—short-term and long-term; sound principles of personnel management; and an understanding and practice of workable principles of leadership. There is an attempt in this chapter to suggest in a practical way some aspects of staff procedures which will maximize the creative leadership ability of each member of the staff and the corporate body of the staff and congregation. Before ending the chapter a word will be said concerning stress and strain, which inevitably arise in the contemporary world as the church staff at-

---

[2] Hutchinson, *How to Think Creatively* (Nashville: Abingdon Press, 1949), p. 38.
[3] *Beyond Management by Objectives.* (New York: American Management Association, 1966), p. 64.

tempts to work in the local congregation as individuals who are witnessing Christians, trained professionals, citizens of a local community, state, and nation, and husbands, wives, and parents.

The Staff in Worship

Worship is central in the Christian community. Consistently it has been stated throughout this work that one of the goals of the church staff is to lead the congregation in worship.

Data received from members of church staffs show approximately one-third of the staffs have some form of worship. This may vary from a prayer by one of the staff members to a formal service in a chapel. The fact that two-thirds of the staffs in the study reported they had no type of staff worship is quite significant. Evidently there is a feeling on the part of the staffs that worship by the staff as a group has little value.

Of the 107 out of 307 staffs that reported they had staff worship, the value of the worship experience was looked upon by the members of the staff differently. Of all persons in all positions on the staff reporting, 86 percent felt the worship experience was valuable or very valuable. Two percent felt the worship was of little value, and 3 percent had some question as to its value. One person felt it was a waste of time. More senior ministers reported staff worship as valuable or very valuable than did other members of the staff. This may reflect a feeling that worship is valuable, but could be made more effective if better planned and shared.

It is a point of interest that the only specific request made by the late Harold Duling, Executive Director of the Department of Religion of the Lilly Endowment, at the time of his announcing to me the grant making possible this study, was in the field of staff worship. Dr. Duling felt staff worship could be a source of staff coordination assisting in solving problems. He asked that this be an item in the study. It is impossible to state from the findings of the data how much correlation there is between staff worship and staff harmony. It is evident, however, that a lack of staff worship may contribute substantially to a lack of clear goals and objectives of the staff at work in the church.

Staff worship can be meaningful and helpful if it is conducted with a degree of regularity, shared by all members, and varied in form. Worship can be at the time of the regular staff meeting and on special occasions. Some staffs have a brief period of worship daily. A staff in a large downtown church in a northwestern city have a five- to ten-minute period of worship each morning at ten o'clock followed by a few minutes of fellowship. All members of the staff, including custodians, participate. The staff in a large church in the Southwest have a twenty-minute period of worship each Monday morning prior to the regular weekly staff meeting. There is a small chapel adjacent to the pastor's office which is used for the place of worship. All staff, including secretaries and custodians, participate. Interviews with staff members in both cases indicate a feeling the worship experiences assist in personal religious growth and add to staff harmony.

The Staff in Fellowship

"All work and no play makes Jack a dull boy" is an ancient and trite saying. Its ancientness and triteness, however, may add to its validity. Church staffs need to develop a fellowship community as the climate in which they get their work done. Persons who of necessity work as closely as church staff members need to know one another on a basis of more than professional relationships. Literature in the field of leadership makes quite clear that any small group working together needs to sense community in its task. Community is not created; it emerges when the conditions are present. When people get to know one another in the context of their family lives, hobbies, attitudes, and opinions, it is most likely they will feel more at ease, be more tolerant, and work better in their professional capacities.

Fellowship within the staff, like worship, must be scheduled. The coffee break has become almost universal in business. It has validity and can be an asset to the entire operation of large or small businesses. Planned parties for all staff and families are valid investments of time. Frequently staff members will say, "But we don't have time for fellowship situations." The truth is they do not have time *not* to have fellowship occasions. A climate of work is important, and the tensions of personality conflicts, disharmony, and misunderstanding can be greatly lessened as people come to know each other on a fellowship basis.

Fellowship situations need to include, as far as possible, families of staff members. Individuals are not whole in a professional role—they are only a part of themselves. They become whole persons when they are involved in their family and community life. No profession needs to involve families like the church professions. The church is a family institution, and as the professional staff involve their families

223

in fellowship, recreation, and at times, in worship, the entire staff will develop a greater appreciation for one another. If wives of professional staff members desire to participate in some staff business or study sessions they should be invited.

The Staff in Nurture

One of the major responsibilities of the church staff is to assist the congregation in nurture. Staffs need to study together. The theological distances between members of the staff are sometimes great. Age differences will frequently be the cause of conservative or liberal points of view. New forms of worship, new and meaningful forms of evangelism, education, and pastoral care all need to be studied.

Staff in nurture can take many forms. Each person can be asked to review a current book for the group. A selected topic may be studied for a thirty-minute period before each weekly staff meeting. A stated time can be set aside once a month for an hour or two of study together. A period can be used when the staff is in retreat.

Seminaries are providing extensive continuing education programs which can be used by the staff. A syllabus on contemporary theology, some phase of the Bible, the church and politics, war, race, or community action could be secured. All staff members can read the literature, and each can participate in leading discussions. Wives or husbands and older children, if they desire, should be involved in the study. One of the most severe criticisms of the church in modern society is the accusation that the ministry does not keep alert to contemporary academic disciplines. The press of work often forces the members of the staff to cut short their study time. It is also quite important that ideas be tried out in conversation.

I can make a personal witness to the value of staff study. A staff in a larger parish in North Missouri set aside an annual six-week period for study together. One morning a week during the six weeks was devoted to discussion of a selected topic with appropriate readings. Leadership was shared by each person in the staff. Educational differences were great, ranging from high school to seminary degrees. Theological differences ranged from a narrow orthodoxy to radical liberalism. Ages ranged from the mid-twenties to the mid-sixties. The experiences of study stand out in my memory as one of the most fruitful in my five years of parish participation. It provided a means not only of refreshing academic disciplines, but of developing a fellowship in common purpose and goal.

It is quite possible that staff meetings, retreat experiences, and staff fellowship can be greatly enlivened as staffs study together.

The Staff in Business Session

Sixty percent of the church staffs in our study indicated they held staff business sessions. Frequency of the meetings ranged from "on call when a need arises" to "a few minutes each day." Most of the staffs met weekly. Approximately 85 percent of the members of the staffs holding business sessions felt the meetings were of vital importance. Approximately 85 percent of the members of staffs not having business sessions felt they needed them.

Business sessions need to be built around: (1) schedule and date clearing, (2) long-range and short-range program planning, (3) problem-solving, (4) conflict-resolving, (5) creative ideas.

Many church staffs focus upon long-range planning during a periodic retreat type meeting annually or more often. The staff, including in some cases wives and families who wish to participate, spend two days together at a camp, motel, or retreat center. Worship, fellowship, business, and study can be combined in this type of experience. An all-day meeting away from the church makes it possible to combine long-range planning with other planning. A staff in a large church in the Southwest has a business session twice a month on Monday afternoon. Once a quarter the staff spends two days in long-range planning in the camp owned by the congregation. Study is a part of the program in the long meetings. Once a month the program director and church business administrator meet with all secretaries to apprise them of all phases of the work of the church. They clear schedules, help with anticipated phone calls, discuss problems, and so on. On various seasonal occasions the entire staff and their families, including custodial and kitchen staff, are together for parties, dinners, and fellowship.

Comparatively few congregations are as large as the church mentioned above. The principles of the staff in worship, fellowship, nurture, and business are present and can be applied whether the staff consists of three people or a hundred. A larger parish staff in Montana, for instance, meets each Monday for a three-hour session. The meeting consists of worship, study, and business. Once a month there is a family get-together for fellowship. It takes planning, fixing of dates, and determination to make staff associations meaningful and fruitful, but the dividends are worth all it costs.

Business sessions need to be conducted with great freedom and cooperative procedure. All the principles of good leadership techniques need to be applied. When the staff meets for business there will always be two levels of interaction within the group. There will be the level of ideas, or the subject matter to be discussed. This is the actual agenda, which has been prepared ahead of time and most likely will be added to as the meeting gets underway. Some writers in leadership would call the actual agenda the "task area," or describe it as "content-oriented" or "problem-oriented." The second level is the social-emotional level. This is the level at which the members of the group attempt to feel one another out, to discover what other members of the group may have in mind in regard to the subject matter—that is, what is each person's desire, what each has to gain in the decision, what axe is there to grind, and how can each come to feel comfortable and free in the discussion. This is the "hidden agenda" in the meeting. It is sometimes described as "process-oriented" or "ego-oriented." It consists of difficult personal relationships and personality conflicts which, if the group is to get its work done effectively, must be worked through. The forces at work within the individual will be behind the hidden agenda—self-concepts; personal values; personal standards; fears; the need for security, recognition, affection, and new experiences; past experiences; invisible "committees" in one's life, such as family and social pressures; the emotional tendencies possessed by each person; and personal goals and beliefs. It may be good at this point for the reader to go back to Chapter 4 and review "The Staff Member: An Individual in a Group." If good principles of personnel management, as have been described in Chapter 3, have been applied, and if good principles of leadership are used, including plenty of opportunities for persons to know one another on a fellowship and worship basis, the hidden agendas will be minimized.

Good group interaction resulting in effective business sessions requires the attainment of a balance between the fulfillment of social and psychological needs of individuals, between content and process, and between problem-orientation and ego-orientation.

Within any group there will be personal interests. This means that each person comes to the group with his own interests in mind. He is defensive of such interests. He may argue for them. He may be closed to altering or compromising with them. Some persons are not flexible in the discussion process. There may be an automatic resistance to change. As one person was heard to say, "There will never be a unanimous decision as long as I'm on this committee!" This type of person is difficult to work with. Patience, respect, and development of group confidence is the only way to discover the maximum potentials of such a person.

There will usually be within the church staff varying degrees of reasoning ability. Some persons have mathematical minds which operate as though solving a problem in geometry. Proposition is laid on proposition, truth upon truth, reason upon reason, until one is able to say, "Therefore—this is the answer." Other people do not reason in this way. They may not be able to articulate ideas clearly. There may be a skipping from one idea to another, or a running off in an irrelevant direction. Such persons can frequently cause confusion in the group and make it difficult to stay with the subject.

Communication has been discussed elsewhere, but it is one of the most difficult phases of staff relationships and a problem in staff meetings. The basic method of communication is language. Words mean different things to different people. Words have emotional overtones. The tone of the voice, the expression on the face, the force with which one speaks—all color the way words are heard. Personal biases, prejudices, and desires enter into both speaking and hearing. Good communication takes time. It is also dependent upon how well persons know and trust one another.

Personal hostility is a major barrier to good staff relationships. There is a tendency for persons to become personally involved and emotionally identified with ideas that are under discussion. When other persons in the group question the validity of a contribution, it is quite possible the person making the contribution may feel the questioning is a personal attack upon himself. It is difficult for such persons to separate issues from personalities. Such persons will most likely further confuse the issue and create an atmosphere of strain that will make group discussion almost impossible. Frequently they will confuse disagreement with personal disrespect and respond as if their egos were being challenged. It may be the person feels he is the final authority on the subject, and to challenge his authority is to challenge him.[4]

As the church staff works together it becomes of vital importance that the leader discover hidden agenda and understand personality problems. The importance of worship, fellowship, and study in a staff cannot be too strongly emphasized as a means of attaining a level of

---

[4] For a full discussion see Haiman, *Group Leadership and Democratic Action,* chap. 4, "The Dynamics of a Group." Also, Leland P. Bradford, "The Case of the Hidden Agenda," *Adult Leadership,* I, 4 (Sept., 1952).

confidence as they attempt to do the business of the church. It is in the realm of personality and emotional problems that sensitivity training is still in the experimental stage. If a staff enters into such training, reliable and tested leaders need to be sought. Training under good direction can be of great value.

The real agenda for a business session can be prepared by the leader in consultation with other members of the staff. A memorandum to each member of the staff before the meeting is a good way to ask each person to suggest items for the agenda.

The principles of leadership and an evaluation of the different methods have been discussed in Chapter 2. At this point an additional word needs to be said in regard to the leadership within the staff meetings.

As far as possible all principles of cooperative leadership need to be applied. In his work, *Group Leadership and Democratic Action,* Franklin S. Haiman summarizes the values of democratic or cooperative leadership under nine headings. The principles are generally known and are listed here without elaboration:

1. People fully understand only those ideas they have helped to formulate.
2. Group decisions receive more support than autocratic edicts.
3. Democratic leadership draws upon all available human resources.
4. It creates self-reliant individuals.
5. It builds a self-sustaining group.
6. It may lead to higher morale.
7. It provides an emotional catharsis for dissenters.
8. It allows for differences, hence progress.
9. It has inherent value as a method.[5]

As a staff works together a stage of maturity will be attained. One fact which must be remembered is that as a new person is added to a staff it becomes a new staff. Orientation must begin again. The new person brings new ideas, past experiences, and all the characteristics mentioned above. The group will again need to develop confidence and maturity as the persons work together. Haiman suggests that a group of persons working together is much like an individual in personal growth. It is, like an infant or newborn baby, uncoordinated and highly dependent upon the leader. As the group grows into what may be compared with adolescence, it struggles with awkwardness and the dependency-independency conflicts as do teen-agers. Emotional

---

[5] *Group Leadership and Democratic Action,* chap. 3.

228

crises are difficult to handle and can be quite disruptive. With increasing patience and working together the group can attain a state of maturity compared with that of a well-oriented adult. Some of the characteristics of a mature group are listed below:

1. Has a clear understanding of its purposes or goals.
2. Makes progress toward its goals with a maximum efficiency and a minimum of wasted effort.
3. Is able to look ahead and plan ahead.
4. Has achieved a high degree of effective inter-communication.
5. Is able to initiate and carry on effective, logical problem-solving.
6. Has achieved an appropriate balance between *established* ways of working together and a *readiness to change* its procedural patterns.
7. Is objective about its own functioning; can face its procedural-emotional problems and intelligently make whatever modifications are called for.
8. Strikes an appropriate balance between group productivity (socio-group functions) and the satisfaction of ego needs (psyche-group functions).
9. Provides for the diffusion and sharing of leadership responsibilities.
10. Achieves an appropriate balance between content and process orientation.
11. Has a high degree of cohesiveness or solidarity but not to the point of exclusiveness or the point of stifling individuality.
12. Makes intelligent use of the differing abilities of its members.
13. Faces reality, and works on the basis of fact rather than fantasy.
14. Provides an atmosphere of psychological freedom for the expression of all feelings and points of view.
15. Is not over-dominated by the leader or by any of its members.
16. Has achieved a healthy balance between cooperative and competitive behavior on the part of its members.
17. Strikes an appropriate balance between emotionality and rationality.
18. Can readily change and adapt itself to the needs of differing situations.
19. Recognizes that means are inseparable from ends.
20. Recognizes the values of and limitations of democratic procedures.[6]

Staff Wives

In the chapter on the associate pastor there is a brief discussion on some of the problems faced by the wife of the associate. It would not be an honest accounting if a further word were not said in regard to staff wives in general. A creative staff can profit greatly by recognizing the potential creative leadership in the wives of members. It is entirely possible for "hidden agenda" and "invisible committees" to be so strong in the lives of staff persons in regard to family life, and particu-

---

[6] *Ibid.,* p. 103.

larly unhappy wives, that work can be seriously hampered. To illustrate: A staff consisting of senior minister, associate minister, minister of education, director of children's work, minister of music, and church business administrator were enjoying dinner along with their wives. The subject of the staff wives was mentioned. Out of the blue came a volley of words obviously filled with emotion and deep resentment from a young wife of one of the staff: "I'm a nobody—just a nobody!" The young lady had a master's degree and had taken considerable work in seminary along with her husband. Now, mother of three small children, with her husband on a church staff and not the senior minister, she felt her education and talents were being mutilated. There is more unrest among minister's wives than appears on the surface, and especially among wives of staff members other than the senior minister.

Some attempts have been made by writers to speak to the subject of the minister's wife. Several references are in the bibliography of this work for further reading. One of the most exhaustive studies was done by William Douglas, a faculty member of the School of Theology of Boston University, under a grant from the Lilly Endowment. It was published in 1965 under the title *Minister's Wives*.[7] One of the most valuable aspects of the Douglas study is the analysis of the types of wives found in the sample of 5,000 wives in the study. Douglas divides wives into 3 major categories: *the teamworker,* 20.6 percent of the total number; *the background supporter,* 63.9 percent; and *the detached,* 15.1 percent; with .4 percent unclassified. The teamworker is described by Douglas as one who feels deeply involved in the life and work of the ministry.

. . . To be a MW [minister's wife] is to be a minister. She and her husband form a team, with division of responsibilities at some points and shared responsibility at others. They are "yoke-fellows" for Christ. They are side by side on the firing line. She feels as much called to witness, to serve, to minister in the broadest sense of that term, as does her husband.[8]

The background supporter is characterized as one who feels a semi-professional leadership, believes firmly in the purposes of the church, considers oneself to be a Christian with responsibility as any other church member, derives much satisfaction from study and learning about the Christian faith, and feels her first responsibility is to be a

___

[7] (New York: Harper, 1965).
[8] *Ibid.,* p. 33.

good wife and mother. She is happy that her husband is a minister and is satisfied with the profession.

Douglas describes the background supporter:

In general, they are more interpersonally oriented and less work-achievement-oriented than are teamworkers. Their religious commitment takes the form more of the disciple than of the apostle: the emphasis is on *following* rather than *leading*, learning rather than witness, and in relation to their husbands there is greater deference than tends to be true for teamworkers. More often concerned about their own leadership abilities than teamworkers, they seldom take a direct leadership role, but rather prefer "hostess-type" activities such as calling, greeting, and entertaining.[9]

The detached minister's wives are divided by Douglas into two major groups: those who are motivated by beliefs in the purpose of the church and desire to fill a position in the church as any laymen; and those who rebel against the demands of the congregation upon their time and energy, and, to some extent, resent the ministry. Obviously the latter are candidates for a good deal of unhappiness. Some of the wives in the first category of the detached have had a long hard struggle accepting the ministry, but they have finally come to accept it and believe in it. In a number of cases husbands have entered the ministry after marriage. The wife feels that she did not marry a minister and resents the necessity of being forced to make the transition.

Douglas makes the observation that, by and large, there is little difference in the wives of members of multiple staff ministries and wives of ministers in parishes of only one minister.

The above analysis provides a framework for church staffs in regard to the place of staff wives. Participation in staff study, retreats, and even business sessions can be left to the judgment of wives. If a wife is a teamworker she should have the opportunity to fulfill her mission in life through staff participation. If she is a detached wife she should enjoy that freedom without feeling the pressure of others in the staff to participate. The background supporter should also have the privilege of participation at will.

The wife of the senior minister needs especially to be conscious of possible friction among staff wives. The congregation usually looks upon the wife of the senior minister with glowing admiration, providing her with attention and gratuities that are not given the wives of other members of the staff. Sharing of honors and frequent get-togeth-

---

[9] *Ibid.*, p. 43.

ers, with the initiative being taken by the wife of the senior minister, will assist in keeping harmony in the group.

Stress

Before closing this chapter some attention must be given to the matter of stress. The creative staff is subject to all the pressures of life in a rapidly changing world. In engineering stress is thought of as the amount of strain, pressure, or tension a particular substance can bear. For instance, how much pressure or strain can a strut in an airplane wing bear before it bends or breaks? Stress in the human body is essentially the same. It is the pressure placed upon the body from work, anxiety, tension, frictions with people, inability to accomplish desired goals, noise, tension arising because of divided loyalties, and so on.

In his monumental work, *The Stress of Life,* Hans Selye defines stress:

> In its medical sense, *stress is essentially the rate of wear and tear in the body.* Anyone who feels that whatever he is doing—or whatever is being done to him—is strenuous and wearing, knows vaguely what we mean by *stress.* The feeling of just being tired, jittery, or ill are subjective sensations of stress.[10]

Selye, a German-educated medical doctor who has spent his life in research in the field of stress on the human body and at this writing is the Director of the Institute of Experimental Medicines and Surgery at the University of Montreal, has established a number of theories in regard to the deterioration of the body as the result of stress. In substance Selye has developed what he calls the *general adaptation syndrome* (G. A. S.), which develops in three stages: (1) the alarm reaction, (2) the stage of resistance, (3) the stage of exhaustion. Certain stressors are present—the common everyday pressures—which attack a part of the glandular system or organs of the body. These are primarily the brain, thyroid and adrenal glands, liver, kidneys, blood vessels, and body cells.

The human body has remarkable adaptive abilities with built-in mechanisms for one part of the body to assist other parts of the body under stress. Eventually, however, the body wears out. The rate of body deterioration may be determined by how well one learns to handle stress. Selye holds to a basic principle that stress is a normal

---

[10] (New York: McGraw-Hill, 1956), p. 3.

part of life. It is the person who learns how to control stress, letting out his energy in such a fashion that exhaustion does not come too soon, who is able to live productively and creatively over a long period of time. Age is both *physiologic* and *chronologic*. "One man may be much more senile in body and mind, and closer to the grave, at forty than another person at sixty." [11] Selye goes on to say, "Vitality is like a special kind of bank account which you can use up by withdrawals, but cannot increase by deposits. Your only control over this most precious fortune is the rate at which you make your withdrawals." [12] Selye suggests that you cannot stop withdrawing the energy, nor can you regulate just enough of this quality of life for survival, but the secret is "the intelligent thing to do is to withdraw generously, but never wastefully." [13]

In "Controlling Executive Stress," Merrill T. Eaton, Professor of Phychiatry at the University of Nebraska, states:

A stress may be defined as a situation including:
1. Hardship, strain, overwork, or fatigue, accompanied by
2. Excessive or persistent noxious emotional states, (e. g. anxiety; anger) which may be related to
3. Some threat of security, self-esteem, or basic goals in living, sometimes involving
4. A need to cope with newly experienced or rapidly changing environmental factors[14]

Stress plays a part in the production of:
1. Psychophysiological disease (e. g., high blood pressure)
2. Psychiatric symptoms (e. g., anxiety)
3. Behavioral disturbances (e. g., alcoholism)
4. Inefficiency
5. Morale problems involving others who are affected by the behavior and attitudes of the person under stress.

In addition to the stresses not connected with his job which may influence the executive's well-being, there are some potential sources of tension which are directly related to his position. These are:
1. Overwork
2. Conflicting obligations
3. Responsibilities
4. Ambiguities of the executive position

---

[11] *Ibid.*, p. 274.
[12] *Ibid.*
[13] *Ibid.*
[14] Reprinted by permission of the publisher from "Executive Stresses Do Exist —But They Can Be Controlled," by Merrill T. Eaton, *Personnel*, March/April 1963. © 1963 by the American Management Association, Inc.

5. The social role of the administrator
6. Insecurity
7. The level of interpersonal tension in the environment.[15]

The ability of the individual to live under the pressures of life is the ability to control stress. Selye uses a term to describe the ability of the body to adapt which he borrowed from the French psychologist Claude Bernard. The word is *homeostasis*. It is derived from two Greek words—*homoios*, meaning like or similar; and *stasis*, meaning position, standing, or the ability to remain the same. Homeostasis, then, is the staying power of the body, or the ability of the human body to adapt organically to constant pressures and changes. It is the steadiness of the body.[16] The breaking point comes, however, when the body can no longer stand the pressures and make adaptations. As an automobile under high speed may have a mechanical breakdown, the body, too, will break.

The members of church staffs, their wives, husbands, and children all are subject to severe stress. In addition to the normal pressures of the everyday run of things, the leadership families in the church are often plagued with guilt when they are unable to solve their own problems. There is a sense of the inadequacy of the gospel, the very center of one's profession, to meet personal needs. The normal question follows, "If I can't find the answers to my own needs, what right have I to attempt to help others in their needs?" Staff members need to apply the same principles in their own lives as they do in ministering to parishioners: Define the needs and attempt to minister to them. One must also recognize that at some stages in ministry one reaches a point where there is no firm answer. Acceptance of that fact alone may relieve the stress, to a certain degree. Anne Roe in *The Psychology of Occupations* uses Maslow's arrangement of the basic needs of the individual in determining the degree of motivation in one's life. The catalogue of needs, however, is applicable to the understanding of the stress points of life. These are: (1) physiological needs, (2) safety needs, (3) the need for belongingness and love, (4) the need for importance, respect, self-esteem, independence, (5) the need for information, (6) the need for understanding, (7) the need for beauty, and (8) the need for self-actualization.[17] The basic needs are in a hierarchy

---

[15] "Controlling Executive Stress." Used by permission of the author.
[16] For a full discussion see *The Stress of Life*, pp. 11-12.
[17] Anne Roe, *The Psychology of Occupations* (New York: Wiley, 1956), p. 25.

of importance, beginning with the purely physical needs for food, drink, sleep and shelter, and reaching to the need for complete self-actualization.

There is an attempt in this work to define problem areas of human relations that emerge in the church staff. These problem areas are spoken to by applying the principles of personnel management, psychology of leadership, and sociology of leadership. All these principles, however, are diagnostic and prescriptive. We are all human beings with strengths and weaknesses. We have personal ambitions, group goals, work-oriented lives, and personal family lives. The creative staff will develop a good relationship in the work-oriented setting, and yet remain good parents, spouses, and citizens in a community.

Some simple and obvious means of minimizing stress may be touched on. Self-discipline is the largest factor in putting them into practice. (1) Rest. Ample sleep is important. (2) Reasonable and regular vacation periods. All families need to get away from routines. (3) Regular days off during the week. With Sunday being the heaviest workday for most of the church staff, it is essential that a schedule of days off be arranged for each member of the staff. One church staff interviewed schedules work so that each member of the staff, including the senior minister, has one weekend per quarter away from the job. (4) Watch the schedules. It is easy to get too many meetings away from the church, too many committee meetings, too many night meetings, too many scheduled counseling sessions together. Church leaders become frantic with running to one thing after another. Selection of engagements should be based on importance and time invested in each. The conscientious religious leader has a tendency to feel that each legitimate call on his time is an opportunity for Christian witness. It is, but the witnesser is a human being with human physical and mental limitations.

The simplest formula for meeting the stresses of life has been stated by Hans Selye:

> Fight always for the highest attainable aim
> But never put up resistance in vain.[18]

---

[18] *The Stress of Life*, p. 300.

13

The Church Reflects the Staff

The ancient saying, "like priest, like people," to a large degree can be applied to the church staff—"like staff, like church." This study began with the basic doctrine that the staff is for the purpose of assisting the congregation to be the church. The staff, in a sense, is a church within itself. It is a company of believers who are working toward the fulfillment of their own Christian experience of worship, nurture, and work in the world. How well the staff fulfills this ministry within itself will determine to a large degree how well the congregation will realize its fulfillment of worship, nurture, and work in the world.

In this book there has been much recorded concerning human relations, communications, leadership, policies, job analyses, right attitudes, and so forth. This is right and essential, for anything that can assist the staff to be more effective is important. Members of the church staff are subject to all the temptations as any other persons. The seven deadly sins of antiquity—pride, covetousness, lust, envy, gluttony, anger, and sloth—find a ready acceptance in contemporary society, and the members of the church staff are subject to these temptations as are other persons. The virtures of antiquity, however, may become the goals of the staff—courage, temperance, wisdom, justice, faith, hope, and love. The church staff is dealing in the highest and noblest attributes of mankind and attempting to live by and convey to others the greatest values in life. The staff is dealing with that intangible quality of man we commonly refer to as spirit. In the Christian context this is the attribute of the human being which places with him the Divine. It is conscience quickened by the Holy Spirit and conditioned by the highest qualities of decency and morality. It is responsibility that causes one to answer in the affirmative the question, "Am I my brother's keeper?"

The noted biologist Edmund W. Sinnott, former Director of the Sheffield Scientific School at Yale University and Dean Emeritus of the Yale Graduate School, discusses in *The Bridge of Life* the relationship of body, mind, and spirit of man.

Mind is the intelligent, rational, thinking part of him [man]. His *self* or *soul* is what makes him an individual person. To these are sometimes added the concepts of the *ego*, the *psyche* and others, each stressing a side of his psychical life. Beyond all, however, and more difficult to understand, is that nebulous, elusive thing men call the *spirit*. Philosophy does not quite know what to do with this and has left discussion of it chiefly to the poets, mystics and men of faith. Psychology never mentions it. Materialism emphatically denies that it exists; but to many people the human spirit is a very precious thing, a warming of the heart, a stirring in the core of being, the place of man's highest ideals where he makes contact with the Divine. It is something real but at the very edge of mystery, something that can be felt but never understood. What a man thinks of the spirit determines his attitude toward his fellow men, his religion and his very concept of God.[1]

The staff is to lead the congregation in meaningful worship. Worship may be in the sanctuary of a great cathedral or in a youth meeting in the mountains, on a lake, or stream. In either case it is the essence of unity within the congregation. It is the central unifying force within the home. A staff that is able to attain a meaningful worship experience within its own group will, in all likelihood, be able to convey the same qualities of worship to the congregation.

Much emphasis is placed in these days upon the value of the small group and face-to-face relationships. The retreat is a means of getting a small group together for a few hours to commune with God and one another. The press of an urban culture causes persons to neglect the sensitivity of the soul, which assists in retaining the value of mankind. In the retreat into nature away from the busy schedule of life one has the opportunity to renew one's commitment to God and gain a new perspective of responsible Christian living.

In some areas of the nation and among some groups in society, corporate worship, and especially the sermon, seems to have fallen into ill repute. The staff needs to study the service of worship. Is it meaningful? Does it meet the needs of the worshiper? Is the congregation schooled in a doctrine of worship, and does it understand the relationship of worship, renewal, and the expression of faith in sound stewardship of all life? Does the sermon speak to human and divine needs in the light of biblical and historical theology? Is the music a means of assisting the congregation in worship? Probably there is no

---

[1] (New York: Simon and Schuster, 1966), pp. 168-69.

point where the staff members' tasks converge as much as in the worshiping congregation. The prophets of doom who predict the extinction of corporate worship and the sermon are wrong. God is still using this experience as one of the most effective means of communicating with his created beings, of teaching, and of keeping men sensitive to his cause. If the service is ineffective it is because of the leaders of the service. Preaching is a powerful instrument of the Spirit. Martin Luther King will be immortalized for his peace marches, but he will also be remembered for his "I Have a Dream" sermon, which stirred the imagination of millions in convicting the conscience of a nation.

The church staff is to lead the congregation in nurture. Nurture consists of teaching and learning the basic tenets of the Christian faith founded in biblical and historical theology. One of the indictments against the Christian church in this day is that church members are biblically and theologically illiterate. This is a strong indictment, but too often we are forced to admit its truth. Hope is on the horizon, however, as one witnesses the numerous study groups emerging in congregations across the nation, especially among young adults. Fellowship is not enough. This can be obtained at the country club, golf course, and bridge club. The church in addition must provide the climate for learning in corporate worship, church school, small study groups, retreats, and in various formal and informal groups. Theology and the relevance of theology to all areas of life are rapidly becoming the center for study. The church staff has the opportunity to assist in training leaders, stimulating various types of learning experiences in all age groups, and leading in teaching-learning experiences.

Probably at no time in modern history has there been such mass confusion concerning morality and immorality. Right and wrong are relative rather than absolute. Yet laymen are greatly confused concerning moral issues and the nature of a Christian society as over against a non-Christian society. Moral questions are not black and white, but gray. The church staff stand as an example of moral stability, and must, even in the midst of grave confusion, be diagnosticians in regard to moral issues. When a new movement invades society the church staff must be able to make some kind of judgment as to whether the movement is a part of a natural and cultural change which must take place if a culture is to progress, or whether the movement is planting the seeds of moral decay. The same judgment must be made in regard to new forms of worship, new art forms, new teaching methods, and new philosophies. Laymen need to be engaged in serious studies to discuss movements, literature, philosophies, and concepts in the light of the Christian ethic.

In their book *The New Morality*,[2] Lunn and Lean credit Monk Gibbon with the following statement:

The truth is that civilization collapses when the essential reverence for absolute values which religion gives disappears. Rome had discovered that in the days of her decadence. Men live on the accumulated Faith of the past as well as on its accumulated self-discipline. Overthrow these and nothing seems missing at first, a few sexual taboos, a little of the prejudice of a Cato, a few rhapsodical impulses—comprehensible, we are told, only in the literature of folklore—these have gone by the board. But something has gone as well, the mortar which held society together, the integrity of the individual soul; then the rats come out of their holes and begin burrowing under the foundations and there is nothing to withstand them.[3]

Finally, the church staff is the stimulating agent to inspire and lead the congregation to be the church in the world. In his high priestly prayer Jesus prayed for the church, not that it might be saved from the world, but that the world through the church would be saved. A church in contemporary society that is not engaged in the moral, social, and political issues of its community, state, nation, and world, is a church that has already sounded its death knell. One of the major criticisms of the church today is that it has been apart from the world instead of a part of the world. No longer can the church be irrelevant to its culture.

One of the most thrilling aspects of the interviewing done with church staffs in the gathering of data for this book was the discovery of work being done by congregations throughout the nation for the betterment of community life or the lifting of a minority group. The criticism of the church has been that it was interested in those programs which would increase its membership or treasury. I discovered many programs that did neither, but were sponsored, sometimes at great cost financially and in manpower, simply as a service to a needy people. I refer to the day school for slum children, primarily Negro and Puetro Rican, in a wealthy New York church; the ministry to American Indians on Vancouver Island; the varied programs of ministering to the narcotics addict and alcoholic in a large church in the Southwest; the teaching of a vocation and way of making a living in the inner city parish. The list could go on. This is the church engag-

---

[2] Arnold Lunn and Garth Lean (London: Blandford Press, 1964).
[3] Gibbon. *Mount Ida* (London: Jonathan Cape, 1948).

ing itself in the world. It may raise controversial issues. It may cross conventional lines. But it is the church being the church.

In many ways the church staff is the change agent in a congregation. The change agent is the instrument which brings about needed transformation. The staff is the agent for change in the life of the individual, the family, every age group in the congrgeation, and the congregation as a whole.

The late Pitirim A. Sorokin, who devoted a major portion of his scholarly life to research and writing in the field of altruistic love, related in his book *The Ways of Power and Love*[4] the chief attributes of the persons who were the great change agents in world history. The persons in his study made the world a better place. Persons under study were Jesus of Nazareth, the Apostle Paul, St. Augustine, Francis of Assisi, Martin Luther, John Wesley, John Woolman, Albert Schweitzer, and other persons of such caliber. In the form of a true sociologist Sorokin gathered data on each of the persons in the study, assimilated the data, and then established what all the persons had in common. He discovered they each had four attributes: (1) love was the central motivating force of life, (2) a complete self-identification with God reflected in reverence, devotion, and obedience, (3) a complete self-identification with a personal standard of morals and self-discipline, (4) a complete self-identification with the problems and ills of the world. In other words, if any of these persons was aware of injustice to any individual or group of individuals he made it his own responsibility to seek justice for the deprived.

The church staff stands as a tower of strength to be the change agent in a congregation and community. It is a disciplined staff working in the power of love for moral integrity, example, and justice in society.

We return in closing, to our original statement concerning the purpose of the church staff. "It [the staff] has its mission in sharing of responsibility, of mutual concern and support of one another as it assists, directs, and participates in a local congregation of Christian believers as they assemble for worship and nurture and are dispersed for work and service in the world."

The creative staff and the creative church fulfill their mission as the body of Christ in and through a needy world by the means of self-sacrifice, self-identification with suffering, and reconciling love—*agape*—without thought of self-glorification, but with self-renunciation

---

[4] (Boston: Beacon Press, 1954.)

in service. From this will come the true *koinonia* (Christian community) under the influence and power of the Holy Spirit. Both staff and congregation will do well to tarry, as the waiting disciples in the upper room, until they are endowed with the Holy Spirit. In that Spirit they will become a releasing agent in the world for the fruits of the Spirit: "love, joy, peace, patience, kindness, goodness, faithfulness, gentleness, self-control." (Galatians 5:22-23 RSV).

Appendix A: Statistics

TABLE 15. SIZE OF CONGREGATION AND PERSONS ON THE CHURCH STAFF BY VARIOUS POSITIONS*

Position on Staff	Size of Congregation							
	Under 400	400 to 699	700 to 999	1,000 to 1,499	1,500 to 1,999	2,000 to 2,999	3,000 to 3,999	4,000 and over
Pastoral Staff	1	1	2	2	3	3	4	5
Education Staff			1	1	1	2	3	3
#Day School Staff			2	3	3	4	5	7
**Music Staff	1	2	2	2	3	3	3	3
Business Administrator				1	1	1	2	2
Secretarial Staff	1	1	1	2	2	3	4	5
Food Service Staff						1	2	3
Buildings and Grounds Staff	1	1	2	2	3	3	5	6

* Figures are compiled from averages. There will be considerable variation by individual congregations.
# Figures are given if there is a day school: 70% of the churches of more than 4,000 members have a day school, while only 7% of churches under 400 have a day school. 26% of churches of 1,500 to 3,000 members have day schools.
** Music staff has the widest variation of any position because of the large number who are part-time employees. Assistants consist of pianists, organists, and various specialists with age-group choirs.

TABLE 16. EDUCATIONAL LEVELS FOR VARIOUS POSITIONS
ON THE CHURCH STAFF

Position in the church staff	Educational levels						
	High School Graduate	Liberal Arts Degree	B.D. Degree	Master's Degree	Ph.D.	Honorary Degree	Special Training*
Pastor	98.79%	97.39%	94.46%	24.42%	10.09%	39.00%	24.79%
Associate Pastor	92.49	91.85	78.28	19.45	3.60	6.00	38.00
Organist-Director	86.00	84.00	5.30	54.26	6.00	2.00	47.81
Director	93.00	83.00	5.00	41.43	3.00	3.00	34.28
Organist	94.00	62.00		26.15			43.07
Director of Education	95.60	83.00	24.00	35.97			40.28
Director of Youth	100.00	73.00	23.00	15.85			34.61
Church Business Administrator	75.00	50.00	7.00	9.00		5.00	58.53
Financial Secretary	64.00	21.00					42.00
Secretary	87.60	16.00		1.12		.56	57.74

* Specialized Training indicates training in a business school, technical school, craft school, college or seminary (less than a degree), church training schools, or short-term course or workshop.

TABLE 17. NUMBER OF YEARS IN PRESENT POSITION FOR EACH
POSITION ON THE CHURCH STAFF

Years	Pastor	Associate Pastor	Director of Music	Choir Director	Organist	Educator	Business Administrator	Secretary
Less than 2 years	12.7%	38.4%	27.60%	23.2%	24.6%	41.7%	27.5%	30.90%
2 to 3 years	21.4	32.1	22.30	18.8	26.2	26.6	22.5	19.00
4 to 5 years	22.7	16.7	11.70	18.8	12.3	14.3	15.0	15.90
6 to 8 years	18.3	7.6	12.70	11.5	13.9	10.7	12.5	17.30
9 to 12 years	10.0	3.1	8.50	13.0	10.7	4.3	10.0	9.30
13 to 15 years	5.6		8.50	8.6		.7	10.0	3.40
16 to 20 years	7.3	.9	4.20	1.4	6.1	1.4	2.5	2.80
21 to 25 years	1.6	.4	1.06	4.3	3.0			.80
26 years or more			3.19		3.0			.28

244

TABLE 18. TOTAL NUMBER OF PERSONS IN THE STUDY
BY DENOMINATION AND POSITION

Position	American Baptist	Southern Baptist	Disciples	Lutheran	Methodist	Presbyterian	Episcopal	Congregational	Total
Pastor	29	19	38	12	107	47	28	27	307
Associate Pastor	11	1	21	9	83	45	31	20	221
Organist-Director	7	4	9	4	34	11	15	10	94
Director	4	4	12	1	25	18	1	5	70
Organist	4	4	9	1	28	9	4	6	65
Director of:									
Education	16	11	13	6	50	18	14	11	139
Adult Work	1				2				3
Youth Work	3	5	4	1	8	4	1		26
Children's Work	2	1	1		6	1		3	14
Church Business Administrator	5	3	4	2	10	7	5	5	41
Finance Secretary	2	1	2		5	3	1		14
Secretary	37	34	36	8	135	64	41		355
TOTAL	121	87	149	44	493	227	141	87	1,849

TABLE 19. SIZE OF COMMUNITY OF BIRTH FOR EACH
POSITION ON THE CHURCH STAFF

Size of Community	Pastor	Associate Pastor	Director of Music	Choir Director	Organist	Educator	Business Administrator	Secretary
Open Country	17.2%	17.2%	8.69%	8.9%	6.15%	15.8%	20.0%	17.1%
Under 500	10.0	7.9	3.26	10.4	4.61	5.7	10.0	7.6
500 to 2,499	13.3	13.0	14.10	11.9	16.90	13.6	17.5	16.8
2,500-9,999	14.0	13.0	13.00	11.9	21.50	13.6	12.5	12.0
10,000-24,999	9.1	11.6	19.50	17.9	7.60	12.9	5.0	10.6
25,000-99,999	10.4	13.9	11.90	20.8	13.80	10.7	12.5	11.2
100,000-499,999	13.3	16.2	17.30	10.4	21.50	16.5	10.0	15.0
500,000 or more	12.3	9.7	11.90	7.4	7.60	10.7	12.5	9.4

TABLE 20. OCCUPATION OF PARENTS FOR EACH POSITION ON THE CHURCH STAFF

Occupation	Pastor	Associate Pastor	Director of Music	Choir Director	Organist	Educator	Business Administrator	Secretary
Professional	38.0%	24.6%	35.4%	25.0%	28.50%	32.8%	17.9%	17.9%
Agricultural	18.8	18.1	7.5	14.0	11.10	23.8	12.8	24.9
Managerial	12.6	19.0	15.0	14.0	14.20	18.6	23.0	13.0
Clerical	3.0	8.3	3.2	3.1	3.17	5.9	2.5	5.7
Sales	7.8	7.9	15.0	15.6	19.00	5.9	20.5	7.9
Crafts or Operative	13.3	15.3	11.8	25.0	11.10	8.9	10.2	21.5
Service	2.3	2.3	2.1		6.30	1.4		3.0
Skilled Labor	3.7	3.2	6.4	1.5	4.70	.7	7.6	3.3
Unskilled Labor	.6	.9	3.2	1.5	1.50	1.4	5.1	2.4

Appendix B

Personnel Policies, Interpreting the Work of the Staff to the Congregation, Job Descriptions

PERSONNEL POLICIES OF CENTRAL CHURCH [1]

I. Full-Time Professional Employees (Ordained Ministers)

Basic Work Schedule

It is recognized that the nature of Church work is such that the position of a minister cannot always be confined rigidly to a definite schedule of hours. It is likewise recognized, however, that a minister should not be bound to his work at the expense of his reasonable obligations to himself, his family, and his community.

In order, therefore, to maintain a high quality of work and to conserve the minister's well-being, it is essential that a reasonable schedule of hours be established and that it be observed as consistently as possible. Working schedules, the preparation and supervision of which are the reponsibility of the minister, should be determined through cooperative staff planning to ensure equitable arrangements for all professional staff members. They should take into account the necessity for study and planning, as well as for recreation, and should allow for any special responsibilities in relation to community-wide interests and activities which are required by the minister's field of work. They should provide for time off each week.

Time off on major holidays—New Year's Day, Memorial Day, July 4th, Labor Day, Thanksgiving, and Christmas—should be scheduled or equivalent time off provided.

---

[1] The following statement of personnel policies is one used by Central Congregational Church, Topeka, Kansas, and is used by permission of the pastor, Arthur H. Kolsti.

Salaries, Wages, and Expense Accounts

Salary schedules and adjustments shall be based upon such items as training, experience, ability, extent of responsibility, amount of supervision required, success on the job, cost of living, and salaries paid in comparable professions.

Salaries and wages shall be reviewed at least annually and adjustments made in the light of changing conditions, the value of services rendered, and the prevailing salary scales paid by churches for similar services. Account shall also be taken of what is fair practice between professional and non-professional workers and between executives and staff associates.

Specific arrangements shall be made for reimbursing ministers for approved Church expenses.

Professional full-time staff members shall not engage in outside remunerative work except for occasional speaking appointments without approval of the Board of Trustees.

Vacations

The minister shall be given an annual vacation with pay of four weeks. The associate minister and the minister of education shall be given an annual vacation with pay of four weeks. For periods of less than a full year's employment, proportional vacation allowance shall be granted.

Leaves of Absence

The sick leave policy of the Church permits salary payment of up to one month per year for the ministers of the Church when absent because of personal illness or very serious illness in the immediate family.

A satisfactory physical examination with an annual checkup shall be made a condition of employment.

At the end of the first year of employment and thereafter, all unused sick leave shall be carried over, and accumulated up to six months. Arrangements for longer absences due to personal illness or other emergency shall be left to the discretion of the Board of Trustees. Sick leave is not cumulative for terminal pay purposes.

The Church grants leaves for military service in accordance with the Universal Military and Service Act of 1951 and any amendment or changes to conform with the law. Ministers who retain a reserve status in any one of the branches of the military and who are required to report for military duty to retain their reserve status are granted leave. All such requests must be duly certified.

Resignation, Release, and Retirement

The Church and the minister shall give each other at least a ninety day notice in case of release or resignation; other full-time professional employees and the Church shall give each other a sixty day notice in case of release or resignation. Failure to give the required notice results in the forfeiture of terminal vacation pay.

When a minister resigns or is released, he shall receive accrued vacation allowance for the current year.

Dismissals occur only in the case of incompetence, misconduct, malfeasance, retrenchment, reorganization, or the will of the congregation. Dismissal for misconduct or malfeasance is without notice or pay in lieu of notice.

In the case of retrenchment or reorganization, in cases where it is mutually advantageous, staff members shall be transferred to other positions of like salary and responsibility. If a transfer cannot be arranged, ninety days' notice and terminal pay shall be given.

The retirement age of ministerial staff members shall be sixty-five, with annual reelection by the Church permissive up to age seventy, when retirement becomes mandatory.

Security Provisions

It is expected that ordained ministers shall be members of the Annuity Fund for Congregational Ministers. The Church shall contribute as dues eleven percent (11%) of salary for each ordained staff member of the Fund.

It is also expected that ordained ministers will have Social Security coverage.

Each full-time professional employee shall make provisions for hospital-medical-surgical insurance coverage for himself and his family. The staff may have a group insurance on a payroll deduction basis.

Workmen's Compensation Insurance is carried by the Church for all of its employees, as provided by Kansas law.

Grievances

The Board of Trustees shall provide the procedure for locating, reviewing, and promptly settling grievances or dissatisfactions. Each minister has a right, in the event of grievances or dissatisfactions, to a hearing before the Board of Trustees or appointed committee upon request.

II. Non-Professional Employees

Basic Work Schedule

A five-day week shall be regarded as a reasonable working schedule except for custodial service.

Vacations and Holidays

Each non-professional employee after one year of full-time service shall be granted an annual vacation of ten working days.

Vacations for periods of service between six months and one year shall be prorated at the rate of one day of vacation for each month of service.

Vacation schedules shall be approved by the Minister or the Board of Trustees.

The following holidays shall be observed: New Year's Day, Memorial Day, July 4, Labor Day, Thanksgiving Day, and Christmas. Should the holiday fall on Sunday, the following Monday will be observed.

Leaves of Absence

No deduction of salary shall be made for absences due to illness, accident, or emergency up to ten working days in any one year. Such leave of time shall not be cumulative from year to year and cannot be used as additional vacation time. In the case of longer absences, the Board of Trustees may take special action.

Resignation or Release

The church shall give an advance notice of at least one pay period or equivalent compensation in case of release, except where release is for "cause." It is expected that an employee will give an advance notice of at least one pay period before voluntarily terminating employment.

Salary Schedules

Salary schedules shall be reviewed annually by the Board of Trustees.

Workmen's Compensation

Workmen's Compensation insurance is provided by the Church.

Retirement

Employees of the Church are covered by Social Security.

General Information

These policies are based on full-time employment. Any policies for part-time employment shall be worked out individually where necessary. Any question regarding a nonprofessional employee's status not covered by these policies shall be referred to the Board of Trustees.

INTERPRETING THE WORK OF THE STAFF TO THE CONGREGATION A SAMPLE BROCHURE [2]

THE FUNCTION OF THE MINISTERIAL STAFF

IN FIRST PRESBYTERIAN CHURCH
EVANSVILLE, INDIANA

MINISTRY belongs to the whole church. All Christians are called to be ministers so it is the privilege of every Christian, by his words and actions, to proclaim the gospel of God's redeeming love. It is the members of the church who by individual and corporate action, call others into the new life of the Kingdom,

---

[2] Used by permission of Joseph W. Baus, pastor of the First Presbyterian Church, Evansville, Indiana.

who nurture each other in faith, train one another in Christian virtue and behavior, and plan and execute the program of the church. It is the members of the church, through their elected representatives, who determine what the policies and program of the church will be, and who direct and control that program.

Because the church is an association of human beings, and because some direction is necessary for human beings to act together in an organization, the church employs a staff. The staff is not to minister for or in place of the members, but to minister to them in order that members may more effectively carry out their ministry in the world. It is the duty of the ministerial staff to lead, guide, supply resources, instruct, initiate, assist, and act as agents in the execution of church policies and programs.

All members of the employed staff are engaged in the ministry to the church. Staff members are in two categories, ordained and lay. The ordained ministers are distinguished from the lay members only in that they are trained and authorized by the denomination to perform certain ecclesiastical functions such as the administration of the sacraments. The staff is not organized as a hierarchy, with some members on a higher level than others, but the distinction is that of function, each having responsibilities which are particularly his.

MINISTER FOR PARISH LIFE

Dr. Joseph W. Baus

This minister's task is the administration and co-ordination of the entire program of the church. He serves as executive for the congregational boards, commissions, and church-wide committees, directs the implementation of the program through the Parish Plan, through congregational societies and organizations, and by all other means suitable and available. His responsibilities include:

Planning public worship services and preaching
Church public relations
Staff personnel relations
Calling and counseling with members about the church program and their personal affairs
The initiation and development of program in the areas of
Stewardship
Community Outreach
World Mission
He is related to the following groups:
Session (Moderator)
Deacons
Building and Planning Committee
Nominating Committee
Budget Committee
Trustees

Parish Council
Stewardship Commission
World Mission Commission
Community Outreach Commission
Public Worship Committee of the Christian Life Commission

A special word need be said about the PREACHING and the CALLING and COUNSELLING responsibilities of all the ordained ministers. Each is fully a minister in his own right, and each takes part in the preaching program of the church. Each calls upon those members who are naturally within the area of his responsibility to see, and each counsels with any persons who seek his help. Each participates in the conduct of public worship and the sacraments, and each is available for the performance of the marriage ceremony.

MINISTER AND FELLOWSHIP AND EVANGELISM

REV. R. WILLIAM GORTON

This minister exercises pastoral concern for persons to the end that they be led into a vital relationship with the church and active participation in its program. He is concerned principally about persons, their needs, and their relationship to Christ.

An important part of his ministry is to the sick and persons with special needs. His responsibilities include:

Calling—on the hospitals
on sick and shut-ins
on newcomers in the community
on prospective members
on new members
on people who have special problems
Initiation and direction of a continuing program of evangelism
Direction and orientation of new members in the church
Initiation and development of program in the area of fellowship
He is related to:
Session
Fellowship Commission
Evangelism Commission

MINISTER FOR CHRISTIAN EDUCATION

REV. WILLIAM IDESON JOHNSON

This minister's task is to administer a program of nurture in Christian faith and discipleship for all members. His responsibilities include:

253

Initiation, direction, and supervision of a program of Christian education for
children
youth
adults
Conduct of a continuing program of leadership development for all phases of the church's work
Teaching and supervising the teaching done by church members and other staff members
He is related to:
Session
Christian Education Commission and its committees

ADMINISTRATIVE ASSISTANT

Mrs. Carl Davis

This staff member's task, working at the direction of the Minister for Parish Life, is to assist the ordained ministers and the elected officers of the church in the administration of the church program, acting as agent for the church boards in the execution of policy and the implementation of program. Her responsibilities include acting as:
Executive Secretary for
Session
Deacons
Board of Trustees
Building and Planning Committee
Budget Committee
Nominating Committee
Church financial secretary
Activities coordinator—keeping a calendar of all events, scheduling rooms and custodial service
Purchasing agent—processing all orders for supplies and equipment
Custodial staff supervisor
Resource person for committees of Session, Deacons, and Trustees

DIRECTOR OF MUSIC

Gilbert R. Wiehe

The staff member's task is the planning and direction of the entire musical program, including the several choirs, music for all public worship services, and the Christian Education program. Other members of the music staff work under his direction. He is also responsible for the initiation and development of program in the Area of Christian Life. He is related in his work to the:
Music Committee
Christian Life Commission
Christian Education Commission

Other members of the music staff are Mrs. Robert Nelson, East Side Choir Director and Organist, and Clifford Kincaid, Downtown Organist.

NURSERY SCHOOL DIRECTOR
Mrs. E. C. Meyers

This staff member's job is the planning, direction, and operation of the week-day Nursery School. She plans curriculum, selects and supervises the teaching staff, prepares the budget, and directs the parent relation and special activities program. She is responsible to the Nursery School Board and also acts as a resource person for the Children's Work Committee of the Christian Education Commission.

OFFICE SECRETARIES
Mrs. Arthur Tiernan— (Johnson)
Mrs. Robert Brooks— (Gorton)
Mrs. George Clemmons— (Baus)

Each secretary works directly with one of the ordained ministers, performing her duties at his direction. These include receiving dictation and typing, mimeographing, filing, keeping his calendar and appointments, and being generally acquainted with the work of the church in the area in which he is responsible. Mrs. Tiernan acts as secretary for various groups in the Christian education department and is responsible for coordination of work within the office; Mrs. Brooks has charge of the membership roll and individual financial accounts and the printing of Tower and Spire; Mrs. Clemmons is responsible for Neighborhood roles and does the secretarial work for the various church organizations.

CUSTODIAL STAFF
Neal Thomas—Downtown and East Side
Archie Kimbrough—Downtown
George Berry—East Side
Mrs. Archie Kimbrough—Housekeeper
William D. Cole—Maintenance Mechanic

The members of the Custodial Staff work at the direction of the Deacon's Building Maintenance Committee to keep the buildings properly heated, clean, and in good repair. They are responsible for having furniture and other equipment in order for activities as scheduled.

JOB DESCRIPTIONS

Senior Minister

1. Preaching—full responsibility for the preaching program with privilege of calling upon associate and others for participation.

2. Plan for and lead in administration of the Sacraments and reception of members.
3. Teaching—
   A. Plan for and share in teaching preparatory membership classes for children and adults.
   B. Occasional class teaching, by invitation, on Sundays when not preaching.
4. Counseling by request and reference.
5. Calling—reports to be made to the parish director.
   A. Hospital and sick at home calls.
   B. Share in shut-in calls.
   C. Share in prospective membership calls—clearing through parish director.
   D. Special calls.
6. Administration of the total program.
   A. Work with commissions, committees, and organizations.
      (1) The chairmen of commissions, committees, and organizations are to have the responsibility of their offices with the counsel and leadership of the senior minister.
      (2) A staff member is to be assigned to work with each group, except those the senior minister will work with, to serve as a representative of the senior minister for his personal guidance.
   B. Meet with staff regularly to coordinate plans, programs, and labors.
   C. Receive reports of all commissions, committees, and organizations within the church.
   D. Supervise other staff members, with certain responsibilities delegated to them.
7. Act as editor of church newsletter, with the assistance of any associate editors.
8. Conduct weddings and funerals by request and reference.
9. Larger church service—district and conference responsibilities, speaking.
10. Community ministry—cooperation in interdenominational and community programs.

Associate Minister

1. Preaching—may be called upon to preach up to 12 times a year.
2. Assist, or lead, when necessary, in the administration of the Sacraments, reception of members, and other services of the church.
3. Teaching—
   A. Assist in planning and teaching preparatory membership classes for children and adults.
   B. No continuing class assignment. Teach occasionally, by invitation, when not preaching.
   C. Assist in creation of new classes as needed.
4. Responsibility, in cooperation with the educational assistant, for the older youth and young adult program.
   A. Counselor for the Senior Methodist Youth Fellowship.
   B. Ministerial recruitment—keep in touch with young people plan-

ning or preparing for full-time Christian service, in cooperation with the Committee on Christian Vocations.

   C. Serve as a resource person in the general education program of the church.

5. Counseling by request and reference.
6. Calling—reports to be made to the senior minister and parish director.

   A. Share in prospective membership calls—assignment by parish director.

   B. Follow-up of funerals, weddings, and convalescence.

   C. Routine calls on members, with special concern for inactives.

   D. Special calls.

7. Administration—

   A. Serve as ministerial representative on the Commission on Missions and the Commission on Christian Social Concerns, Christian Vocations Committee, and with The Methodist Men and Boy Scouts.

   B. Building and Maintenance—

      (1) Direct supervision, with the cooperation of the House and Property Committee, of Janitorial Staff, with responsibility to fix hours of work, assignment of duties, and follow up to see work is completed.

      (2) Purchase building and janitorial supplies.

      (3) Supervise the upkeep of the buildings and grounds in cooperation with the House and Property Committee.

      (4) See that opening and closing of the building are properly attended to.

8. Conduct weddings, funerals, and other services by request and reference.
9. General availability to assist in work of church.
10. Larger church service—district and conference responsibilities, speaking.
11. Community ministry—cooperation in interdenominational and community programs.

Director or Minister of Education

Agreement of the _____ Church, (city and state) and _____ concerning the position of Director of Christian Education, as determined by the Session of the Church and effective (date). (See session minutes of (date) .)

The position of Director of Christian Education in the _____ Church of (city) shall be described as follows:

The Director shall be responsible to the Minister and the Session, and shall serve both and report to the Session monthly through the Council of Christian Education. She shall have general oversight of the program of Christian Education with responsibility for:

1) Nursery and Preschool services of the church.
2) Elementary, Secondary, Young Adult, and Adult programs.
3) Leadership enlistment and training with the assistance of the Council of Christian Education, and planning for the use of the curriculum and other needed materials.

4) Program promotion and interpretation of missions and other special emphases approved by the Session.

5) Coordinate the services of the Department of Christian Education with other departments of the church, e.g., music, women's and men's work.

6) Establish a system of rolls and registers.

7) Order all materials and supplies provided for by the Christian Education budget.

8) Assist the Council in the preparation and interpretation of the Christian Education budget, and in the effective promotion of the total church budget program through the Christian Education programs.

9) Schedule use of the church facilities and arrange for reservations of other facilities outside the church properties, e.g., camps, retreats.

10) Coordinate the total youth work of the church; act as resource leader for advisors and youth in organization and program planning and implementation.

11) Advise and consult with the minister on all the above, recognizing his responsibility for the total church program, and as a staff member cooperate in carrying out the policies and program approved by the Session. The minister and Session in turn promise counsel, support, and assistance to the Director in an effort to advance the program wherever possible.

In pursuit of these duties it is understood that the position as outlined cannot be defined in terms of a fixed schedule of hours per week. It is understood that a forty-hour week will be required at the very minimum. The Director will be present generally in the church each morning from 8:30 to 12:00 noon and from 1:00 to 3:00 p.m. with the exception of one day off each week, and when required by the program will meet here or elsewhere and at other times necessary to the completion of the duties outlined.

The Director shall have three week's vacation (21 days) with pay each summer. The dates of said vacation shall be set at a time other than the period scheduled for the vacation church school and the minister's vacation. Time spent as a conference leader for Presbytery or Synod shall not be charged against the aforementioned vacation.

During the course of each year the Director is expected to attend selected training opportunities offered by the denomination or other satisfactory programs to gain new insights and inspiration for the work. To that end a sum of $300.00 is available to cover expenses so incurred. Approval for attendance and the expenditure of the funds shall be issued by the Council of Christian Education.

The salary of the Director shall be $———— plus $———— for car allowance, and is payable semi-monthly. The Session will make an annual review of this remuneration and present its recommendations to the Board of Trustees prior to announcement of the church budget.

The parties involved, the church through the Session and the Director, agree to give thirty (30) days' notice of intention to terminate or change this agreement. In the fond hope and prayer that God will bless both parties, and enable all concerned to express Christian love and understanding and advance God's kingdom through good example we the undersigned affix our signatures.

Director of Christian Education	Chairman of the Session

Minister of Christian Education and Evangelism

Section I. Relations with the Department of Christian Education and Its Program

a. The Minister of Education and Evangelism shall be the professional staff person responsible for the Christian Education ministry in _____ Church, the program of which is denominational in its orientation and cooperative with the educational program of the official bodies of the denomination.

b. The Minister of Christian Education shall be the administrative officer of the Department of Christian Education of the church. He will meet with the Department in the formulation of its policy and program; shall supervise its work; provide creative leadership for the various aspects of the church's ministry of Christian Education; work with the committees of the Department on a regular basis; and shall assist in the recruitment and training of workers who function within the Department of Christian Education, especially in the youth work of the church.

c. The Minister of Christian Education shall mobilize the resources within the church and those provided by the denomination, and shall utilize them creatively in order to discover the answers for our own peculiar and particular needs as a church, especially in the light of our transitional situation.

d. In keeping with previous policy, the Minister of Christian Education shall be available for leadership of denominational nature, but only upon a "time available" basis and in cooperation with other professional staff members of the church.

e. The Minister of Christian Education shall coordinate the Sunday evening program as it has been developed in the church.

f. While it is difficult to ascertain specific fractions of time that will be involved in the ministry of Christian Education of our church under the present call, the magnitude of the program would indicate that the largest portion of time should be devoted to this ministry, perhaps half of working hours. Work with the Departments of Evangelism and Membership and remaining duties might take up the remaining half. Office hours shall be maintained on a regular basis commensurate with the schedule of other staff members. Days off shall be arranged in cooperation with the other members.

g. This work arrangement may be changed upon mutual agreement between the Department of Christian Education and its Minister in cooperation with the Staff Relations Committee of the Diaconate and provisions within its policy.

Section II. Work Arrangement with the Department of Evangelism

a. The policies and program of the Department of Evangelism shall be led and administered by the Minister of Christian Education and Evangelism according to previous practice and experience of the Department with Mr. _____.

b. He shall be the administrative officer of the Department and shall meet with the Department in the formulation of policy and program. He shall meet with the committees of the Department in producing program outlined by the Department.

c. Special projects of evangelism shall be under his direction unless otherwise arranged with the professional staff and Department.

d. The Minister of Christian Education and Evangelism shall be responsible for visiting prospects for membership and visitors to the church. These may be assigned to other professional staff members for primary contacts according to mutual agreement.

Section III. Work Arrangement with the Department of Membership

a. The Minister of Christian Education and Evangelism shall be the resource leader available from the professional staff to the Department of Membership although not the administrative officer of the Department.

b. The Minister of Christian Education and Evangelism shall meet with the Department and shall supervise the "at-homers" roll of the Department, and assist the Deaconess in her work.

c. He shall assist the men of the Membership Department in their responsibility, acting in an advisory capacity for them.

Section IV. Work Arrangement in Relation to the Pastor

a. The Minister of Christian Education and Evangelism shall assist the pastor in administration of the total program of the church and will function in keeping with the policies of the Staff Relations Committee and the Diaconate.

b. The Minister of Christian Education and Evangelism shall not be assistant pastor or assistant to the pastor. He shall be a professional person in his own right, and is expected to relate to the pastor and the functions of the pastorate in a manner that will fulfill the needs of the church, and this by mutual agreement and arrangement with the pastor.

c. The Minister of Christian Education and Evangelism shall be acting pastor during absence of the pastor from the field.

Director of Children's Work (DCW)

Basically, the duty of the DCW is to serve on the staff in such a way as to guide the church in bringing Christ and his teachings to the children in ways that *they* might comprehend.

This would involve specific things such as:

    1. Leading in developing policies for the Children's Division's educational program in line with policies of the church. Active ex officio member of the Commission on Education.

2. Leading in coordinating and unifying the various educational activities for the children into an integrated program of Christian education—e.g., vacation church school, day camp, field trips, etc.
3. Interpreting the objectives and program of education for children to the church as a whole, i.e., a program of relating parents to goals and procedures of the various departments.
4. Supervising entire education program for both children's divisions—preschool and elementary (birth to and through sixth grade).
5. Leading in adopting curriculum in harmony with the policy of the church, e.g., preparing the Divisions for curriculum change, etc.
6. Developing a plan for discovering, enlisting and training workers for the work in the Divisions, i.e., administrating a worker recruitment program, providing periodical leadership-training agencies, helping department superintendents prepare for monthly planning sessions, attending planning sessions as a resource person for persistent leadership training in both individual and group contact.
7. Helping the Commission understand facility needs, both in building and equipment.
8. Helping church groups realize their responsibility for reaching more children.
9. Enlisting co-workers in program of promotion and publicity work of the Children's Divisions.
10. Evaluating teaching and establishing a long-range educational program for the children.

The DCW is responsible directly to the Associate Minister in charge of Education, who in turn is responsible for the DCW's work. The DCW's position is one of *full-time* responsibility for work with children, and she is not required to function in additional unrelated tasks such as those of receptionist, typist, secretary, etc.; at the same time she should feel free to serve in any capacity in which the church will benefit from assistance as long as work with children is primary. Along with other professional staff members, the DCW is expected to lend wholehearted support to all ministries of the church, helping to set the example for the children to follow. Salary is to be _____ as set in the _____ budget, including a two-week vacation to be taken during the conference year.

Minister of Music

_____ Church has a full-time Minister of Music (organist and director). There are five choirs in the church—two sanctuary choirs, high school, junior, and primary choirs—and two handbell choirs (Junior Bell Choir and High School Bell Choir). There are five professional, paid section leaders—four in the four-part choir and one, a soprano, in the two-part choir.

The weekly services for which the Minister of Music is responsible are these:

8:30 A.M. Sunday—Chapel Service
9:40 A.M. Sunday—Young People's Church Chapel Service
(October through Palm Sunday)

11:00 A.M. Sunday—Morning Service in the Sanctuary
5:00 P.M. Sunday—Evening Bells Worship Service
(December through Easter)

A fundamental policy concerning music.

1. The importance of music in this church is recognized. We require organ, voices, and chimes in a skillful blend. Our services of worship are such that only the highest level of Christian music will express the ideals which we cherish. Much needs to be done in making our general membership more aware of the religious values in our music. The hymns in every service are an opportunity for every member to share in creating the sort of music that will give more power to our public witness for Christ. Singing of hymns in which a large number of members share is an effective element in the total music of the church. Anthems and other special numbers are of Christian significance, both in words and music.

2. We re-emphasize that our music is part of the total program of our church and is related to all else in the church. The music needs to be integrated with the actual functioning of each department in the whole church life, in addition to the choirs, using the Woman's Council, the church school, the various guilds, the Youth Fellowship Sunday evening meetings, the Men of _____, and every other part of the total church for an emphasis on the Christian values in our music. Our minister is the chief executive officer of the congregation, and one of his duties is to guide such correlation of the music, with the cooperation of the professional, employed organist and choir director.

In addition to his work with the choirs, the Minister of Music is expected to teach each year a course in the January Leadership Training School. A subject best suited to the needs and opportunities of the particular year within the field of music or worship in the church should be selected. The Minister of Music acts largely as his own enlistment agency in recruiting members of this class.

The work schedule of the Minister of Music is long, but not more than he would have in a combination college and church position or if he also had private students. Sunday's schedule begins with the preparation for the day at eight o'clock, continuing through one o'clock after refreshment time; it resumes again at four o'clock or before and is over at the completion of the Sunday evening program at about eight o'clock.

A normal week-day begins at eight o'clock in the morning. Two afternoons of each week are the minimum that should be spent in calls—cultivation of present choir and church members and recruitment of others. About seventy-five calls per month should be the average for the Minister of Music. Three evenings a week at home is the ideal we are striving for, though any one week may not reach this goal. One day off a week is provided for the Minister of Music.

In part our Minister of Music must be a teacher of and about music, helping people to understand its meaning and arousing intelligent enthusiasm for his part of the total church program. He is responsible for securing new singers in the choirs. He leads the effort to secure a fine attendance at the Evening Bells Worship Services.

Though no direct secretarial assistance is provided, the Minister of Music is freed from the chores of running the mimeograph machine, addressing letters, licking stamps, and answering all phone calls coming into the church.

A goal of twenty hours each week of practice and study should be set. Perhaps other duties will cut into this, but this should be the goal, along with the important job of calling on the congregation.

The month of July is the appropriate month for vacation for the Minister of Music, but frequently this has been changed when necessary to serve the church.

All weddings and funerals at the church where organ music is requested are the privilege of the Minister of Music. He is paid extra for weddings. The Minister of Music attends all wedding rehearsals, conducting them in the chapel.

Though his concern is chiefly with the Ministry of Music, the Minister of Music is one of five ministers of the church, working with the whole church, with all ages of individuals in the church. He must promote the total work above any selfish, departmental considerations. He works with the minister, the assistant minister, the minister of education, and the minister of administration in all ways possible. In turn these four encourage the Minister of Music and persuade him to pull his full share of the load.

The Minister of Music is responsible for (but does not necessarily furnish himself) all the music of the congregation—sacred and social. He must be a fine craftsman in both organ and conducting—yet he must not use his skills in either for his own personal glorification. A sense of dedication to the ideals of the church is required above all, and the personality of the Minister of Music must quietly merge into the background of the work he is doing and the music he is creating.

The Minister of Music must appeal to youth—but he cannot become too intimate with any one of them; he must remain friendly, yet somewhat removed from them. He must be a true and loyal friend to all adults—for it is with them he must work most and upon them he must depend for counsel, support, assistance, and encouragement.

The Minister of Music is a musician—but he is more a minister, and he must remain loyal to all the ministry holds important and sacred.

This memorandum is in part a description of the work to be done by all the ministers of the church and cannot be considered apart from them. We believe in an approximate equality of effort by all five of our ministers with similar hours and pattern of labor.

Business Manager

Age: Mature person.
Salary:
Qualifications: Christian; morally sound.
                 Executive qualities; ability to organize.
                 Ability to direct and work harmoniously with others.
                 Office management and fund-raising experience desirable.
                 No serious deformities.
                 Preferably not member of this church at time of employment.
                 Not eligible to hold an elective office of church.
                 Ability to speak before groups, large or small.

Duties: Staff status on same level with associate pastors.

Supervise and coordinate the work of all personnel other than pastoral, music, and Christian education directors. Responsible for hiring and discharging all personnel under business manager's jurisdiction.

Responsible for keeping of proper books and records in connection with the business of the church; must audit all bills and issue checks; act as purchasing agent for the church; encourage economy in expenditures; be responsible for preparations of all reports; keep petty cash and supper money boxes.

Adhere to policies and budgets of the church as directed by the proper boards and committees.

Schedule all weddings, meetings, receptions, and meals held in the church.

Supervise collection of pledges, other income, and accounts. Supervise maintenance of property.

Handle publicity releases; supervise church publications. Assist in budget-planning and in planning fund-raising drives.

Attend meetings of boards and committees as required.

Employment: Employed or discharged with approval of both boards through the Advisory Committee.

Vacation: 2 weeks after 9 months' employment. 3 weeks after 10 years. 4 weeks after 20 years.

Retirement: January 1 following 65th birthday.

Chief Secretary and Office Manager

The secretary to the senior minister shall work exclusively for the senior minister and under his direction only.

The Chief Secretary is the permanent host or hostess of the church. She shall be responsible for the following:

Schedule all interviews, conferences, and meetings for the senior minister.

Handle all the senior minister's correspondence, files, records, and dictation.

Receive calls concerning the scheduling of weddings, baptisms, and funerals and schedule these events in consultation with the ministers.

Keep the Session records and church register of membership, such as a list of persons:

joining	baptized
dismissed	married
suspended	church officers
deceased	church pastors—associates and assistants

Make up annual report for the General Assembly.

Prepare *Presbyterian* subscriptions, making deletions, additions, and address changes.

Attend Session meetings when new members are received. Handle the correspondence and telephoning to assure their attendance at classes and confirmation services. Attend worship services when new members are received and ascertain that all persons received by the Session reach the stage of public reception.

Prepare lists of new members received by the Session for the use of minister, deacons, and friendship callers.

Prepare letters of dismissal and record them in Church Register.

Prepare monthly list of recommended membership actions to dismiss, suspend, restore, etc., and report to the Session through the Moderator.

Investigate and secure correct addresses of all members. In case of removal, follow up with prepared letters to individuals concerned and the church in the new community. After appropriate time, transfer such persons to nonresident roll, and, subject to further lack of action, place on list for membership action "recommend to suspend."

Prepare baptismal and membership certificates and have them signed by the proper persons.

Maintain such lists as are necessary for immediate reference to personnel statistics as required for the Annual Report.

Friendship Callers shall report to Chief Secretary on calls made so she can pass the information on to the proper persons.

Type sermons, meditations, communion forms, prayers, service forms, etc.

Schedule the use of rooms and buildings for church groups and for non-church organizations under the direction of the senior minister as representative of the Session.

Prepare and maintain the monthly and weekly schedule of events.

Prepare basic documents for Audit Committee.

Maintain a regular inventory of office supplies, prepare lists of needed supplies, and order them through the proper channels.

Supervise volunteer assistance when and where needed.

Notify ministers, deacons, and other concerned persons about illness, death, problems, etc.

Dispatch promptly all incoming mail to the recipients.

Maintain desk file of names and addresses and telephone numbers of all members.

Contact responsible person concerning the flowers in the sanctuary and greeters for services.

Supervise all church organizational mailings.

Office Secretary

The Office Secretary shall be directly responsible to the Chief Secretary and shall work under her direction only.

She shall be responsible for the following:

Gathering information, typing the stencils, proofreading and mimeographing the church newsletter and the Sunday bulletins.

Preparing the weekly newspaper and radio publicity and seeing that it reaches the proper office on time.

Writing all thank-you notes regarding flowers, memorials, and special services.

Operating the mimeograph, ditto, folding and addressograph machines for *all* work requiring the use of these machines for *all* departments of the church.

All miscellaneous correspondence, typing, filing, and any assistance required by the Chief Secretary. This includes secretarial work for the ministers and other members of the program staff and assistance at the telephone and reception desk as needed.

Recruiting all the needed volunteer assistants.

Sending notices of meeting dates and times to the church officers.

Maintaining the addressograph plates and mailing file.

Sending names, addresses, and telephone numbers of new members and interested persons to the appropriate organizations.

Annually preparing the church directory for printing or mimeographing.

Annually preparing and mimeographing the annual report for the congregational meeting.

Taking all telephone reservations and cancellations for camp conferences, breakfasts, luncheons, dinners of a church-wide nature.

Maintaining a file of the members of the church serving in the armed forces and a list or file of college students.

Supervising the volunteer help in preparing the "guest letters" each Monday to visitors attending services the previous day. This involves assigning cards to the Friendship Callers and keeping the list current. The Friendship Callers shall report the nature and content of their calls to the Chief Secretary for her to channel and refer to proper persons.

All the mechanical work regarding mailings, church bulletin inserts, etc., and general filing and clerical work as required by the Chief Secretary or Financial Secretary.

Membership Secretary

The membership secretary, as a member of the church staff, under the authority of the minister, is directly responsible to the secretary to the minister. Her specific duties are to:

1. Maintain an accurate, up-to-date card file of the entire church membership including preparatory and unbaptized children in each family.
2. Maintain a book of historical data recording new members, births, baptisms, marriages, and deaths.
3. Keep current a set of membership books with a page of detailed data on each family in the membership.
4. Maintain a card file indicating phases of church work in which members are interested in serving; make this information available to appropriate department chairmen of the church.
5. Keep current several loose-leaf copies of a complete membership directory for desk use by the staff.
6. Maintain an up-to-date card file on prospective church members; make this information available to the Commission on Membership and Evangelism.
7. Maintain current addressograph file, which includes the complete church membership, prospective members, youth organizations and college students, and personnel of the Official Board.

8. Inform the financial secretary and ministers immediately of any change in the membership or changes of address, and the educational secretary of changes involving children and youth.

9. Under the direction of the associate minister who is in charge of membership, make the various arrangements for membership classes. Prior to the forming of a new class, work with him in determining (from the prospective membership file) those who should receive letters of invitation to membership, and write letters to those persons for the minister's signature; make available necessary material for orientation classes; handle all correspondence, for the signature of the minister, regarding new members.

10. After new members have been received, give their names to the various organizations and groups within the church who, in turn, invite these persons to join them; also, give the names of children in the family to the educational secretary.

11. Mail out notices of meetings of the Commission on Membership and Evangelism; receive the minutes from the commission secretary and be responsible for typing and distributing copies to the members of the commission.

12. Furnish correct names of the entire membership, alphabetically arranged, with addresses and telephone numbers for the annual membership directory; proofread the directory with the office secretary for correctness; furnish day-by-day changes for inclusion until the actual mimeographing is done; help to assemble the directory.

13. Prior to a baptismal service, do the initial telephone work with the parents; write letters to the parents for the minister's signature; secure necessary data for the certificates, and prepare the certificates.

14. Prepare for the minister's signature and send a booklet of condolence to members of a family where a death has occurred.

15. Type the following correspondence for the minister's signature:
    a. Letters of thanks to flower donors
    b. Letters to visitors at worship services
    c. Congratulatory letters to members after births, special recognition, etc.
    d. Other miscellaneous correspondence as directed

16. Inform editor of church paper of news items of interest regarding the membership, such as births, baptisms, weddings, new members, illnesses, etc.; type all general material for the church paper in conjunction with the editor; handle mailing of the church paper.

17. Maintain a complete file of correspondence regarding the membership.

18. Upon request, furnish statistical data for Church and Annual Conference and other reports for Official Board, Executive Committee, and other meetings.

19. Type the pastor's sermons from the tape recorder.

20. Assist the financial secretary in handling the Sunday offering, go to the bank with her to receive it, assist in counting and recording it properly, and accompany her when making deposits.

21. Deliver the altar flowers to the ill and shut-ins when requested.

22. Assist with the general office work load as directed.

23. Use good judgment in keeping confidential staff and congregational matters.
24. Handle objectively any comments of commendation or criticism by members of the congregation and/or staff in order to maintain a happy, wholesome atmosphere regarding all aspects of the administration of the church.

In summarizing, she should contribute a gracious spirit to the cooperative efforts of the staff in serving the people effectively.

Bookkeeper

General Duties

1. Supervise and assist in opening Sunday's offering; prepare it for deposit.
2. Handle all mail pertaining to Finance Office, taking advice from the Finance Committee concerning legal matters.
3. Post detailed analysis of all receipts weekly.
4. Audit and prepare bills for payment monthly. Pay church notes and insurance premiums.
5. Figure payroll and supervise writing checks to employees.
6. Bill classes and departments that owe church for food or nursery time.
7. Issue purchase orders for church expenditures. Sell tickets at dinner meetings.

Records

1. Keep a detailed record of the payroll.
2. At the end of each quarter make a report to the Department of Internal Revenue listing salaries and deductions.
3. At the end of the year send W-2 forms to employees and the Revenue Department.
4. Prepare annual audit of salaries to Workmen's Compensation Insurance.
5. Keep detailed account of all money placed in trust through the church for specific distribution.

Reports

1. Submit to the church a summary of all receipts and expenditures for the month.
2. Furnish the Finance Committee a detailed report of the status of pledges each month.

Statements

1. At the end of the month total gifts of each account, denoting present standing, either past due, overpaid, or exactly current.
2. Send statements each month to all overdue accounts.
3. Send annual statements to all who contribute to the church.
4. Furnish auditor with detailed report of all receipts and expenditures for the year.

Church Hostess

I

(Name) is to be employed by the church at the rate of $_____ per month for ten months of the calendar year—July and August being excluded.

II

_____ will be expected to do the following things:

(a) Prepare the Sunday evening meal for the Wesley Foundation (the college-age group) meeting in the church. It is understood the young people will collect the money and pay Mrs. _____, and that out of the funds she will pay for the food, turning over whatever balance there is to the church office. The young people will set the tables and clear them and do the dishes following the meal.

(b) The hostess is to care for all the church kitchens. This means she is to be responsible for seeing that everything is kept in its place and that all kitchens are clean; that towels, etc., are prepared for the laundry and are counted upon return. She is to work closely with the custodian. In the maintenance of supplies she will work with a committee of the Women's Society of Christian Service.

(c) Mrs. _____ will work with the Women's Society of Christian Service and with all other groups that may be using the kitchens. This does not mean that she must be at the church every time the kitchens are used. It does mean that she is responsible for the protection of such kitchen equipment as the ovens, disposal, and dishwasher. She should be assured that someone is at hand who knows how to operate this equipment if she is absent.

(d) A committee of the Women's Society, represented by one woman, will act as supervisor to the Hostess.

III

The hostess will be considered a member of the church staff and will be expected to attend staff meetings unless excused. This is required for her benefit so that she may see her work in terms of the total program of the church.

_____

Church Hostess

_____

Pastor

Custodian Contract

Agreement between the custodian and the Committee on Lay Personnel of the _____ Church pertaining to the duties of the custodian and the responsibilities of the Church.

In order to clarify the duties of the custodian, to protect him from unreasonable requirements, and to assure the complete understanding of regular requirements by both the custodian and the Board of Trustees, this agreement is deemed necessary.

I. Responsibility

The custodian is the employee of the Committee on Lay Personnel of The ———— United Methodist Church. Requirements for his services shall be from the Board of Trustees or from their authorized representative, and from no other person or group of persons. It is to be expected, however, that the custodian will act as a Christian gentleman and will strive to perform his duties cheerfully and with a willingness to cooperate with all persons whenever possible. In the event of differences or misunderstandings, the decision of the Board of Trustees, subject to the Church Conference, shall be final in all cases.

II. Pay and Privileges

The custodian shall be paid by the Treasurer of the Church, by check, which when properly endorsed, shall constitute a true and lawful receipt of payment for services rendered. The position of custodian is covered by the Federal Insurance Contributions Act as provided by the Social Security Administration of the United States Government, and contributions as required for participation in that plan shall be deducted from his gross earnings. The rate of pay shall be mutually agreed upon at the time of employment and may be adjusted from time to time by the recommendation of the Finance Commission and the approval of the Official Board of the Church. The custodian shall receive one week's vacation with pay after one year of service, and two week's vacation with pay after three years of service. The time taken as vacation shall be acceptable to the Board of Trustees.

III. General Duties and Activities

The custodian shall:
1. Sweep and dust the meeting rooms of the Church (including sanctuary) weekly.
2. Clean the hallways, toilets, and vestibules weekly.
3. Arrange chairs in classrooms as required weekly. (Exception: When ———— Hall or other classrooms are used for gatherings on Saturday, the custodian is not required to arrange chairs in that area for the Sunday immediately following, except in the case of weddings or other occasions when the custodian receives additional compensation for this effort.)
4. Provide for comfortable heating as required for scheduled functions.
5. Empty all waste and garbage receptacles at least weekly.
6. Replace all broken and defective electric light bulbs, tubes, fuses, and starters as needed.
7. Place hymnals or song books in required locations for scheduled services.
8. Provide for the general satisfactory appearance of the Church through judicious and thoughtful care, giving special attention to general neatness and cleanliness. Keep exterior neat and clean by sweeping, mowing, and removing snow and ice when required.

9. Scrub and wax tiled floors periodically. They must be maintained by weekly buffing.
10. Put in place and remove communion tables when needed.
11. Wash all windows that are accessible at least twice a year.
12. Watch for and eliminate fire and safety hazards. If action is required, notify the Chairman of the Board of Trustees.
13. Arrange for laundering, dry cleaning, and other services that require pick-up and delivery of materials from and to the Church.
14. Remove flowers from vases if not sent to the sick or shut-in by others.
15. Place and remove parking lot and curb signs as needed for special occasions.
16. Lock and unlock the Church up to a period of four weeks upon resignation of the hired security personnel in the event that a new employee is not obtainable immediately.

IV. Responsibilities of the Church and Its Organizations

The Church and its organizations shall:
1. Provide all necessary dusting, cleaning, scrubbing, and waxing supplies and materials.
2. Provide replacement parts and supplies, such as light bulbs.
3. Provide equipment for proper and effective cleaning, mowing, snow removal, etc.
4. Provide satisfactory waste and garbage receptacles.
5. Provide for all major repair and maintenance requiring professional services.
6. Provide for maintenance of the organ (except normal cleaning and dusting).
7. Notify the custodian at least one week in advance of activities in which church facilities are to be used. All such schedules should be cleared through the church office.
8. Any group that uses the church for a dinner of any kind is responsible for seeing that the furniture necessary for the occasion is set up and returned to the proper place afterward; that the kitchen is properly cleaned; that all tables are wiped clean, unless the custodian is hired for this at time-and-a-half rate.

V. Special Duties
1. The custodian shall be responsible for arranging the sanctuary, reception area, and grounds upon the occasion of a wedding. For such services rendered and for returning all these areas to their proper condition, he shall receive not less than $7.50 per ceremony for a member's wedding and not less than $10 for a non-member's wedding. This fee is to be paid by the couple involved.
2. In the case of wedding receptions the custodian shall not be responsible for the arrangement of furniture and the returning of said furniture to its proper place unless he is contracted for this service by the group putting on the reception. For this service he must be paid a sum of $8.50. This fee may be paid entirely or in part by the wedding couple, or it may be borne entirely or in part from the remuneration the Church group receives for preparing the reception.

271

If the custodian is asked to take this responsibility for a reception and is unable to do so himself, it shall be his responsibility to secure someone else for the task, subject to approval of the Trustees.

In every case the group in charge of the reception is responsible for cleaning up the kitchen.

3. The custodian shall receive no extra compensation for services attendant upon use of the Church for the funeral of any member.

4. The custodian shall receive no additional compensation for extra services resulting from the following activities:
   a. Communion
   b. Christmas activities
   c. Daily Vacation Bible School
   d. Children's Day
   e. Scheduled meetings such as:
      (1) missionary conference
      (2) prayer mission
      (3) evangelistic campaign
      (4) financial canvass
   f. Small receptions in parlor, as for:
      (1) new members
      (2) farewells
      (3) missionary reception or commissionings
   g. W.S.C.S. Birthday Party

The foregoing duties, responsibilities, and other concerns have been jointly agreed upon by the custodian and the Committee on Lay Personnel of the _____ Church and have been approved by the Official Board. In witness whereof, we do attach thereto our signatures and further agree, the Lord being our helper, to perform the several duties described herein to the best of our abilities.

Signed:

_____	_____
Custodian	For Committee on Lay Personnel
_____	_____
Date	Chairman, Official Board

272

Appendix C: Representative Theories of Learning

TABLE 21. REPRESENTATIVE THEORIES OF LEARNING

Theory of Learning	Assumption Concerning the Basic Nature of Man	Psychological System or Outlook	Basis of Transfer	Key Persons	Contemporary Exponents
1. Mental discipline	bad-active (mind substance)	faculty psychology	exercised faculties, transfer automatic	St. Augustine John Calvin J. Edwards	many Hebraic-Christian fundamentalists
2. Mental discipline	neutral-active (mind substance)	classicism	cultivated mind or intellect	Plato Aristotle	M. J. Adler St. John's College
3. Natural unfoldment	good-active (natural)	romantic naturalism	recapitulation, no transfer	J. J. Rousseau F. Froebel	extreme progressivists
4. Apperception	neutral-passive (mental)	structuralism	apperceptive mass	J. F. Herbart E. B. Titchener	many teachers and administrators
5. S-R bond	neutral-passive (physical or mental)	connectionism	identical elements	E. L. Thorndike	J. M. Stephens A. I. Gates
6. Conditioning (with no reinforcement)	neutral-passive (physical)	behaviorism	conditioned responses	J. B. Watson	E. R. Guthrie
7. Reinforcement and conditioning	neutral-passive (organism)	reinforcement	reinforced, or conditioned, responses	C. L. Hull	B. F. Skinner K. W. Spence
8. Insight	active (natural)	Gestalt psychology	transposition of insights	M. Wertheimer K. Koffka	W. Köhler
9. Goal insight	neutral-interactive	configurationalism	tested insights	B. H. Bode	E. E. Bayles
10. Cognitive-field	neutral-interactive (psychological)	field psychology or relativism	continuity of life spaces, experience or insights	Kurt Lewin E. C. Tolman J. S. Bruner	R. G. Barker A. W. Combs H. F. Wright

From Morris L. Bigge, *Learning Theories for Teachers* (New York: Harper, 1964), pp. 12-13.

Bibliography

The bibliographies are listed by academic disciplines and topics rather than by chapter topic and sequence. The topics may be helpful in pursuing various phases of the subject matter further and when the book is used as a text.

There is much overlapping of books in the various fields, though in order to save space there is little cross-referencing.

Doctrine of the Church: Ministry and Laity

Ayres, Francis O. *The Ministry of the Laity*. Philadelphia: Westminster Press, 1962.

Barr, Browne. *Parish Back Talk*. Nashville: Abingdon Press, 1964.

Berger, Peter. *The Noise of Solemn Assemblies*. Garden City, N. Y.: Doubleday, 1961.

Berkhof, Hendrikus. *The Doctrine of the Holy Spirit*. Richmond, Va.: John Knox Press, 1964.

Berton, Pierre. *The Comfortable Pew*. Philadelphia: Lippincott, 1965.

Bovet, Theodor. *That They May Have Life*. Translated by John A. Baker. London: Darton, Longman & Todd, 1964.

Clark, M. Edward, William L. Malcomson, and Warren Lane Molton (eds.) *The Church Creative*. Nashville: Abingdon Press, 1967.

Congar, Yves M.J., O. P. *Lay People in the Church*. Translated by Donald Attwater. London: Bloomsbury, 1957.

Dewar, Lindsay. *The Holy Spirit and Modern Thought*. London: A. R. Mowbrey & Co., 1959.

Dittes, James E. *The Church in the Way*. New York: Scribner's, 1967.

Fichter, Joseph H. *America's Forgotten Priests—What They are Saying*. New York: Harper, 1968.

Fuller, Reginald H., and Brian K. Rice. *Christianity and the Affluent Society*. Grand Rapids: Eerdmans, 1966.

Gibbs, Mark and T. Ralph Morton. *God's Frozen People*. Philadelphia: Westminster Press, 1965.

Glasse, James D. *Profession: Minister*. Nashville: Abingdon Press, 1968.

Grimes, Lewis Howard. *The Church Redemptive*. Nashville: Abingdon Press, 1958.

————. *Realms of our Calling*. New York: Friendship Press, 1965.

————. *The Rebirth of the Laity*. Nashville: Abingdon Press, 1962.

Gustafson, James M. "The Clergy in the United States." *Daedalus, Journal of the American Academy of Arts and Science*. Fall 1963, pp. 724-44.

Holmes, William A. *Tomorrow's Church, a Cosmopolitan Community*. Nashville: Abingdon Press, 1968.

Hughes, Everett C. "Professions." *Daedalus*. Fall 1963, pp. 655-68.

Johnson, Robert Clyde (ed.). *The Church and Its Changing Ministry*. Philadelphia: The United Presbyterian Church, 1961.

Kirkpatrick, Dow (ed.). *The Doctrine of the Church*. Oxford Institute on Methodist Theological Studies. (Prepared under the direction of the World Methodist Council.) Nashville: Abingdon Press, 1964.

Kraemer, Hendrik. *A Theology of the Laity*. Philadelphia: Westminster Press, 1959.

Lee, Robert (ed.). *The Church and the Exploding Metropolis*. Richmond, Va.: John Knox Press, 1965.

Lindsay, Thomas M. *The Church and the Ministry in the Early Centuries*. London: Hodder & Stoughton, 1902.

Neill, Stephen Charles and Hans-Ruedi Weber, (eds.). *The Layman in Christian History*. Philadelphia: Westminster Press, 1963.

Niebuhr, H. Richard. *The Purpose of the Church and Its Ministry*. New York: Harper, 1956.

————, and Daniel D. Williams, (eds.). *The Ministry in Historical Perspectives*. New York: Harper, 1956.

Norwood, Frederick A. *Church Membership in the Methodist Tradition*. Nashville: Methodist Publishing House, 1958.

Oates, Wayne E. *The Christian Pastor*. (Revised and enlarged edition.) Philadelphia: Westminster Press, 1964.

Paton, David M. (ed.). *The Parish Communion To-day*. (The report of the 1962 Conference of Parish and People.) London: S.P.C.K., 1962.

Raines, Robert A. *New Life in the Church*. New York: Harper, 1961.

Robinson, John A. T. *On Being the Church in the World*. Philadelphia: Westminster Press, 1962.

Schaller, Lyle E. *Planning for Protestantism in Urban America*. Nashville: Abingdon Press, 1965.

Shoemaker, Samuel M. *Beginning Your Ministry*. New York: Harper, 1963.

Smart, James D. *The Rebirth of the Ministry*. Philadelphia: Westminster Press, 1960.

Smith, Charles Merrill. *How to Become a Bishop Without Being Religious*. Garden City, N. Y.: Doubleday, 1965.

Southard, Samuel. *Pastoral Authority in Personal Relationships*. Nashville: Abingdon Press, 1969.

Stevenson, William. *The Story of the Reformation*. Richmond, Va.: John Knox Press, 1964.

Thielicke, Helmut. *The Trouble With the Church*. Translated and edited by John W. Doberstein. New York: Harper, 1965.

Trueblood, Elton. *The Incendiary Fellowship*. New York: Harper, 1967.

Vincent, John J. *Christ and Methodism.* Nashville: Abingdon Press, 1965.

Webber, George W. *The Congregation in Mission.* Nashville: Abingdon Press, 1964.

————. *God's Colony in Man's World.* Nashville: Abingdon Press, 1960.

Wilson, Gregory. *The Stained Glass Jungle.* Garden City, N. Y.: Doubleday, 1962.

Leadership, Group Dynamics, Communications, and Human Relations

Anderson, Philip A. *Church Meetings That Matter.* Philadelphia: United Church Press, 1966.

Biggers, John D. *Human Relations in Modern Business.* Englewood Cliffs, N. J.: Prentice-Hall, 1949.

Bion, W. R. "Experience in Groups: I," *Human Relations.* I, 3 (1948), pp. 314-20.

————. "Group Dynamics: A Re-View." *International Journal of Psychoanalysis.* (1952) pp. 33, 235-47.

Bradford, Leland P. (ed.), Jack R. Gibbs, and Kenneth D. Benne. *T-Group Theory and Laboratory Method.* New York: Wiley, 1964.

Cartwright, Dorwin and Alvin Zander. *Group Dynamics: Research and Theory.* 2nd edition. New York: Harper, 1960.

Chase, Stuart in collaboration with Marian Tyler Chase. *Roads to Agreement: Successful Methods in the Science of Human Relations.* New York: Harper, 1951.

Dubin, Robert (ed.). *Human Relations in Administration.* Englewood Cliffs, N. J.: Prentice-Hall, 1961.

Gable, Lee J. *Encyclopedia for Church Group Leaders.* New York: Association Press, 1959.

Gardner, John W. *Excellence: Can We Be Equal and Excellent Too?* New York: Harper, 1961.

————. *Self Renewal: The Individual and the Innovative Society.* New York: Harper, 1964.

Greenewalt, Crawford H. *The Uncommon Man.* New York: McGraw-Hill, 1959.

Haiman, Franklyn S. *Group Leadership and Democratic Action.* Boston: Houghton Mifflin, 1951.

Hemphill, John K. "Relations Between the Size of the Group and the Behavior of 'Superior' Leaders," *Journal of Social Psychology.* Vol. 32, 1950, pp. 11-22.

Hendry, Charles E., and Murray G. Ross. *New Understandings of Leadership.* New York: Association Press, 1957.

Knowles, Malcolm and Hulda. *Introduction to Group Dynamics.* New York: Association Press, 1959.

Le Bon, Gustave. *The Crowd.* Introduction by Robert K. Merton. New York: Viking Press, 1960.

Lewin, Kurt. *Field Theory in Social Science.* Dorwin Cartwright (ed.). New York: Harper, 1951.

Lifton, Walter M. *Working With Groups—Group Process and Individual Growth.* New York: Wiley, 1966.

Loomis, Charles P. and Zona K. *Modern Social Theories*. Princeton, N.J.: Van Nostrand, 1965.

McCormick, Charles P. *The Power of People: Multiple Management Up to Date*. New York: Harper, 1949.

Maier, Norman R. F. *Principles of Human Relations*. New York: Wiley, 1952.

Naess, Arne. *Communication and Argument: Elements of Applied Semantics*. Trans. by Alastair Hannay. Towtowa, N. J.: Bedminster, 1966.

Shartle, Carroll L. *Executive Performance and Leadership*. Englewood Cliffs, N. J.: Prentice-Hall, 1956.

Smith, William S. *Group Problem-Solving Through Discussion*. Indianapolis: Bobbs-Merrill, 1965.

Stock, Dorothy and Herbert A. Thelen. *Emotional Dynamics and Group Culture*. New York University Press, 1958.

Tead, Ordway. *The Art of Leadership*. New York: McGraw-Hill, 1935.

Thelen, Herbert A. *Dynamics of Groups at Work*. The University of Chicago Press, 1967.

Trecker, Harleigh B. and Audrey R. *How to Work With Groups*. New York: Association Press, 1952.

Administration

Bassett, Glenn A. *Management Styles in Transition*. New York: American Management Association, 1967.

Batten, J. D. *Beyond Management By Objectives*. American Management Association, 1967.

————. *Tough-Minded Management*. American Management Association, 1963.

Bellows, Roger. *Creative Leadership*. Englewood Cliffs, N. J.: Prentice-Hall, 1959.

————, Thomas Q. Gilson and George S. Odiorne. *Executive Skills*. Englewood Cliffs, N. J.: Prentice-Hall, 1962.

Brady, Raymond (ed.). *What Makes a "Best Managed" Company?* Dunn and Bradstreet Publications Corp., 1965.

Dimock, Marshall E. *A Philosophy of Administration*. New York: Harper, 1958.

Ditzen, Lowell R. *The Minister's Desk Book*. West Nyack, N.Y.: Parker Publishing Co., 1968.

Drucker, Peter. *The Effective Executive*. New York: Harper, 1967.

Editors of *Fortune*. *The Executive Life*. Garden City, N. Y.: Doubleday, 1956.

Ginzberg, E. (ed.). *What Makes an Executive?* New York: Columbia University Press, 1955.

Hardwick, C. T. and B. F. Landuyt. *Administration Strategy*. New York: Simmons-Boardman Publishing Corp., 1961.

Judy, Marvin T. *The Cooperative Parish in Nonmetropolitan Areas*. Nashville: Abingdon Press, 1967.

————. *The Larger Parish and Group Ministry*. Abingdon Press, 1959.

Kenrick, Bruce. *Come Out the Wilderness*. New York: Harper, 1962.

Lindgren, Alvin J. *Foundations for Purposeful Church Administration*. Nashville: Abingdon Press, 1965.

McCormick, Charles P. *The Power of People: Multiple Management Up to Date.* New York: Harper, 1949.

McPherson, Joseph H. "What Is Creativity in Industry Today?" *AMA Management Bulletin,* No. 4 (1960), pp. 1-7.

Moore, Paul, Jr. *The Church Reclaims the City.* New York: Seabury Press, 1963.

Neuner, John J. W. and B. Lewis Keeling. *Administrative Office Management.* 5th ed. Dallas: South-Western Publishing Company, 1966.

Paul, Leslie. *The Deployment and Payment of the Clergy.* Westminster, SWI: Church Information Office, 1964.

Spangler, Selden B. "The Role of Creativity in Industry Today." *AMA Management Bulletin.* No. 4 (1960), pp. 1-7.

Steiner, Gary A. (ed.). *The Creative Organization.* The University of Chicago Press, 1965.

Tead, Ordway. *Administration: Its Purpose and Performance.* New York: Harper, 1959.

————. *The Art of Administration.* New York: McGraw-Hill, 1951.

————. *Democratic Administration.* New York: Association Press, 1945.

Terry, George R. *Principles of Management.* Homewood, Ill.: Richard D. Irwin, 1964.

Creativity

Allen, Myron S. *Morphological Creativity: The Miracle of Your Hidden Brain Power.* Englewood Cliffs, N. J.: Prentice-Hall, 1962.

Anderson, Harold H. (ed.). *Creativity and Its Cultivation.* New York: Harper, 1959.

Andrews, Michael F. (ed.). *Creativity and Psychological Health.* Syracuse University Press, 1961.

Carner, Charles. "Are We Rejecting Our Creative Children?" *Today's Health.* February, 1964.

Crawford, Robert P. *The Technique of Creative Thinking.* New York: Hawthorne Books, 1954.

————. *Think for Yourself.* Wells, Vt.: Fraser Publishing Co., 1964.

Crutchfield, Richard S. "The Creative Process." Conference on *The Creative Person.* Lake Tahoe: University of California, 1961.

Farber, Seymour M. and Roger H. L. Wilson (eds.). *Man and Civilization Conflict and Creativity.* New York: McGraw-Hill, 1961.

Ghiselin, Brewster (ed.). *The Creative Process.* Berkeley: University of California Press, 1952.

Gruber, Howard E., Glenn Terrell, and Michael Wertheimer (eds.). *Contemporary Approaches to Creative Thinking.* New York: Atherton Press, 1962.

Guilford, J. P. "Creativity," *American Psychologist.* Vol. 5 (1950), pp. 444-54.

Hutchinson, Eliot Dale. *How to Think Creatively.* Nashville: Abingdon Press, 1949.

McPherson, Joseph H. "What Is Creativity in Industry Today?" *AMA Management Bulletin,* No. 4 (1960), pp. 9-14.

Ojemann, Ralph H. (ed.). *Recent Research on Creative Approaches to En-*

vironmental Stress. Iowa City: State University of Iowa, Department of Publications, 1964.

Osborn, Alex F. *Applied Imagination.* New York: Scribner's, 1963.

Parnes, Sidney J. and Harold F. Harding (eds.) . *A Source Book for Creative Thinking.* New York: Scribner's, 1962.

Spangler, Selden B. "The Role of Creativity in Industry Today." *AMA Management Bulletin,* No. 4 (1960) , pp. 1-7.

Spearman, Charles E. *Creative Mind.* London: Nisbett Co., 1930.

Taylor, Calvin W. and Frank Barron (eds.) . *Scientific Creativity: Its Recognition and Development.* New York: Wiley, 1963.

Stress and Tension

Allen, Myron S. *Morphological Creativity: The Miracle of Your Hidden Brain Power.* (Chap. 7, "Frustration," pp. 124-42.) Englewood Cliffs, N. J.: Prentice-Hall, 1962.

Anderson, Camilla M. *Beyond Freud.* (Chap. 7, "Stress," pp. 117-37.) New York: Harper, 1957.

————. *Saints, Sinners and Psychiatry.* (Chap. 2, "The Footprints of Anxiety.") Philadelphia: Lippincott, 1950.

Bellows, Roger. *Creative Leadership.* (Section Four: "Tension, Conflict, and Leadership," pp. 151-92.) Englewood Cliffs, N. J.: Prentice-Hall, 1959.

Bowers, Margaretta K., M.D. *Conflicts of the Clergy.* New York: Thomas Nelson, 1963.

Chase, Stuart in collaboration with Marian Tyler Chase. *Roads to Agreement.* (Chap. 2, "Levels of Conflict.") New York: Harper, 1951.

Dubin, Robert (ed.) . *Human Relations in Administration.* (Section on "The Executive—Executives' Job Fatigue," pp. 101 ff.) Englewood Cliffs, N. J.: Prentice-Hall, 1961.

Eaton, Merrill T., M.D. "Controlling Executive Stress." Lincoln: University of Nebraska, College of Medicine. (Mimeographed.)

————. "Maintaining Health Despite Executive Tensions and Pressures." Lincoln, Nebraska: University of Nebraska, College of Medicine. (Mimeographed.)

Editors of *Fortune. The Executive Life.* (Chap. 5, "How Executives Crack Up," pp. 268-89.) Garden City, N.Y.: Doubleday, 1956.

Hicks, Clifford B. "Jet-Age Blues," *Today's Health* (Chicago) , November, 1966, p. 19.

Irwin, Theodore. *What the Executive Should Know About Tension.* Larchmont, N. Y.: American Research Council, 1966.

Mowrer, O. Hobert. *The Crisis in Psychiatry and Religion.* Princeton: Van Nostrand, 1961.

Ojemann, Ralph H. (ed.) . *Recent Research on Creative Approaches to Environmental Stress.* Iowa City: State University of Iowa Department of Publications, 1964.

Ratcliff, J. D. "Stress—The Cause of All Diseases?" *The Reader's Digest,* January, 1955.

Rethlingshafer, Dorothy. *Motivation as Related to Personality.* (Chap. 12, "Tension.") New York: McGraw-Hill, 1963.

Roche Laboratories. *Aspects of Anxiety.* Philadelphia: Lippincott, 1965.
Selye, Hans, M.D. *The Stress of Life.* New York: McGraw-Hill, 1956.
Tournier, Paul (ed.). *Fatigue in Modern Society.* Translated by James H. Faraey. Richmond, Va.: John Knox Press, 1965.
————. *The Healing of Persons.* Trans. by Edwin Hudson. (Chaps. 8 and 9, "Flight" and "Overwork and Idleness," pp. 95-125.) New York: Harper, 1965.

Staff Personnel and Positions

Anderson, Martin, *Multiple Ministries.* Minneapolis: Augsburg, 1965.
Bigge, Morris L. *Learning Theories for Teachers.* New York: Harper, 1964.
Butts, R. Freeman and Lawrence A. Cremin. *A History of Education in American Culture.* New York: Holt, Rinehart & Winston, 1953.
Carpenter, William Whitney and James Walter Pierson. *Relationship: The Foundation of a Team Ministry.* Unpublished dissertation. The School of Theology at Claremont, 1965.
Chamberlin, J. Gordon. *Freedom and Faith: New Approaches to Christian Education.* Philadelphia: Westminster Press, 1965.
Cremin, Lawrence A. *The Transformation of the School.* New York: Knopf, 1962.
Denton, Wallace. *The Role of the Minister's Wife.* Philadelphia: Westminister Press, 1962.
Ditzen, Lowell Russell. *Handbook for the Church Secretary.* Englewood Cliffs, N. J.: Prentice-Hall, 1963.
Douglas, William. *Ministers' Wives.* New York: Harper, 1965.
Douglas, Winifred. *Church Music in History and Practice.* New York: Scribner's, 1962.
Ely, Virginia S. *The Church Secretary.* Chicago: Moody Press, 1956.
Gray, Robert N. *Church Business Administration: An Emerging Profession.* Enid, Oklahoma: Phillips University Press, 1968.
Henderlite, Rachel. *The Holy Spirit in Christian Education.* Philadelphia: Westminster Press, 1964.
Hooper, William Loyd. *Church Music in Transition.* Nashville: Broadman Press, 1963.
Howse, W. L. *The Church Staff and Its Work.* Nashville: Broadman Press, 1959.
LaPiere, Richard. *The Freudian Ethic.* New York: Duell, Sloan & Pearce, 1959.
Lobsenz, Norman. *The Minister's Complete Guide to Successful Retirement.* New York: Channel Press, 1955.
Lovelace, Austin C. and William C. Rice. *Music and Worship in the Church.* Nashville: Abingdon Press, 1960.
Mathis, William S. *The Pianist and Church Music.* Nashville: Abingdon Press, 1962.
Miller, Randolph Crump. *Education for Christian Living.* Englewood Cliffs, N. J.: Prentice-Hall, 1963.
Mitchell, Kenneth R. *Psychological and Theological Relationships in the Multiple Staff Ministry.* Philadelphia: Westminster Press, 1966.

Oden, Marilyn Brown. *The Minister's Wife: Person or Position?* Nashville: Abingdon Press, 1966.

Person, Peter P. *The Minister in Christian Education.* Grand Rapids: Baker Book House, 1960.

Phenix, Philip H. *Education and the Worship of God.* Philadelphia: Westminster Press, 1966.

————. *Philosophy of Education.* New York: Holt, Rinehart & Winston, 1958.

————. *Realms of Meaning.* New York: McGraw-Hill, 1964.

Roe, Anne. *The Psychology of Occupations.* New York: Wiley, 1956.

Routley, Erik. *Music Leadership in the Church.* Nashville: Abingdon Press, 1967.

Smart, James D. *The Creed in Christian Teaching.* Philadelphia: Westminster Press, 1962.

————. *The Teaching Ministry of the Church.* Philadelphia: Westminster Press, 1954.

Squire, Russel N. *Church Music.* St. Louis: Bethany Press, 1962.

Sweet, Herman J. *The Multiple Staff in the Local Church.* Philadelphia: Westminster Press, 1963.

Sydnor, James R. *Planning for Church Music.* Nashville: Abingdon Press, 1961.

Taylor, Marvin J. (ed.). *An Introduction to Christian Education.* Nashville: Abingdon Press, 1966.

Wiest, Elam G. *How to Organize Your Church Staff.* Old Tappan, N. J.: Fleming H. Revell, 1962.

Motivation and Renewal

Angell, Robert Cooley. *Free Society and Moral Crisis.* Ann Arbor: University of Michigan Press, 1965.

Barrois, George A. (ed.). *Pathways of the Inner Life.* New York: Bobbs-Merrill, 1956.

Braybrooke, Neville (ed.). *Teilhard de Chardin: Pilgrim of the Future.* New York: Seabury Press, 1964.

Brother Lawrence. *The Practice of the Presence of God.* Old Tappan, N. J.: Fleming H. Revell, 1958.

Casteel, John L. *Renewal in Retreats.* New York: Association Press, 1959.

————. (ed.). *Spiritual Renewal Through Personal Groups.* New York: Association Press, 1957.

Clark, Walter Houston. *The Oxford Group.* New York: Bookman Associates, 1951.

Come, Arnold B. *Human Spirit and Holy Spirit.* Philadelphia: Westminster Press, 1966.

Deshler, G. Byron. *The Power of the Personal Group.* Nashville, Tennessee: Tidings, n.d.

Dewar, Lindsay. *The Holy Spirit and Modern Thought.* New York: Harper, 1960.

Frankl, Viktor E. *Man's Search for Meaning.* Part One translated by Ilse Lasch. New York: Washington Square Press, 1963.

Fromm, Erich. *The Art of Loving.* New York: Harper, 1956.

Jones, Marshall R. (ed.). *Nebraska Symposium on Motivation.* Lincoln: University of Nebraska Press, 1955.

Kelly, Thomas R. *Holy Obedience,* William Penn Lecture 1939. Philadelphia: Book Committee, Religious Society of Friends, 1939.

Kilpack, Gilbert. *The Idea of a Retreat.* Wallingford, Pennsylvania: Pendle Hill Pamphlets.

Lunn, Arnold and Garth Lean. *The New Morality.* London: Blanford Press, 1964.

Magee, Raymond J. (ed.). *Call to Adventure.* Nashville: Abingdon Press, 1967.

Maslow, A. H. *Motivation and Personality.* New York: Harper, 1954.

————. *Religions, Values, and Peak-experiences.* Columbus: Ohio State University Press, 1964.

Merton, Thomas. *Life and Holiness.* New York: Herder and Herder, 1963.

Parker, William R. and Elaine St. Johns. *Prayer Can Change Your Life.* Englewood Cliffs, N. J.: Prentice-Hall, 1957.

Raynolds, Robert. *The Choice to Love.* New York: Harper, 1959.

Robinson, H. Wheeler. *The Christian Experience of The Holy Spirit.* New York: Harper, 1928.

Sinnott, Edmund W. *The Bridge of Life.* New York: Simon and Schuster, 1966.

Skoglund, John E. *Worship in the Free Churches.* Valley Forge, Pennsylvania: Judson Press, 1965.

Sorokin, Pitirim A. *The Ways of Power and Love.* Chicago: Regnery, 1967.

Steere, Douglas V. *Time to Spare.* New York: Harper, 1949.

Teilhard de Chardin, Pierre. *The Divine Milieu.* New York: Harper, 1960.

Underhill, Evelyn. *Light of Christ.* London: Longmans, Green & Co., 1945.

Van Dusen, Henry P. *Spirit, Son and Father.* New York: Scribner's, 1958.

White, James F. *The Worldliness of Worship.* New York: Oxford University Press, 1967.

Winward, Stephen F. *The Reformation of Our Worship.* Richmond, Va.: John Knox Press, 1965.

Wyon, Olive. *The School of Prayer.* New York: Macmillan, 1963.

Mimeographed papers. Available from Bridwell Library, Perkins School of Theology, Southern Methodist University, Dallas, Texas 75222. Copyright, Marvin T. Judy, 1964.

Tead, Ordway. "Personality in Church Administration."

Sartain, Aaron Q. "Personnel Management and the Church Staff."

Jumper, Andrew A. "The Pastor as Director of the Church Staff."

Fitch, Carroll B. "The Church Business Administrator."

Thornton, Randolph. "The Professional Christian Educator on the Church Staff."

Young, Carlton R. "The Professional Musician on the Church Staff."

Index